My Experiments with Truth

or

Evolution of the Science of Satyagraha

– M. K. Gandhi

My Experiments with Truth
An Autobiography by Mahatma Gandhi,
Navajivan Press,
Ahmedabad, 1927

Revised Edition 2025

ISBN: 978-81-8382-332-6

'How peculiar it is that someone as non-violent as Gandhi, who was very inspired by the Gita, was on the side of Krishna, who is making Arjuna fight a war and kill people – when Arjuna is saying may be he shouldn't kill.'

– Nobel Laureate Amartya Sen
(Outlook, 17 Aug. 09)

Published by:
Lotus Press Publishers & Distributors
4735/22, Prakash Deep Building, Ansari Road,
Darya Ganj, New Delhi-10002
Ph.: 41325510, 23280047, 9811594448
E-Mail: lotuspress1984@gmail.com
www.lotuspress.co.in

Printed at: **Lotus Press Publishers & Distributors**, New Delhi-110002

My Experiments with Truth

or

Evolution of the Science of Satyagraha

Mahatma Gandhi

Welcome
to A Super
Classic of
Modern
Times

'Gandhi's self-told unique story of his making into a Mahatma from an England-educated Bar-at-Law who offered hope for reform without destruction to the world'.

INDIA BOOKVARSITY
LOTUS CHOICES
Editor: Mahendra Kulasrestha

'...the greatest person since Buddha... 'his great contribution was the theory and practice of non-violence...usage of moral weapons to achieve practical results.'

—**John Gunther**

'From my background, I gained my regulating Christian ideals; from Gandhi I learned my operational technique.'

—**Martin Luther King**

'In Gandhi's teachings and writings, I think you will find no lies, no meanness, no slander, no dogmatism, no hypocrisy, no fear, no arrogance, no false pride, no hatred, no claims of infallibility.... He followed Buddha in employing the actions and arguments of love for dynamic ends.... Like Buddha, it was Gandhi's urge to liberate man.'

—**Edgar P. Show**

Edited by:
Mahendra Kulasrestha

Initiated and Published by:
SAURABH SEHGAL,
LOTUS PRESS Publishers & Distributors
New Delhi, India.

Lotus PRESS
4735/22, Prakash Deep Building,
Ansari Road, Daryaganj,
New Delhi-110002

Editorspeak

LET OTHERS SPEAK

'I believe that **Gandhi held the most enlightened views of all the political men of his times....** The problem of bringing peace to the world on a supranational basis will be solved only by employing Gandhi's method on a large scale.

'I believe Gandhi would have been Gandhi even without Thoreau and Tolstoy.'

—**Albert Einstein**

'In the life and death of Mahatma Gandhi we have seen reenacted in our time the supreme drama of humanity. He was a political leader and he was a seer, and **perhaps never before on so grand a scale has anyone sought to shape the course of events in the world** as it is by the example of a spirit which was not of the world as it is.

'Gandhi was the political leader transformed in the renewing of his mind. He was not "conformed to this world" yet he sought to govern turbulent masses of men who were still very much conformed to this world and have not been transformed.

'He died by violence because he was staking his life in order to set the example of non-violence.'

—**Walter Lippman**

'Gandhi was a devoted Hindu, and a philosophic Hindu can be at home with many religions, as he notably proved. **He admired and used much of the Bible and many Christian hymns.** He rejected, however, the orthodox Christian notion of redemption by the sacrifice of Christ on the ground that

God was too good to require the sacrifice of His son as a condition of forgiving erring human beings.'

—Norman Thomas

'Gandhi held no office, commanded no soldiers, yet paralysed India with a word. Men simply stopped work, crippling the offices, factories, mines, railways, ignoring the courts, paying no taxes, inviting arrest by tens of thousands, filling the jails until there was no room for more... He spent over 2000 days in prisons, reading, meditating, and drove the British frantic with his final, bloodless weapon: fasting. Nothing so haunted Whitehall as the nightmare of what might happen in this idolatrous land if the "Seditious Fakir", as Churchill called him, died in the protest fast.'

—Leo Rosten

'I saw a picture of the home for untouchable boys that Gandhi had founded on the outskirts of Delhi, and of the bare little room on the second floor that he used when he went there to stay with them. I saw the room when we were in Delhi, and **I stood at the entrance awed by the thought of the power of the man who had lived there.** All there was in that room is still there—a rug, a rolled up pad that was used at night as a bed, a pillow.'

—Eleanor Roosevelt

'.... he stands out almost hauntingly as a man who while small and ascetic was also of infectious agility and energy, totally serious yet of a pervasive gaiety, always himself yet attuned to each counter-player... Outstanding throughout his life was Gandhi's locomotor restlessness, a not uncommon characteristic of great men.

'Animated by a gay teasing.... **this is how the Mahatma teased the Viceroy in his own place.** After the brutal events of the Great Salt March which Lord Irwin described as "the most dramatic personal encounter between a Viceroy and an Indian leader".... When Gandhi was handed a cup of tea, he poured a bit of salt (tax free) into it out of a small paper hidden in his shawl and remarked smilingly, "to remind us of the famous Boston Tea Party."

—**Erik H. Erikson**

'The Marxists, those monks of politics, were shocked by his intimacy with rich men like Birla and Tata, just as the Pharisees of their days were shocked by Christ's sitting at table with bartenders. **It is true that Gandhi "compromised" with the rich**, those untouchables of the class struggle, **but he also "compromised" with the poor**, spending at least as much time in the 'untouchables' quarters.... He seems to have regarded the capitalist as well as the garbage-man as his social equal.'

—**Dwight Macdonald**

'There has never been anybody quite like the Mahatma either in presence or in practice. He was unique beyond all that the world has known. **When he was needed, he came as a new creation, straight from the hand of God**.'

—**John Haynes Holmes**

'The horror of Gandhi's murder lies not in the political motives behind it or in its consequences for Indian polity or for the future of non-violence; **the horror lies simply in the fact that any man could look into the face of this extraordinary person and deliberately pull a trigger**.'

—**Mary McCarthy**

Gandhi said to Rajkumari Amrit Kaur on Jan 28, 1948:

'If I am to die by the bullet of a mad man, I must do so smiling. There must be no anger within me. God must be in my heart and on my lips.

'And you promise me one thing: should such a thing happen, you are not to shed one tear.'

• •

Though leaders and great men of the world have many biographies written about their lives and deeds, an autobiography penned by himself always holds a very special place in socio-political literature. In India we are lucky to possess one such of not only our own but the entire world's greatest man of the twentieth century, 'Munia' in his early childhood, 'Bhai' Gandhi in South Africa, and 'Mahatma' Gandhi after he was active in India. It was originally written in Gujerati and published in 'Navjivan' for a few years, then translated into English by his able secretary Mahadev Desai, and vetted by experts, finally published in book form in 1927.

It soon became very popular not only because it was very honest—detailing Gandhi's bad habits, including his lust for his wife, but also because it was very well written and readable like a novel — and because such fact is always more exciting than fiction, also because honest writing is not the done thing in our culture; it made its mark as a pathbreaking contribution. No other national leader seem to have produced a similar work. Perhaps Netaji Subhas wrote an autobiographical work but if suffered its writer's fate and was lost to society.

The present writer may note that he collected Nehru's letters to his wife Kamala and edited them in the early nineties, when he worked as consultant to the Indira Gandhi Memorial Trust. This he undertook at the instance of N.K. Seshan, the then Secretary of the Trust, and one who worked with Nehru since the freedom movement and was especially devoted to him. The letters were in Hindi because Kamalaji didn't know English—though Nehru did write a few letters in English perhaps to teach her English. I got the final work translated into English. The work presented a most tentalising and honest picture of the life of the other great of the Congress movement and his family, while he passed his days in prisons. A work of about 300 pages, it still has to see the light of day in any of the languages. Alas!

Another work I'd like to mention in this tradition is P.V. Narasimha Rao's autobiographical novel, 'The Insider,' which was penned chiefly to expose the Congress leaders' culture of corruption ever since it started ruling in the country. The work is not only very courageous, it has high literary merit, because the author was essentially a man of letters. I had the honour to publish it in Hindi and also translate almost one-third of this work of over 800 pages. It had a remarkable sense of humour, a rarity in Indian writing, all the more striking from a glum-looking person famous for his silent pouting lips, like PVNR. I used to dictate the translation to my steno, while doing other office work, and on occasions we burst out laughing over his unequalled descriptions. I was fortunate to be in the old man's good books, and he talked on a variety of subjects with me. I was struck by his understanding of national issues and his subtility of expression. Unfortunately, his party did not give him his due—he was the party's saviour and would have revived it completely— and, being a sick man, he could not contribute the second part of the work, and passed away. 'The Insider' did make its mark most effectively, but did not get its rightful due—I hold the view that it belongs to the Noble Prize category.

Returning to 'Munia-to-Bhai-to-Mahatma' Gandhi, here is a work all of us interested in contemporary history, polity, economics, social development, and especially, fighting against terrorism—the horror of present times—must read. There is a regular movement these days to develop leaders to 'Lead India', fast growing courtesy the *Times of India* and internet groups like the Jago Party, etc., to change the national situation. Well, here is a work which guides such matters in every respect and in great detail. It is also essential to understand the real Gandhi and his 'truth' which is more relevant today.

As I write these lines, as if as a Godsend, I find in the current issue of *Outlook* a rather detailed account of a group functioning in Palestine for quite some time now, trying to solve their problems on the lines set by Gandhi. This is the first time that such a report has appeared, and that too because an American, Robert Hirschfield, is researching to write a book on the movement. They hold non-violent protests every Friday; an NGO known as Holy Land Trust has been active in the area since the eighties; its leader Mubarak Awad is called 'Abu Gandhi'. There are a few other NGOs also, such as MEND, Wiam, etc., working in this field. What attracted me most is their regular courses in non-violent behaviour: 'over the course of three days, 50 or more participants learn to recognise and express their anger; non-violent conflict-resolution; and strategies for civil disobedience.' Perhaps our own Gandhiites can learn these from them.

It seems that the movement is not very successful, because it is not regarded as 'manly'. The fact remains that Gandhi himself faltered in the face of Islam, and here is a problem which needs further study and rethinking of strategy, especially in this regard, also because present-day terrorism is chiefly related to it.

It is reported that Arun Gandhi, one of Gandhi's grandsons, was associated with this movement but his strident remarks regarding the Jews, compelled him to resign from the group he had helped develop. In this connection I would like to point out that Gandhi himself favoured the right of the Jews to settle down in these lands. While talking to the famous journalist Louis Fischer in 1946 in Delhi, he made these remarks, which I quote verbatim: 'It is the same in Palestine. The Jews have a good case. I told Sydney Silverman, British M.P., the Jews have a prior claim because they were there first. Jesus was a Jew. He was the first flower of Judaism.' So, beware those who blindly oppose the unfortunate community of Jews and their instrument of survival, Judaism!

I would like to complete Gandhi's statement which, though not relevant to the present subject, is illuminating. He says: 'Jesus was a Jew. He was the finest flower of Judaism. You can see that from the four stories of the four apostles. They had untutored minds, Paul was not a jew, he was a Greek, he had an oratorial mind, and he distorted Jesus. Jesus possessed a great force, the love force, but Christianity became disfigured when it went to the west. It became the religion of kings.' How perceptive and correct!

It may also be reported in passing, that **people had started thinking of taking Gandhi to the UNO**. David Sheean, the foreign correspondent of the *Paris Tribune*, visited him in Delhi just two days before his killing. He says,' .... (this) was one of the reasons that had brought me to him,' and he did talk about it, but Gandhi said,' perhaps, if I were spared for more years of service....' Perhaps he knew that two days later, he will not be.

Now because this is a big book of more than 400 pages,

and reading habits are declining rapidly, I've tried to condense it, and edit it, even presenting the significant parts in bold letters to attract attention, and also illustrating it with suitable photographs. I strongly feel that the book should be made compulsory reading in our educational institutions in various short, medium and larger editions.

This autobiography of Gandhi, in his own words, **basically presents the evolution of the Science of Satyagraha**—a fact quite ignored by the publishers—which makes it a yet more significant work like Karl Marx's *Das Capital*. I've tried to give it due prominence by presenting it as a subtitle.

The work presents the story till 1920, when the first major Satyagraha was launched in India and Gandhi had become a major leader of the Congress party. The later story he doesn't relate because it is well known. He also omits the satyagraha in S. Africa which he wrote in detail in *The History of Satyagraha in South Africa*, which, if need be, can be looked up.

I look at this work as a guide book to the 21st century which is passing through unexpected and undeserved terrorist turmoil the world over.

I'll close this note with perhaps the most comprehensive assessment of Gandhi and his contribution to India and the world, by one of the most versatile scholar of our times, author of the 8-vol. *Story of Civilisation* and *Story of Philosophy*—a great favourite of the present writer, a work the like of which was never penned on this hoary subject, translated into a dozen languages of the world and sold in billions in about four decades: Will Durant.

'... We are free to accept and honour Gandhi for his astonishing record of achievements. **First**, though leaping far ahead of the moral consciousness of mankind, which is yet tribal and national, he has helped the international organisation of industries and states to prepare us for the large morality in which the code of conduct between gentlemen will be applied to the conduct of nations. **Second**, he has lifted religion upto a plane where the most unscrupulous statesman must reckon with it as a great force. **Third**, he has for a generation kept a great revolutionary movement from all but sporadic violence; he has refused to unleash the mob; in this way he has a boon to all humanity, which is so sensitive now to disorder anywhere. He has approached one of the fundamental principles of statesmanship to persuade radicals that change must be gradual to be permanent, and to persuade conservatives that change must be. **Fourth**, he has educated his people, he has aroused them, as no man before in their history, to the evils of untouchability, temple prostitution, child marriage, unmarriageable widows, and the traffic in opium. **Fifth**, by the power of imagination and the word, given to India a psychological unity never possessed by it before, making all these races, languages and creeds feel and think alike, as the prelude to action. **Sixth**, he has given to his countrymen what they needed above everything else—pride.'

•••

India, Dare to be Worthy of Your Gandhi!

Rabindranth Tagore once said: 'Perhaps he will not succeed, perhaps he will fail as the Buddha failed and as Christ failed to wean men from their iniquities but he will always be remembered as one who made his life a lesson for all ages to come.'

Now after 60 years of his tragic demise it may be said that he himself did certainly not fail, but his men who came into power, did grievously fail him.

Perhaps in the same context another great writer Pearl S. Buck said: 'There is no weapon, no bomb so powerful as the force of a great good spirit. India will live and become great in our world, only as her people use this priceless force, the force of non-violence, which the life of Gandhi exemplified for them.... oh India, dare to be worthy of your Gandhi.'

Still another author, Edgar P. Snow says: 'Now the world question is: Can Gandhi's technique be applied without Gandhi? Surely the first answer must come from India itself where the Master's teachings are specific and clear.'

Authorspeak

EXPERIMENTS IN THE SCIENCE OF SATYAGRAHA

Four or five years ago, at the instance of some of my nearest coworkers, I agreed to write my autobiography.

It is not my purpose to attempt a real autobiography. I simply want to tell the story of my numerous experiments with truth, and as my life consists of nothing but those experiments, it is true that the story will take the shape of an autobiography. I believe, or at any rate flatter myself with the belief, that a connected account of all these experiments will not be without benefit to the reader. My experiments in the political field are now known. I should certainly like to narrate my experiments in the spiritual field which are known only to myself, and from which I have derived such power as I possess for working in the political field.

What I want to achieve,—what I have been striving and pining to achieve these thirty years,—is self-realization, to see God face to face, to attain Moksha live and move and have my being in pursuit of the goal. All that I do by way of speaking and writing, and all my ventures in the political field, are directed to this same end. But as I have all along believed that what is possible for one is possible for all, my experiments have not been conducted in the closet, but in the open.

I have gone through deep self-introspection, searched myself through and through, and examined and anlaysed every psychological situation. Yet I am far from claiming any finality or infallibility about my conclusions. One claim I do indeed make and it is this. For me they appear to be absolutely correct, and seem for the time being to be final. For if they were not, I should base no action on them.

My purpose being to give an account of various practical applications of these principles, I have given the chapters I propose to write the title of *The Story of My Experiments with Truth*. These will of course include experiments with non-violence, celibacy and other principles of conduct believed to be distinct from truth. But for me, truth is the sovereign principle, which includes numerous other principles. This truth is not only truthfulness in word, but truthfulness in thought also, and not only the relative truth of our conception, but the Absolute Truth, the Eternal Principle, that is God. I worship God as Truth only. I have not yet found Him, but I am seeking after Him. I am prepared to sacrifice the things dearest to me in pursuit of this quest. Even if the sacrifice demanded be my very life, I hope I may be prepared to give it. Often in my progress I have had faint glimpses of the Absolute Truth, God, and daily the conviction if growing upon me that He alone is real and all else is unreal. Let those, who wish, realize how the conviction has grown upon me; let them share my experiments and share also my conviction if they can.

I am not writing this autobiography to please critics. Writing it is itself one of the experiments with truth.

I hope and pray that no one will regard the advice interspersed in the following chapters as authoritative. The experiments narrated should be regarded as illustrations, in the light of which every one may carry on his own experiments according to his own inclination and capacity. I trust that to this limited extent the illustrations will be really helpful; because I am not going either to conceal or understate any ugly things that must be told. I hope to acquaint the reader fully with all my faults and errors. **My purpose is to describe experiments in the science of Satyagraha,** not to say how good I am. In judging myself I shall try to be as harsh as truth, as I want others also to be. Measuring myself by that standard I must exclaim with Surdas:

Where is there a wretch

So wicked and loathsome as I?

I have forsaken my Maker,

So faithless have I been.

For it is an unbroken torture to me that I am still so far from Him Who, as I fully know, governs every breath of my life, and Whose offspring I am. I know that it is the evil passions within that keep me so far from Him, and yet I cannot get away from them.

1925 **—M.K. Gandhi**

Contents

1. Boyhood (From Birth till 18)
19

2. Studies in England (Age 18-21)
53

3. Failure in India (Age 22-23)
94

4. Three Turbulent Years in S. Africa (Age 23-26)
107

5. Promoting the S. Africa Cause in India
156

6. With Family in S. Africa
166

7. At the Congress Session in India
191

8.In South Africa
211

9. Return to India with the Grand New Weapon of Satyagraha
257

Bapu ji
12.4.1930

1

BOYHOOD

(FROM BIRTH TILL AGE 18)

The Gandhis belong to the Bania caste and seem to have been originally grocers. But for three generations, from my grandfather, they have been Prime Ministers in several Kathiawad States. Uttamchand Gandhi, *alias* Ota Gandhi, my grandfather, must have been a man of principle. State intrigues compelled him to leave Porbandar, where he was Diwan, and to seek refuge in Junagadh. There he saluted the Nawab with the left hand. Someone, noticing the apparent discourtesy, asked for an explanation, which was given thus: 'The right hand is already pledged to Porbandar.'

Ota Gandhi married a second time, having lost his first wife. He had four sons by his first wife and two by his second wife. I do not think that in my childhood I ever felt or knew that these sons of Ota Gandhi were not all of the same mother. The fifth of these six brothers was Karamchand Gandhi, *alias* Kaba Gandhi, and the sixth was Tulsidas Gandhi. Both these brothers were Prime Ministers in Porbandar, one after the other. Kaba Gandhi was my father. He was a member of the Rajasthanik Court. It is now extinct, but in those days it was a very influential body for settling disputes between the chiefs and their fellow clansmen. He was for some time Prime Minister in Rajkot and then in Vankaner. He was a pensioner of the Rajkot State when he died.

Kaba Gandhi married four times in succession, having lost his wife each time by death. He had two daughters by his first and second marriages. His last wife, Putlibai, bore him a daughter and three sons, I being the youngest.

My father was a lover of his clan, truthful, brave and generous, but short-tempered. To a certain extent he might have been given to carnal pleasures. For he married for the fourth time when he was over forty. But he was incorruptible and had earned a name for strict impartiality in his family as well as outside. His loyalty to the State was well known. An Assistant Political Agent spoke insultingly of the Rajkot Thakore Saheb, his chief, and he stood up to the insult. The Agent was angry and asked Kaba Gandhi to apologize. This he refused to do and was therefore kept under detention for a few hours. But when the Agent saw that Kaba Gandhi was adamant, he ordered him to be released.

My father never had any ambition to accumulate riches and left us very little property.

The outstanding impression my mother has left on my memory is that of saintliness. She was deeply religious. She would not think of taking her meals without her daily prayers. Going to Haveli—the Vaishnava temple—was one of her daily duties. As far as my memory can go back, I do not remember her having ever missed the Chaturmas. She would take the hardest vows and keep them without flinching. Illness was no excuse for relaxing them. I can recall her once falling ill when she was observing the Chandrayana vow, but the illness was not allowed to interrupt the observance. To keep two or three consecutive fasts was nothing to her. Living on one meal a day during Chaturmas was a habit with her. Not content with that she fasted every alternate day during one Chaturmas. During another Chaturmas she vowed not to have food without seeing the sun. We children on those days would stand, staring at the sky, waiting to announce the appearance of the sun to our mother. Everyone knows that at the height of the rainy season the sun often does not condescend to show his face. And I remember days when, at his sudden appearance, we would rush and announce it to her. She would run out to see with her own eyes, but by that time the fugitive sun would be gone, thus depriving her of her meal. "That does not matter," she would say cheerfully, "God did not want me to eat today." And then she would return to her round of duties.

My mother had strong commonsense. She was well informed about all matters of State, and ladies of the court thought highly of her intelligence. Often I would accompany her, exercising the privilege of childhood, and I still remember many lively discussions she had with the widowed mother of the Thakore Saheb.

Of these parents I was born at Porbandar, otherwise known as Sudamapuri, on the 2nd October, 1869.

I passed my childhood in Porbandar. I recollect having been put to school. It was with some difficulty that I got through the multiplication tables. The fact that I recollect nothing more of those days than having learnt, in company with other boys, to call our teacher all kinds of names, would strongly suggest that my intellect must have been sluggish, and my memory raw.

A Shy, Honest Boy

I must have been about seven when my father left Porbandar for Rajkot to become a member of the Rajasthanik Court. There I was put into a primary school, and I can well recollect those days, including the names and other particulars of the teachers who taught me. As at Porbandar, so here, there is hardly anything to note about my studies. **I could only have been a mediocre student.** From this school I went to the suburban school and thence to the high school, having already reached my twelfth year. I do not remember having ever told a lie, during this short period, either to my teachers or to my school-mates. I used to be very shy and avoided all company. My books and my lessons were my sole companions. To be at school at the stroke of the hour and to run back home as soon as the school closed,—that was my daily habit. I literally ran back, because I could not bear to talk to anybody. I was even afraid lest anyone should poke fun at me.

There is an incident which occurred at the examination during my first year at the high school and which is worth recording. Mr. Giles, the Educational Inspector, had come on a visit of inspection. He had set us five words to write as a spelling exercise. One of the words was 'kettle'. I had misspelt it. **The teacher tried to prompt me with the point of his boot, but I would not be prompted.** It was beyond me to see that he wanted me to copy the spelling from my neighbour's slate, for I had thought that the teacher was there to supervise us against copying. The result was that all the boys, except myself, were found to have spelt every word correctly. Only I had been stupid. The teacher tried later to bring this stupidity home to me, but without effect. I never could learn the art of 'copying'.

Yet the incident did not in the least diminish my respect for my teacher. I was by nature, blind to the faults of elders. Later I came to know of many other failings of this teacher, but my regard for him remained the same. For I had learnt to carry out the orders of elders, not to scan their actions.

Two other incidents belonging to the same period have always clung to my memory. As a rule I had a distaste for any reading beyond my school books. The daily lessons had to be done, because I disliked, being taken to task by my teacher as much as I disliked deceiving him. Therefore, I would do the lessons, but often without my mind in them. Thus when even the lessons could not be done properly, there was of course no question of any extra reading. But somehow my eyes fell on a book purchased by my father. It was *Shravana Pitribhakti Nataka* (a play about Shravana's devotion to his parents). I read it with intense interest. There came to our place about the same time itinerant showmen. One of the pictures I was shown was of Shravana carrying, by means of slings fitted for his shoulders, his blind parents on a pilgrimage. The book and the picture left an indelible impression on my mind. 'Here is an example for you to copy,' I said to myself. The agonized lament of the parents over Shravana's death is still fresh in my memory. The melting tune moved me deeply, and I played it on a concertina which my father had purchased for me.

There was a similar incident connected with another play. Just about this time, I had secured my father's permission to see a play performed by a certain dramatic company. This play—*Harishchandra*—captured my heart. I could never be tired of seeing it. But how often should I be permitted to go? It

Gandhi Album–1

haunted me and I must have acted Harishchandra to myself times without number. 'Why should not all be truthful like Harishchandra?' was the question I asked myself day and night. To follow truth and to go through all the ordeals Harishchandra went through was the one ideal it inspired in me. I literally believed in the story of Harishchandra. The thought of it all often made me weep. My commonsense tells me today that Harishchandra could not have been a historical character. Still both Harishchandra and Shravana are living realities for me, and I am sure I should be moved as before if I were to read those plays again today.

Married at 13

Much as I wish that I had not to write this chapter, I know that I shall have to swallow many such bitter draughts in the course of this narrative. And I cannot do otherwise, if I claim to be a worshipper of Truth. It is my painful duty to have to record here my marriage at the age of thirteen. As I see the youngsters of the same age about me who are under my care, and think of my own marriage, I am inclined to pity myself and to congratulate them on having escaped my lot. I can see no moral argument in support of such a preposterously early marriage.

Let the reader make no mistake. I was married, not betrothed. It appears that I was betrothed thrice, though without my knowledge. I was told that two girls chosen for me had died in turn, and therefore I infer that I was betrothed three times. I have a faint recollection, however, that the third betrothal took place in my seventh year. But I do not recollect having been informed about it. In the present chapter I am talking about my marriage, of which I have the clearest recollection.

It will be remembered that we were three brothers. The first was already married. The elders decided to marry my second brother, who was two or three years my senior, a cousin, possibly a year older, and me, all at the same time. In doing so there was no thought of our welfare, much less our wishes. It was purely a question of their own convenience and economy.

It was only through these preparations that we got warning of the coming event. I do not think it meant to me anything more than the prospect of good clothes to wear, drum beating, marriage processions, rich dinners and a strange girl to play with. The carnal desire came later. I propose to draw the curtain over my shame, except for a few details worth recording.

So my brother and I were both taken to Porbandar from Rajkot. There are some amusing details of the preliminaries to the final drama—e.g., smearing our bodies all over with turmeric paste—but I must omit them.

My father was a Diwan, but nevertheless a servant, and all the more so because he was in favour with the Thakore Saheb. The latter would not let him go until the last moment. And when he did so, he ordered for my father special stage coaches, reducing the journey by two days. But the fates had willed otherwise. Porbandar is 120 miles from Rajkot,—a cart journey of five days. My father did the distance in three, but the coach toppled over in the third stage, and he sustained severe injuries. He arrived bandaged all over. Both his and our interest in the coming event was half destroyed, but the ceremony had to be gone through. For how could the marriage dates be changed? However, I forgot my grief over my father's injuries in the childish amusement of the wedding.

I was devoted to my parents. But no less was I devoted to the passions that flesh is heir to. I had yet to learn that all happiness and pleasure should be sacrificed in devoted service to my parents. And yet, as though by way of punishment for my desire for pleasures, an incident happened, which has ever since rankled in my mind and which I will relate later.

My father put on a brave face in spite of his injuries, and took full part in the wedding. I can picture to myself, even today, how we sat on our wedding dais, how we performed the Saptapadi, how we, the newly wedded husband and wife, put the sweet Kansar into each other's mouth, and how we began to live together, and oh! that first night. Two innocent children all unwittingly hurled themselves into the ocean of life. My brother's wife had thoroughly coached me about my behaviour on the first night. I do not know who had coached my wife. I have never asked her about it, nor am I inclined to do so now.

The reader may be sure that we were too nervous to face each other. We were certainly too shy. How was I to talk to her, and what was I to say? The coaching could not carry me far. But no coaching is really necessary in such matters. The impressions of the former birth are potent enough to make all coaching superfluous. We gradually began to know each other, and to speak freely together. We were the same age. But I took no time in assuming the authority of a husband.

Playing the Husband

About the time of my marriage, little pamphlets costing a pice, or a pie (I now forget how much), used to be issued, in which conjugal love, thrift, child marriages, and other such subjects were discussed. Whenever I came across any of these, I used to go through them cover to cover, and it was a habit with me to forget what I did not like, and to carry out in practice whatever I liked. Lifelong faithfulness to the wife, inculcated in these booklets as the duty of the husband, remained permanently imprinted on my heart. Furthermore, the passion for truth was innate in me, and to be false to her was therefore out of the question. And then there was very little chance of my being faithless at that tender age.

But the lesson of faithfulness had also an untoward effect. 'If I should be pledged to be faithful to my wife, she also should be pledged to be faithful to me,' I said to myself. The thought made me a jealous husband. Her duty was easily converted into my right to exact faithfulness from her, and if it had to be exacted, I should be watchfully tenacious of the right. I had absolutely no reason to suspect my wife's fidelity, but **jealousy does not wait for reasons. I must needs be for ever on the lookout regarding her movements, and therefore she could not go anywhere without my permission. This sowed the seeds of a bitter quarrel between us.** The restraint was virtually a sort of imprisonment. And Kasturbai was not the

Gandhi Album–2

Gandhi at 7

Gandhi at 14

Gandhi at 21, called to the bar, Inner Temple, London

girl to brook any such thing. She made it a point to go out whenever and wherever she liked. More restraint on my part resulted in more liberty being taken by her, and in my getting more and more cross. Refusal to speak to one another thus became the order of the day with us, married children.

I think it was quite innocent of Kasturbai to have taken those liberties with my restrictions. How could a guileless girl brook any restraint on going to the temple or on going on visits to friends? If I had the right to impose restrictions on her, had not she also a similar right? All this is dear to me today. But at that time I had to make good my authority as a husband!

Let not the reader think, however, that ours was a life of unrelieved bitterness. For my severities were all based on love. I wanted to *make* my wife an ideal wife. My ambition was to *make* her live a pure life, learn what I learnt, and identify her life and thought with mine.

I do not know whether Kasturbai had any such ambition. She was illiterate. By nature she was simple, independent, persevering and, with me at least, reticent. She was not impatient of her ignorance and I do not recollect my studies having ever spurred her to go in for a similar adventure. I fancy, therefore, that my ambition was all one-sided. My passion was entirely centred on one woman, and I wanted it to be reciprocated. But even if there were no reciprocity, it could not be all unrelieved misery because there was active love on one side at least.

I must say **I was passionately fond of her. Even at school I used to think of her, and the thought of nightfall and our subsequent meeting was ever haunting me. Separation was unbearable. I used to keep her awake till late in the night with my idle talk.** If with this devouring passion there had not been in me a burning attachment to duty, I should either have fallen a prey to disease and premature death, or have sunk into a burdensome existence. But the appointed tasks had to be gone through every morning, and lying to anyone was out of the question. It was this last thing that saved me from many a pitfall.

I have already said that Kasturbai was illiterate. **I was very anxious to teach her, but lustful love left me no time. For one thing, the teaching had to be done against her will, and that too at night. I dared not meet her in the presence of the elders, much less talk to her.** Kathiawad had then, and to a certain extent has even today, its own peculiar, useless and barbarous Purdah. Circumstances were thus unfavourable. I must therefore confess that most of my efforts to instruct Kasturbai in our youth were unsuccessful. And when I awoke from the sleep of lust, I had already launched forth into public life, which did not leave me much spare time. **I failed likewise to instruct her through private tutors. As a result Kasturbai can now with difficulty write simple letters and understand simple Gujarati.** I am sure that, had my love for her been absolutely untainted with lust, she would be a learned lady today, for I could then have conquered her dislike for studies. I know that nothing is impossible for pure love.

I have mentioned one circumstance that more or less saved me from the disasters of lustful love. There is another worth noting. Numerous examples have convinced me that God ultimately saves him whose motive is pure. Along with the cruel custom of child marriages, Hindu society has another custom which to a certain extent diminishes the evils of the former. Parents do not allow young couples to stay together long. The child-wife spends more than half her time at her father's place. Such was the case with us. That is to say, during the first five years of our married life (from the age of 13 to 18), we could not have lived together longer than an aggregate period of three years. We would hardly have spent six months together, when there would be a call to my wife from her parents. Such calls were very unwelcome in those days, but they saved us both. **At the age of eighteen I went to England, and this meant a long and healthy spell of separation.** Even after my return from England we hardly stayed together longer than six months. For I had to run up and down between Rajkot and Bombay. Then came the call from South Africa, and that found me already fairly free from the carnal appetite.

At the High School

I have already said that I was learning at the high school when I was married. We three brothers were learning at the same school. The eldest brother was in a much higher class, and the brother who was married at the same time as I was, only one class ahead of me. **Marriage resulted in both of us wasting a year.** Indeed the result was even worse for my brother, for he gave up studies altogether.

My studies were continued. I was not regarded as a dunce at the high school. I always enjoyed the affection of my teachers. Certificates of progress and character used to be sent to the parents every year. I never had a bad certificate. In fact I even won prizes after I passed out of the second standard. In the fifth and sixth I obtained scholarships of rupees four and ten respectively, an achievement for which I have to thank good luck more than my merit.

My own recollection is that I had not any high regard for my ability. I used to be astonished whenever I won prizes and scholarships. But I very jealously guarded my character. The least little blemish drew tears from my eyes. When I merited, or seemed to the teacher to merit, a rebuke, it was unbearable for me. I remember having once received corporal punishment. I did not so much mind the punishment, as the fact that it was considered my desert. I wept piteously. That was when I was in the first or second standard.

There was another such incident during the time when I was in the seventh standard. Dorabji Edulji Gimi was the headmaster then. He was popular among boys, as he was a disciplinarian, a man of method and a good teacher. He had made gymnastics and cricket compulsory for boys of the upper standards. **I disliked both. I never took part in any exercise, cricket or football, before they were made compulsory.** My shyness was one of the reasons for this aloofness, which I now see was wrong.

I may mention, however, that I was none the worse for abstaining from exercise. That was because I had read in books about the benefits of long walks in the open air, and having

Gandhi Album–3

Gandhi (4th from left) as Barrister in S. Africa

Gandhi at 30 (5th from left, second row) organised an Ambulance Corps of 1100 persons on the outbreak of Boer War.

liked the advice, I had formed a habit of taking walks, which has still remained with me. These walks gave me a fairly hardy constitution.

The reason of my dislike for gymnastics was my keen desire to serve as nurse to my father. As soon as the school closed, I would hurry home and begin serving him. Compulsory exercise came directly in the way of this service. I requested Mr. Gimi to exempt me from gymnastic, so that I might be free to serve my father. But he would not listen to me. Now it so happened that one Saturday, when we had school in the morning, I had to go from home to the school for gymnastics at 4 o'clock in the afternoon. I had no watch, and the clouds deceived me. Before I reached the school the boys had all left. The next day Mr. Gimi, examining the roll, found me marked absent. Being asked the reason for absence, I told him what had happened. He refused to believe me and ordered me to pay a fine of one or two annas (I cannot now recall how much).

I was convicted of lying! That deeply pained me. How was I to prove my innocence? There was no way. I cried in deep anguish. I saw that a man of truth must also be a man of care. This was the first and last instance of my carelessness in school. I have a faint recollection that I finally succeeded in getting the fine remitted. The exemption from exercise was of course obtained, as my father wrote himself to the headmaster saying that he wanted me at home after school.

But though I was none the worse for having neglected exercise, I am still paying the penalty of another neglect. I do not know whence I got the notion that good handwriting was not a necessary part of education, but I retained it until I went to England. When later, especially in South Africa, I saw the beautiful handwriting of lawyers and young men born and educated in South Africa, I was ashamed of myself and repented of my neglect. I saw that bad hanwriting should be regarded as a sign of an imperfect education. I tried later to improve mine, but it was too late. I could never repair the neglect of my youth. Let every young man and woman be warned by my example.

Two more reminiscences of my school days are worth recording. I had lost one year because of my marriage, and the teacher wanted me to make good the loss by skipping a class—a privilege usually allowed to industrious boys. I therefore had only six months in the third standard and was promoted to the fourth after the examinations which are followed by the summer vacation. **English became the medium of instruction in most subjects from the fourth standard. I found myself completely at sea.** Geometry was a new subject in which I was not particularly strong, and the English medium made it still more difficult for me. The teacher taught the subject very well but I could now follow him. Often I would lose heart and think of going back to the standard, feeling that the packing of two years' studies into a single year was too ambitious. But this would discredit not only me, but also the teacher. So the fear of the double discredit kept me at my post. When, however, with much effort I reached the thirteenth proposition of Euclid, the utter simplicity of the subject was suddenly revealed to me. A subject which only required a pure and simple use of one's reasoning powers could not be difficult.

Samskrit, however, proved a harder task. In Samskrit everything had to be learnt by heart. This subject also was commenced from the fourth standard. As soon as I entered the sixth I became disheartened. The teacher was a hard taskmaster, anxious, as I thought, to force the boys. There was a sort of rivalry going on between the Samskrit and the Persian teachers. The Persian teacher was lenient. The boys used to talk among themselves that Persian was very easy and the Persian teacher very good and considerate to the students. The 'easiness' tempted me and one day I sat in the Persian class. The Samskrit teacher was grieved. He called me to his side and said: 'How can you forget that you are the son of a Vaishnava father? Won't you learn the language of your own religion? If you have any difficulty, why not come to me? I want to teach you students Samskrit to the best of my ability. As you proceed further, you will find in it things of absorbing interest. You should not lose heart. Come and sit again in the Samskrit class.'

This kindness put me to shame. I could not disregard my teacher's affection. Today I cannot but think with gratitude of Krishnashankar Pandya. For if I had not acquired the little Samskrrt that I learnt then, I should have found it difficult to take any interest in our sacred books. In fact I deeply regret that I was not able to acquire a more thorough knowledge of the language, because **I have since realized that every Hindu boy and girl should possess sound Samskrit learning.**

Eating Meat

Amongst my few friends at the high school I had, at different times, two who might be called intimate. One of these friendships did not last long, though I never forsook my friend. He forsook me, because I made friends with the other. This latter friendship I regard as a tragedy in my life. It lasted long. I formed it in the spirit of a reformer.

This companion was originally my elder brother's friend. They were classmates. I knew his weaknesses, but I regarded him as a faithful friend. My mother, my eldest brother, and my wife warned me that I was in bad company. I was too proud to heed my wife's warning. But I dared not go against the opinion of my mother and my eldest brother. Nevertheless I pleaded with them saying, 'I know he has the weaknesses you attribute to him, but you do not know his virtues. He cannot lead me astray, as my association with him is meant to reform him. For I am sure that if he reforms his ways, he will be a splendid man. I beg you not to be anxious on my account.'

A wave of 'reform' was sweeping over Rajkot at the time when I first came across this friend. He informed me that many of our teachers were secretly taking meat and wine. He also named many well-known people of Rajkot as belonging to the same company. There were also, I was told, some high-school boys among them.

I was surprised and pained. I asked my friend the reason and he explained it thus. **'We are a weak people because we**

Gandhi Album–4

Gandhi (seated in the middle) with members of Anglo-Indian Association, Transvaal—1912.

Gandhi (seated, left) at Johannesburg

do not eat meat. The English are able to rule over us, because they are meateaters. You know how hardy I am, and how great a runner too. It is because I am a meateater. Meateaters do not have boils or tumours, and even if they sometimes happen to have any, these heal quickly. There is nothing like trying.'

All these pleas on behalf of meateating were not advanced at a single sitting. They represent the substance of a long and elaborate argument which my friend was trying to impress upon me from time to time. My elder brother had already fallen. He therefore supported my friend's argument. I certainly looked feeble-bodied by the side of my brother and this friend. This friend's exploits cast a spell over me. He could run long distances and extraordinarily fast. He was an adept in high and long jumping. He could put up with any amount of corporal punishment.

Moreover, I was a coward. I used to be haunted by the fear of thieves, ghosts, and serpents. I did not dare to stir out of doors at night. Darkness was a terror to me. It was almost impossible for me to sleep in the dark, as I would imagine ghosts coming from one direction, thieves from another and serpents from a third. I could not therefore bear to sleep without a light in the room. How could I disclose my fears to my wife, no child, but already at the threshold of youth, sleeping by my side? I knew that she had more courage than I, and I felt ashamed of myself. She knew no fear of serpents and ghosts. She could go out anywhere in the dark.

A doggerel of the Gujarati poet Narmad was in vogue amongst us schoolboys, as follows:

Behold the mighty Englishman
He rules the Indian small,
Because being a meateater
He is five cubits tall.

All this had its due effect on me. I was beaten. It began to grow on me that meateating was good, that it would make me strong and daring, and that, if the whole country took to meateating, the English could be overcome.[1]

A day was thereupon fixed for beginning the experiment. It had to be conducted in secret. The Gandhis were Vaishnavas. My parents were particularly staunch Vaishnavas. They would regularly visit the Haveli. The family had even its own temples. Jainism was strong in Gujarat, and its influence was felt everywhere and on all occasions. I was extremely devoted to my parents. I knew that the moment they came to know of my having eaten meat, they would be shocked to death. Moreover, my love of truth made me extra-cautious. I wished to be strong and daring and wanted my countrymen also to be such, so that we might defeat the English and make India free. The word 'Swaraj' I had not yet heard. But I knew what freedom meant.

So the day came. We went in search of a lonely spot by the river, and there I saw, for the first time in my life—meat. There was baker's bread also. I relished neither. **The goat's meat was as tough as leather. I simply could not eat it.** I was sick and had to leave off eating.

I had a very bad night afterwards. A horrible nightmare haunted me. **Every time I dropped off to sleep it would seem as though a live goat were bleating inside me, and I would jump up full of remorse.** But then I would remind myself that meateating was a duty and so become more cheerful.

My friend was not a man to give in easily. He now began to cook various delicacies with meat and dress them neatly. And for dining, no longer was the secluded spot on the river chosen, but a State house, with its dining hall, and tables and chairs, about which my friend had made arrangements in collusion with the chief cook there. This bait had its effect. **I got over my dislike for bread, forswore my compassion for the goats, and became a relisher of meat-dishes,** if not of meat itself.

This went on for about a year. But not more than half a dozen meat-feasts were enjoyed in all; because the State house

1. The same thing happened in Japan. The Emperor Meiji thought similarly, and the day he started eating meat, the whole country, men in particular, started doing so. (Ed.)

was not available every day, and there was the obvious difficulty about frequently preparing expensive savoury meat-dishes. I had no money to pay for this 'reform'. My friend had therefore always to find the wherewithal.

Whenever I had occasion to indulge in these surreptitious feasts, dinner at home was out of the question. My mother would naturally ask me to come and take my food and want to know the reason why I did not wish to eat. I would say to her, 'I have no appetite today; there is something wrong with my digestion.' It was not without compunction that I devised these pretexts. I knew I was lying, and lying to my mother. I also knew that, if my mother and father came to know of my having become a meateater, they would be deeply shocked. This knowledge was gnawing at my heart.

Therefore I said to myself: 'Though it is essential to eat meat, and also essential to take up food 'reform' in the country, yet **deceiving and lying to one's father and mother is worse than not eating meat. In their lifetime, therefore, meateating must be out of the question. When they are no more and I have found my freedom, I will eat meat openly.**

This decision I communicated to my friend, and I have never since gone back to meat. My parents never knew that two of their sons had become meateaters.

I abjured meat out of the purity of my desire not to lie to my parents, but I did not abjure the company of my friend. My zeal for reforming him had proved disastrous for me, and all the time I was completely unconscious of the fact.

Visiting a Brothel

The same company would have led me into faithlessness to my wife. But I was saved by the skin of my teeth. My friend once took me to a brothel. He sent me in with the necessary instructions. It was all prearranged. The bill had already been paid. I went into the jaws of sin, but God in His infinite mercy protected me against myself. **I was almost struck blind and dumb in this den of vice. I sat near the woman on her bed, but I was tongue-tied. She naturally lost patience with me, and showed me the door, with abuses and insults.** I then

Gandhi Album–5

Gandhi as leader of Satyagrah movement—1914

felt as though my manhood had been injured, and wished to sink into the ground for shame. But I have ever since given thanks to God for having saved me.

I can recall four more similar incidents in my life, and in most of them my good fortune, rather than any effort on my part, saved me. From a strictly ethical point of view, all these occasions must be regarded as moral lapses; for the carnal desire was there, and it was as good as the act. But from the ordinary point of view, a man who is saved from physically committing sin is regarded as saved. And I was saved only in that sense. There are some actions from which an escape is a godsend both for the man who escapes and for those about him. Man, as soon as he gets back his consciousness of right, is thankful to the Divine mercy for the escape. As we know that a man often succumbs to temptation, however much he may resist it, we also know that Providence often intercedes and saves him in spite of himself. How all this happens,—how far a man is free and how far a creature of circumstances,—how far freewill comes into play and where fate enters on the scene,—all this is a mystery and will remain a mystery.

But to go on with the story. Even this was far from opening my eyes to the viciousness of my friend's company. I therefore had many more bitter draughts in store for me, until my eyes were actually opened by an ocular demonstration of some of his lapses quite unexpected by me. But of them later.

One thing, however, I must mention now, as it pertains to the same period. One of the reasons of my differences with my wife was undoubtedly the company of this friend. I was both a devoted and a jealous husband, and **this friend fanned the flame of my suspicions about my wife. I never could doubt his veracity. And I have never forgiven myself the violence of which I have been guilty in often having pained my wife by acting on his information.** Perhaps only a Hindu wife would tolerate these hardships, and that is why I have regarded woman as an incarnation of tolerance. A servant wrongly suspected may throw up his job, a son in the same case may leave his father's roof, and a friend may put an end to the friendship. The wife, if she suspects her husband, will keep quiet, but if the husband suspects her, she is ruined. Where is she to go? A Hindu wife may not seek divorce in a law-court. Law has no remedy: for *her.* And I can never forget or forgive myself for having driven my wife to that desperation.

The canker of suspicion was rooted out only when I understood Ahimsa in all its bearings. I saw then the glory of Brahmacharya and realized that the wife is not the husband's bondslave, but his companion and his helpmate, and an equal partner in all his joys and sorrows—as free as the husband to choose her own path. **Whenever I think of those dark days of doubts and suspicions, I am filled with loathing of my folly and my lustful cruelty, and I deplore my blind devotion to my friend.**

Smoking, Stealing Money, Gold....

A relative and I became fond of smoking. Not that we saw any good in smoking, or were enamoured of the smell of a cigarette. We simply imagined a sort of pleasure in emitting clouds of smoke from our mouths. My uncle had the habit and when we saw him smoking, we thought we should copy his example. But we had no money. So **we began pilfering stumps of cigarettes thrown away by my uncle.**

The stumps, however, were not always available, and could not emit much smoke either. So **we began to steal coins from the servant's pocket money in order to purchase Indian cigarettes.** But the question was where to keep them. We could not of course smoke in the presence of elders. We managed somehow for a few weeks on these stolen coins. In the meantime we heard that the stalks of a certain plant were porous and could be smoked like cigarettes. We got them and began this kind of smoking.

But we were far from being satisfied with such things as these. Our want of independence began to smart. It was unbearable that we should be unable to do anything without the elders' permission. At last, **in sheer disgust, we decided to commit suicide!**

But how were we to do it? From where were we to get the poison? We heard that Dhatura seeds were an effective poison. Off we went to the jungle in search of these seeds, and got them. Evening was thought to be the auspicious hour. We went to Kedarji Mandir, put ghee in the temple-lamp, had the *darshan* and then looked for a lonely corner.

But our courage failed us. Supposing we were not instantly killed? And what was the good of killing ourselves? Why not rather put up with the lack of independence? But we swallowed two or three seeds nevertheless. We dared not take more. Both of us fought shy of death, and decided to go to Ramji Mandir to compose ourselves, and to dismiss the thought of suicide.

I realized that it was not as easy to commit suicide as to contemplate it. And since then, whenever I have heard of someone threatening to commit suicide, it has had little or no effect on me.

The thought of suicide ultimately resulted in both of us bidding good-bye to the habit, of smoking stumps of cigarettes and of stealing the servant's coins for the purpose of smoking.

But much more serious than this theft was the one I was guilty of a little later. I pilfered the coins when I was twelve or thirteen, possibly less. The other theft was committed when I was fifteen. In this case **I stole a bit of gold out of my meateating brother's armlet.** This brother had run into a debt of about twenty-five rupees. He had on his arm an armlet of solid gold. It was not difficult to clip a bit out of it.

Confessing to Father

Well, it was done, and the debt cleared. But this became more than I could bear. I resolved never to steal again. I also made up my mind to confess it to my father. But I did not dare to speak. Not that I was afraid of my father beating me. No. I do not recall his ever having beaten any of us. I was afraid of the pain that I should cause him. But I felt that the risk should be taken; that there could not be a cleansing without a clean confession.

I decided at last to write out the confession, to submit it

to my father, and ask his forgiveness. I wrote it on a slip of paper and handed it to him myself. In this note not only did I confess my guilt, but I asked adequate punishment for it, and closed with a request to him not to punish himself for my offence. I also pledged myself never to steal in future.

I was trembling as I handed the confession to my father. He was then suffering from a fistula and was confined to bed. His bed was a plain wooden plank. I handed him the note and sat opposite the plank.

He read it through, and pearl-drops trickled down his cheeks, wetting the paper. For a moment he closed his eyes in thought and then tore up the note. He had sat up to read it. He again lay down. I also cried. I could see my father's agony. If I were a painter I could draw a picture of the whole scene today. It is still so vivid in my mind.

Those pearl-drops of love cleansed my heart, and washed my sin away. Only he who has experienced such love can know what it is. As the hymn says:

'Only he
Who is smitten with the arrows of love,
Knows its power.'

A Lesson in Ahimsa

This was for me, an object lesson in Ahimsa. Then I could read in it nothing more than a father's love, but today I know that it was pure Ahimsa. When such Ahimsa becomes all-embracing, it transforms everything it touches. There is no limit to its power.

This sort of sublime forgiveness was not natural to my father. I had thought that he would be angry, say hard things, and strike his forehead. But he was so wonderfully peaceful, and I believe this was due to my clean confession. A clean confession, combined with a promise never to commit the sin again, when offered before one who has the right to receive it, is the purest type of repentance. I know that my confession made my father feel absolutely safe about me, and increased his affection for me beyond measure.

My Lust During Father's Death

The time of which I am now speaking is my sixteenth year. My father, as we have seen, was bed-ridden, suffering from a fistula. My mother, an old servant of the house, and I were his principal attendants. I had the duties of a nurse, which mainly consisted in dressing the wound, giving my father his medicine, and compounding drugs whenever they had to be made up at home. Every night I massaged his legs and retired only when he asked me to do so or after he had fallen asleep. I loved to do this service. I do not remember ever having neglected it. All the time at my disposal, after the performance of the daily duties, was divided between school and attending on my father. I would only go out for an evening walk either when he permitted me or when he was feeling well.

This was also the time when my wife was expecting a baby,—a circumstance which, as I can see today, meant a double shame for me. For one thing I did not restrain myself, as I should have done, whilst I was yet a student. And secondly, this carnal lust got the better of what I regarded as my duty to study, and of what was even a greater duty, my devotion to my parents, Shravana having been my ideal since childhood. Every night whilst my hands were busy massaging my father's legs, my mind was hovering about the bed-room,—and that too at a time when religion, medical science and commonsense alike forbade sexual intercourse. (Note that this was a very strong idea in those times. *Ed.*) I was always glad to be relieved from my duty, and went straight to the bed-room after doing obeisance to my father.

At the same time my father was getting worse every day. Ayurvedic physicians had tried all their ointments, Hakims their plasters, and local quacks their nostrums. An English surgeon had also used his skill. As the last and only resort he had recommended a surgical operation. (Another idea of those times—*Ed.*) But the family physician came in the way. He disapproved of an operation being performed at such an advanced age. The physician was competent and well known, and his advice prevailed. The operation was abandoned, and

Gandhi Album–6

Gandhi on his return to India in 1915 (age 46) with Kasturba.

Gandhi in Karachi—1916

various medicines purchased for the purpose were of no account. I have an impression that, if the physician had allowed the operation, the wound would have been easily healed. The operation also was to have been performed by a surgeon who was then well known in Bombay. But God had willed otherwise. When death is imminent, who can think of the right remedy? My father returned from Bombay with all the paraphernalia of the operation, which were now useless. He despaired of living any longer. He was getting weaker and weaker, until at last he had to be asked to perform the necessary functions in bed. But up to the last he refused to do anything of the kind, always insisting on going through the strain of leaving his bed. The Vaishnavite rules about external cleanliness are so inexorable.

Such cleanliness is quite essential no doubt, but Western medical science has taught us that all the functions, including a bath, can be done in bed with the strictest regard to cleanliness, and without the slightest discomfort to the patient, the bed always remaining spotlessly clean. I should regard such cleanliness as quite consistent with Vaishnavism. But my father's insistence on leaving the bed only struck me with wonder then, and I had nothing but admiration for it.

The dreadful night came. My uncle was then in Rajkot. I have a faint recollection that he came to Rajkot having had news that my father was getting worse. The brothers were deeply attached to each other. My uncle would sit near my father's bed the whole day, and would insist on sleeping by his bedside after sending us all to sleep. No one had dreamt that this was to be the fateful night. The danger of course was there.

It was 10-30 or 11 p.m. I was giving the massage. My uncle offered to relieve me. I was glad and went straight to the bed-room. My wife, poor thing, was fast asleep. But how could she sleep when I was there? I woke her up. In five or six minutes, however, the servant knocked at the door. I started with alarm. 'Get up,' he said. 'Father is very ill.' I knew of course that he was very ill, and so I guessed what 'very ill' meant at that moment. I sprang out of bed.

'What is the matter? Do tell me!'

'Father is no more.'

So all was over! I had, but to wring my hands. I felt deeply ashamed and miserable. I ran to my father's room. I saw that, **if animal passion had not blinded me, I should have been spared the torture of separation from my father during his last moments.** I should have been massaging him, and he would have died in my arms. But now it was my uncle who had this privilege. He was so deeply devoted to his elder brother that he had earned the honour of doing him the last services! My father had forebodings of the coming event. He had made a sign for pen and paper, and written: 'Prepare for the last rites.' He had then snapped the amulet off his arm and also his gold necklace of *tulasi*-beads and flung them aside. A moment after this he was no more.

The shame, to which I have referred in a foregoing chapter, was this shame of my carnal desire even at the critical hour of my father's death, which demanded wakeful service. It is a blot I have never been able to efface or forget, and I have always thought that, although my devotion to my parents knew no bounds and I would have given up anything for it, yet it was weighed and found unpardonably wanting because my mind was at the same moment in the grip of lust. **I have therefore always regarded myself as a lustful, though a faithful, husband.** It took me long to get free from the shackles of lust, and I had to pass through many ordeals before I could overcome it.

Before I close this chapter of my double shame, I may mention that the poor mite that was born to my wife scarcely breathed for more than three or four days. Nothing else could be expected.

Entry into Religion

Being born in the Vaishnava faith, I had often to go to the temple, Haveli. But it never appealed to me. I did not like its glitter and pomp. Also I heard rumours of immorality being practised there, and lost all interest in it. Hence I could gain nothing from the Haveli.

But what I failed to get there I obtained from my nurse, an old servant of the family, whose affection for me I still recall. I have said before that there was in me a fear of ghosts and spirits. Rambha, for that was her name, suggested, as a remedy for this fear, the repetition of Ramanama. I had more faith in her than in her remedy, and so at a tender age I began repeating Ramanama to cure my fear of ghosts and spirits. This was of course, shortlived, but the good seed sown in childhood was not sown in vain. I think it is due to the seed sown by that good woman Rambha that today Ramanama is an infallible remedy for me.

Just about this time, a cousin of mine who was a devotee of the *Ramayana* arranged for my second brother and me to learn *Rama-Raksha*. We got it by heart, and made it a rule to recite it every morning after the bath. The practice was kept up as long as we were in Porbandar. As soon as we reached Rajkot, it was forgotten. For I had not much belief in it. I recited it partly because of my pride in being able to recite *Rama-Raksha* with correct pronunciation.

What, however, left a deep impression on me was the reading of the *Ramayana* before my father. During part of his illness my father was in Porbandar. There every evening he used to listen to the *Ramayana*. The reader was a great devotee of Rama—Ladha Maharaj of Bileshvar. It was said of him that he cured himself of his leprosy not by any medicine, but by applying to the affected parts *bilva* leaves which had been cast away after being offered to the image of Mahadev in Bileshvar temple, and by the regular repetition of Ramanama. His faith, it was said, had made him whole. This may or may not be true. We at any rate believed the story. And it is a fact that when Ladha Maharaj began his reading of the *Ramayana* his body was entirely free from leprosy. He had a melodious voice. He would sing the Dohas and Chopais (quatrains), and explain them, losing himself in the discourse and carrying his listeners along with him. I must have been thirteen at that time, but I quite remember being enraptured by his reading. That laid the foundation of my deep devotion to the *Ramayana*.

Gandhi Album–7

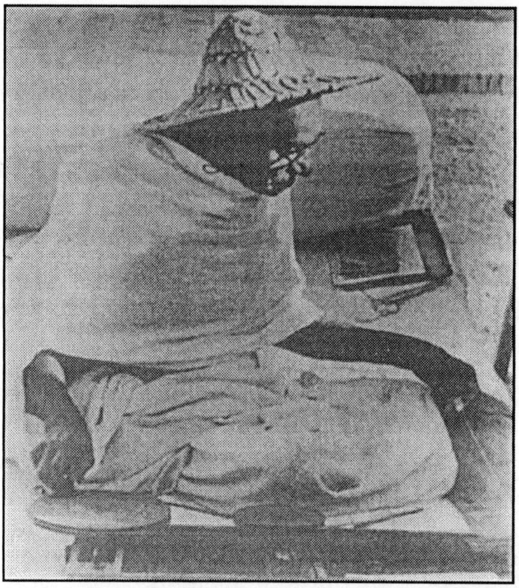

Gandhi at Charkha

Protest march against Salt Tax—1930

Today **I regard the *Ramayana* of Tulasidas as the greatest book in all devotional literature.**

A few months after this we came to Rajkot. There was no *Ramayana* reading there. The *Bhagavat,* however, used to be read on every Ekadashi day. Sometimes I attended the reading, but the reciter was uninspiring. Today I see that the *Bhagavat* is a book which can evoke religious fervour. I have read it in Gujarati with intense interest. But when I heard portions of the original read by Pandit Madan Mohan Malaviya during my twenty-one days' fast, I wished I had heard it in my childhood from such a devotee as he is, so that I could have formed a liking for it at an early age.

In Rajkot, however, I got an early grounding in toleration for all branches of Hinduism and sister religions. For my father and mother I would visit the Haveli as also Shiva's and Rama's temples, and would take or send us youngsters there. Jain monks also would pay frequent visits to my father, and would even go out of their way to accept food from us—non-Jains.

He had, besides, Musalman and Parsi friends, who would talk to him about their own faiths, and he would listen to them always with respect, and often with interest. Being his nurse, I often had a chance to be present at these talks. **These many things combined to inculcate in me a toleration for all faiths.**

Only Christianity was at the time an exception. I developed a sort of dislike for it. And for a reason. In those days **Christian missionaries used to stand in a corner near the high school and hold forth, pouring abuse on Hindus and their gods. I could not endure this.** (A noteworthy statement.—Ed.) I must have stood there to hear them once only, but that was enough to dissuade me from repeating the experiment. About the same time, I heard of a well-known Hindu having been converted to Christianity. It was the talk of the town that, when he was baptized, he had to eat beef and drink liquor, that he also had to change his clothes, and that thenceforth he began to go about in European costume including a hat. These things got on my nerves. Surely, thought I, a religion that compelled one to eat beef, drink liquor, and change one's own clothes did hot deserve the name. I also heard that the new convert had already begun abusing the religion of his ancestors, their customs and their country. All these things created in me a dislike for Christianity.

But the fact that I had learnt to be tolerant to other religions did not mean that I had any living faith in God. I happened, about this time, to come across *Manusmriti* which was amongst my father's collection. The story of the creation and similar things in it did not impress me very much, but on the contrary, made me incline towards atheism.

There was a cousin of mine, still alive, for whose intellect I had great regard. To him I turned with my doubts. But he could not resolve them. He sent me away with this answer: 'When you grow up, you will be able to solve these doubts yourself. These questions ought not to be raised at your age.' I was silenced, but was not comforted. Chapters about diet and the like in *Manusmriti* seemed to me to run contrary to daily practice. To my doubts as to this also, I got the same answer.

But one thing took deep root in me—**the conviction that morality is the basis of things, and that truth is the substance of all morality.**

•••

Gandhi Album–8

Gandhi at the Round Table Conference, London, 1931, after his release from Yervada prison

2

Studies in England

(Age 18-21)

I passed the matriculation examination in 1887. It then used to be held at two centres, Ahmedabad and Bombay. The general poverty of the country naturally led Kathiawad students to prefer the nearer and the cheaper centre. The poverty of my family likewise dictated to me the same choice. This was my first journey from Rajkot to Ahmedabad and that too without a companion.

My elders wanted me to pursue my studies at college after the matriculation. There was a college in Bhavnagar as well as in Bombay, and as the former was cheaper, **I decided to go there and join the Samaldas College. I went, but found myself entirely at sea.** Everything was difficult. I could not follow, let alone taking interest in, the professors' lectures. It was no fault of theirs. The professors in that College were regarded as first-rate. But I was so raw. **At the end of the first term, I returned home.**

Bat at-Law Very Easy

We had in Mavji Dave, who was a shrewd and learned Brahmin, an old friend and adviser of the family. He had kept up his connection with the family even after my father's death. He happened to visit us during my vacation. In conversation with my mother and elder brother, he inquired about my studies. Learning that I was at Samaldas College, he said: 'The times are changed. And none of you can expect to succeed to your father's *gadi* without having had a proper education. Now as this boy is still pursuing his studies, you should all look to him to keep the *gadi.* It will take him four or five years to get his B.A. degree, which will at best qualify him for a sixty rupees' post, not for a Diwanship. If like my son he went in for law, it would take him still longer, by which time there would be a host of lawyers aspiring for a Diwan's post. I would far rather that you sent him to England. **My son Kevalram says it is very easy to become a barrister. In three years' time he will return.** Also expenses will not exceed four to five thousand rupees. Think of that barrister who has just come back from England. How stylishly he lives! He could get the Diwanship for the asking. **I would strongly advise you to send Mohandas to England this very year.** Kevalram has numerous friends in England. He will give notes of introduction to them, and Mohandas will have an easy time of it there.

Joshiji—that is how we used to call old Mavji Dave—turned to me with complete assurance, and asked: 'Would you not rather go to England than study here?' Nothing could have been more welcome to me. I was fighting shy of my difficult studies. So I jumped at the proposal and said that the sooner I was sent the better. It was no easy business to pass examinations quickly. Could I not be sent to qualify for the medical profession?

My brother interrupted me: 'Father never liked it. He had you in mind when he said that we Vaishnavas should have nothing to do with dissection of dead bodies. Father intended you for the bar.'

Joshiji went away, and I began building castles in the air.

My elder brother was greatly exercised in his mind. How was he to find the wherewithal to send me? And was it proper to trust a young man like me to go abroad alone?

My mother was sorely perplexed. She did not like the idea of parting with me. This is how she tried to put me off: 'Uncle,' she said, 'is now the eldest member of the family. He should first be consulted. If he consents we will consider the matter.'

My brother had another idea. He said to me: 'We have a certain claim on the Porbandar State. Mr. Lely is the

Administrator. He thinks highly of our family and Uncle is in his good books. It is just possible that he might recommend you for some State help for your education in England.'

I liked all this and got ready to start off for Porbandar. **There was no railway in those days. It was a five days' bullock-cart journey.**

I have already said that I was a coward. But at that moment my cowardice vanished before the desire to go to England, which completely possessed me. **I hired a bullock-cart as far as Dhoraji, and from Dhoraji I took a camel in order to get to Porbandar a day quicker.** This was my first camel-ride.

I arrived at last, did obeisance to my uncle, and told him everything. He thought it over and said: 'I am not sure whether it is possible for one to stay in England without prejudice to one's own religion. From all I have heard, I have my doubts. When I meet these big barristers, I see no difference between their life and that of Europeans. They know no scruples regarding food. Cigars are never out of their mouths. They dress as shamelessly as Englishmen. All that would not be in keeping with our family tradition. I am shortly going on a pilgrimage and have not many years to live. At the threshold of death, how dare I give you permission to go to England, to cross the seas? But I will not stand in your way. It is your mother's permission which really matters. If she permits you, then godspeed! Tell her I will not interfere. You will go with my blessings.'

'I could expect nothing more from you,' said I. 'I shall now try to win Mother over. But would you not recommend me to Mr. Lely?'

'How can I do that?' said he. 'But he is a good man. You ask for an appointment telling him how you are connected. He will certainly give you one and may even help you.'

I wrote to Mr. Lely, who asked me to see him at his residence. He saw me as he was ascending the staircase; and saying curtly, 'Pass your B.A. first and then see me. No help can be given you now,' he hurried upstairs. I had made elaborate preparations to meet him. I had carefully learnt up a few sentences and had bowed low and saluted him with both hands. But all to no purpose!

I returned to Rajkot from Porbandar and reported all that had happened. I consulted Joshiji, who of course advised even incurring a debt if necessary. I suggested the disposal of my wife's ornaments, which could fetch about two to three thousand rupees. My brother promised to find the money somehow.

My mother, however, was still unwilling. She had begun making minute inquiries. Someone had told her that young men got lost in England. Someone else had said that they took to meat; and yet another that they could not live there without liquor. 'How about all this?' she asked me. I said: 'Will you not trust me? I shall not lie to you. I swear that I shall not touch any of those things. If there were any such danger, would Joshiji let me go?' 'I can trust you,' she said. 'But how can I trust you in a distant land? I am dazed and know not what to do. I will ask Becharji Swami.'

Becharji Swami was originally a Modh Bania, but had now become a Jain monk. He too was a family adviser like Joshiji. He came to my help, and said: 'I shall get the boy solemnly to take the three vows, and then he can be allowed to go.' He administered the oath and **I vowed not to touch wine, woman and meat.** This done, my mother gave her permission.

The high school had a send-off in my honour. It was an uncommon thing for a young man of Rajkot to go to England. I had written out a few words of thanks. But I could scarcely stammer them out. I remember how my head reeled and how my whole frame shook as I stood up to read them.

With the blessings of my elders, I started for Bombay. This was my first journey from Rajkot to Bombay. My brother accompanied me.

But on arrival there friends told my brother that the Indian Ocean was rough in June and July, and as this was my first voyage, I should not be allowed to sail until November.

Gandhi Album–9

Gandhi in London

Someone also reported that a steamer had just been sunk in a gale.

This made my brother uneasy, and he refused to take the risk of allowing me to sail immediately. Leaving me with a friend in Bombay, he returned to Rajkot to resume his duty. He put the money for my travelling expenses in the keeping of a brother-in-law, and left word with some friends to give me whatever help I might need.

Time hung heavily on my hands in Bombay. I dreamt continually of going to England.

Caste and Religions Objections

Meanwhile my caste-people were agitated over my going abroad. No Modh Bania had been to England up to now, and if I dared to do so, I ought to be brought to book! A general meeting of the caste was called and I was summoned to appear before it. I went. How I suddenly managed to muster up courage I do not know. Nothing daunted, and without the slightest hesitation, I came before the meeting. The Sheth—the headman of the community—who was distantly related to me and had been on very good terms with my father, thus accosted me:

'In the opinion of the caste, your proposal to go to England is not proper. Our religion forbids voyages abroad. We have also heard that it is not possible to live there without compromising our religion. One is obliged to eat and drink with Europeans!'

To which I replied: 'I do not think it is at all against our religion to go to England. I intend going there for further studies. And I have already solemnly promised to my mother to abstain from three things you fear most. I am sure the vow will keep me safe.'

'But we tell you,' rejoined the Sheth, 'that it is *not* possible to keep our religion there. You know my relations with your father and you ought to listen to my advice.'

'I know those relations,' said I. 'And you are as an elder to me. But I am helpless in this matter. I cannot alter my resolve to go to England. My father's friend and adviser, who is a learned Brahmin, sees no objection to my going to England, and my mother and brother have also given me their permission.'

'But will you disregard the orders of the caste?'

'I am really helpless. I think the caste should not interfere in the matter.'

This incensed the Sheth. He swore at me. I sat unmoved. So the Sheth pronounced his order: **'This boy shall be treated as an outcaste from today**. Whoever helps him or goes to see him off at the dock shall be punishable with a fine of one rupee four annas.'

The order had no effect on me, and I took my leave of the Sheth.

But I wondered how my brother would take it. Fortunately, he remained firm and wrote to assure me that I had his permission to go, the Sheth's order notwithstanding.

As I was worrying over my predicament, I heard that a Junagadh vakil was going to England, for being called to the bar, by a boat sailing on the 4th of September. I met the friends to whose care my brother had commended me. They also agreed that I should not let go the opportunity of going in such company. There was no time to be lost. I wired to my brother for permission, which he granted. I asked my brother-in-law to give me the money. But he referred to the order of the Sheth and said that he could not afford to lose caste.

I then sought a friend of the family and requested him to accommodate me to the extent of my passage and sundries, and to recover the loan from my brother. The friend was not only good enough to accede to my request, but he cheered me up as well. I was so thankful. With part of the money I at once purchased the passage. Then I had to equip myself for the voyage. There was another friend who had experience in the matter. He got clothes and other things ready. Some of the clothes I liked and some I did not like at all. The necktie, which I delighted in wearing later; I then abhorred. The short jacket I looked upon as immodest.

A berth was reserved for me by my friends in the same cabin as that of Sjt. Tryambakrai Mazmudar, the Junagadh vakil. They also commended me to him. He was an experienced man of mature age and knew the world. I was yet a stripling of eighteen without any experience of the world. Sjt. Mazmudar told my friends not to worry about me.

I sailed at last from Bombay on the 4th of September.

In London

I did not feel at all sea-sick. But as the days passed, I became fidgety. I felt shy even in speaking to the steward. **I was quite unaccustomed to talking English,** and except for Sjt. Mazmudar all the other passengers in the second saloon were English. I could not speak to them. For I could rarely follow their remarks when they came up to speak to me, and even when I understood I could not reply. I had to frame every sentence in my mind, before I could bring it out. I was innocent of the use of knives and forks and had not the boldness to inquire what dishes on the menu were free of meat. **I therefore never took meals at table but always had them in my cabin, and they consisted principally of sweets and fruits which I had brought with me.** Sjt. Mazmudar had no difficulty, and he mixed with everybody. He would move about freely on deck, while I hid myself in the cabin the whole day, only venturing up on deck when there were but few people. Sjt. Mazmudar kept pleading with me to associate with the passengers and to talk with them freely. He told me that lawyers should have a long tongue, and related to me his legal experiences. **He advised me to take every possible opportunity of talking English, and not to mind making mistakes** which were obviously unavoidable with a foreign tongue. But nothing could make me conquer my shyness.

An English passenger, taking kindly to me, drew me into conversation. He was older than I. He asked me what I ate, what I was, where I was going, why I was shy, and so on. He also advised me to come to table. He laughed at my insistence on abjuring meat, and said in a friendly way when we were in the Red Sea: 'It is all very well so far but you will have to revise

Gandhi Album–10

Gandhi with Romain Rolland—1931

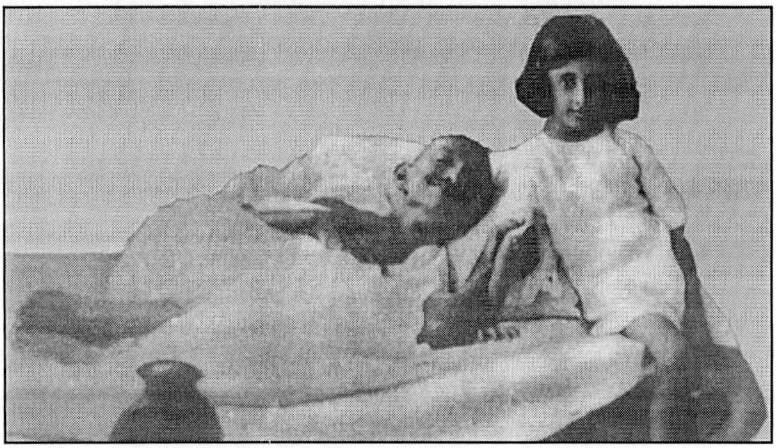

Gandhi with Indira as a girl

your decision in the Bay of Biscay. And it is so cold in England that one cannot possibly live there without meat.'

'But I have heard that people *can* live there without eating meat,' I said.

'Rest assured it is a fib,' said he. 'No one, to my knowledge, lives there without being a meateater. Don't you see that I am not asking you to take liquor, though I do so? But I do think you should eat meat, for you cannot live without it.'

'I thank you for your kind advice, but I have solemnly promised to my mother not to touch meat, and therefore I cannot think of taking it. If it be found impossible to get on without it, I will either go back to India than eat meat in order to remain there.'

We entered the Bay of Biscay, but I did not begin to feel the need either of meat or liquor. I had been advised to collect certificates of my having abstained from meat, and I asked the English friend to give me one. He gladly gave it and I treasured it for some time. But when I saw later that one could get such a certificate in spite of being a meateater, it lost all its charm for me. If my word was not to be trusted, where was the use of possessing a certificate in the matter?

However, we reached Southampton, as far as I remember, on a Saturday. On the boat I had worn a black suit, the white flannel one, which my friends had got me, having been kept especially for wearing when I landed. I had thought that white clothes would suit me better when I stepped ashore, and therefore I did so in white flannels. Those were the last days of September, and I found I was the only person wearing such clothes. I left in charge of an agent of Grindlay and Co. all my kit, including the keys, seeing that many others had done the same and I must follow suit.

I had four notes of introduction: to Dr. P. J. Mehta, to Sjt. Dalpatram Shukla, to Prince Ranjitsinhji and to Dadabhai Naoroji. Someone on board had advised us to put up at the Victoria Hotel in London. Sjt. Mazmudar and I accordingly went there. The shame of being the only person in white clothes was already too much for me. And when at the hotel I was told that I should not get my things from Grindlay's the next day, it being a Sunday,' I was exasperated.

Dr. Mehta, to whom I had wired from Southampton, called at about eight o'clock the same evening. He gave me a hearty greeting. He smiled at my being in flannels. As we were talking, I casually picked up his top-hat, and trying to see how smooth it was, passed my hand over it the wrong way and disturbed the fur. Dr. Mehta looked somewhat angrily at what I was doing and stopped me. But the mischief had been done. **The incident was a warning for the future. This was my first lesson in European etiquette,** into the details of which Dr. Mehta humorously initiated me. 'Do not touch other people's things,' he said. 'Do not ask questions as we usually do in India on first acquaintance; do not talk loudly; never address people as 'sir' whilst speaking to them as we do in India; only servants and subordinates address their masters that way.' And so on and so forth. He also told me that it was very expensive to live in a hotel and recommended that I should live with a private family. We deferred consideration of the matter until Monday.

Sjt. Mazmudar and I found the hotel to be a trying affair. It was also very expensive. There was, however, a Sindhi fellow-passenger from Malta who had become friends with Sjt. Mazmudar, and as he was not a stranger to London, he offered to find rooms for us. We agreed, and on Monday, as soon as we got our baggage, we paid up out bills and went to the rooms rented for us by the Sindhi friend. I remember my hotel bill came to £3, an amount which shocked me. And I had practically starved in spite of this heavy bill! For I could relish nothing. When I did not like one thing, I asked for another, but had to pay for both just the same. The fact is that all this while I had depended on the provisions which I had brought with me from Bombay.

I was very uneasy even in the new rooms. I would continually think of my home and country. My mother's love always haunted me. At night the tears would stream down my cheeks, and home memories of all sorts made sleep out of the question.

It was impossible to share my misery with anyone. And even if I could have done so, where was the use? I knew of nothing that would soothe me. Everything was strange—the people, their ways, and even their dwellings. I was a complete novice in the matter of English etiquette and continually had to be on my guard. There was the additional inconvenience of the vegetarian vow. Even the dishes that I could eat were tasteless and insipid. England I could not bear, but to return to India was not to be thought of. Now that I had come, I must finish the three years, said the inner voice.

My Choice

Dr. Mehta went on Monday to the Victoria Hotel expecting to find me there. He discovered that we had left, got our new address, and met me at our rooms. Through sheer folly I had managed to get ringworm on the boat. For washing and bathing we used to have sea-water, in which soap is not soluble. **I, however, used soap, taking its use to be a sign of civilization,** with the result that instead of cleaning the skin it made it greasy. This gave me ringworm. I showed it to Dr. Mehta, who told me to apply acetic acid. I remember how the burning acid made me cry. Dr. Mehta inspected my room and its appointments and shook his head in disapproval. 'This place won't do,' he said. 'We come to England not so much for the purpose of studies as for gaining experience of English life and customs. And for this you need to live with a family. But before you do so, I think you had better serve a period of apprenticeship with—.I will take you there.'

I gratefully accepted the suggestion and removed to the friend's rooms. He was all kindness and attention. He treated me as his own brother, initiated me into English ways and manners, and accustomed me to talking the language. My food, however, became a serious question. I could not relish boiled vegetables cooked without salt or condiments. The landlady was at a loss to know what to prepare for me. We had oatmeal porridge for breakfast, which was fairly filling, but I always starved at lunch and dinner. The friend continually reasoned with me to eat meat, but I always pleaded my vow and then

Gandhi Album–11

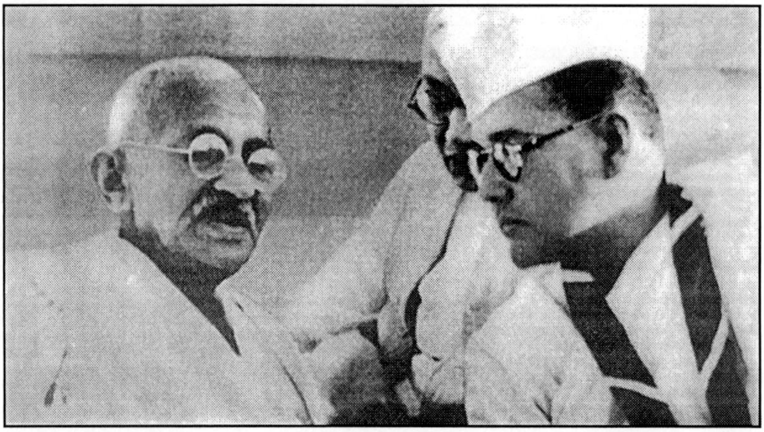

Gandhi with Subhas Chandra Bose—1938

Gandhi with Rabindranath Tagore at Santiniketan, the rural university started by the latter, Kasturba is also with him

remained silent. Both for luncheon and dinner we had spinach and bread and jam too. I was a good eater and had a capacious stomach; but I was ashamed to ask for more than two or three slices of bread, as it did not seem correct to do so. Added to this, there was no milk either for lunch or dinner. The friend once got disgusted with this state of things, and said: 'Had you been my own brother, I would have sent you packing. What is the value of a vow made before an illiterate mother, and in ignorance of conditions here? It is pure superstition to stick to a promise. You confess to having eaten and relished meat. You took it where it was absolutely unnecessary, and will not where it is quite essential. What a pity!'

But I was adamant.

Day in and day out the friend would argue, but I had an eternal negative to face him with. The more he argued, the more uncompromising I became. Daily I would pray for God's protection and get it. Not that I had any idea of God. It was faith that was at work—faith of which the seed had been sown by the good nurse Rambha.

One day the friend began to read to me Bentham's *Theory of Utility.* I was at my wit's end. The language was too difficult for me to understand. He began to expound it. I said: 'Pray excuse me. These abstruse things are beyond me. I admit it is necessary to eat meat. But I cannot break my vow. Please give me up as foolish or obstinate.'

The friend looked at me in surprise. He closed the book and said: 'All right. I will not argue any more.' I was glad. He never discussed the subject again.

That is how I served my apprenticeship for a month. The friend's house was in Richmond, and it was not possible to go to London more than once or twice a week. Dr. Mehta and Sjt. Dalpatram Shukla therefore decided that I should be put with some family. Sjt. Shukla hit upon an Anglo-Indian's house in West Kensington and placed me there. The landlady was a widow. I told her about my vow. The old lady promised to look after me properly, and I took up my residence in her house. Here too I practically had to starve. I had sent for sweets and other eatables from home, but nothing had yet come. I was still as shy as ever and dared not ask for more than was put before me. She had two daughters. They insisted on serving me with an extra slice or two of bread. But little did they know that nothing less than a loaf would have filled me.

But I had found my feet now. I had not yet started upon my regular studies. I had just begun reading newspapers, thanks to Sjt. Shukla. In India I had never read a newspaper. But here I succeeded in cultivating a liking for them by regular reading. I always glanced over *The Daily News, The Daily Telegraph,* and *The Pall Mall Gazette.* This took me hardly an hour. I therefore began to wander about. I launched out in search of a vegetarian restaurant. The landlady had told me that there were such places in the city. I would trot ten or twelve miles each day, go into a cheap restaurant and eat my fill of bread, but would never be satisfied. During these wanderings I once hit on a vegetarian restaurant in Farringdon Street. The sight of it filled me with the same joy that a child feels on getting a thing after its own heart. Before I entered I noticed books for sale exhibited under a glass window near the door. I saw among them Salt's *Plea for Vegetarianism.* This I purchased for a shilling and went straight to the dining room. This was my first hearty meal since my arrival in England. God had come to my aid.

I read Salt's book from cover to cover and was very much impressed by it. From the date of reading this book, I may claim to have become a vegetarian by choice.

Learning to Dance, Play Violin. . .

My faith in vegetarianism grew on me from day to day. Salt's book whetted my appetite for dietetic studies. I went in for all books available on vegetarianism and read them. One of these, Howard Williams' *The Ethics of Diet,* was a 'biographical history of the literature of humane dietetics from the earliest period to the present day.' It tried to make out, that all philosophers and prophets from Pythagoras and Jesus down to those of the present age were vegetarians. Dr. Anna Kingsford's *The Perfect Way in Diet* was also an attractive book. Dr. Allinson's writings on health and hygiene were likewise very helpful. He advocated a curative system based on regulation of the dietary of patients.

Meanwhile my friend had not ceased to worry about me. When he came to know that I had begun to interest myself in books on vege-tarianism, he was afraid lest these studies should muddle my head; that I should fritter my life away in experiments, forgetting my own work, and become a crank. He one day invited me to go to the theatre. Before the play we were to dine together at the Holborn Restaurant, to me a palatial place. The friend had planned to take me to this restaurant evidently imagining that modesty would forbid any questions. The first course was soup. I wondered what it might be made of, but dare not ask the friend about it. I therefore summoned the waiter. My friend saw the movement and sternly asked across the table what was the matter. With considerable hesitation I told him that I wanted to inquire if the soup was a vegetable soup. 'You are too clumsy for decent society,' he passionately exclaimed. 'If you cannot behave yourself, you had better go. Feed in some other restaurant and await me outside.' This delighted me. Out I went. There was a vegetarian restaurant close by, but it was closed. So I went without food that night.

That was the last friendly tussle we had. It did not affect our relations in the least. But I decided that I should assure him that I would be clumsy no more, but try to become polished and make up for my vegetarianism by cultivating other accomplishments which fitted one for polite society. And for this purpose I undertook the all too impossible task of becoming an English gentleman.

The clothes after the Bombay cut that I was wearing were, I thought, unsuitable for English society, and I got new ones at the Army and Navy Stores. I also went in for a chimney-pot hat costing ninteen shillings—an excessive price in those days. Not content with this, I wasted ten pounds on an evening suit made in Bond Street, the centre of fashionable life in London; and got my good and noble-hearted brother to send me a double watch-chain of gold. It was not correct to wear a ready-made tie and I learnt the art of tying one for myself. While in

Gandhi Album–12

Gandhi with Dr Rajendra Prasad, who became the first President of India

Gandhi with Mohammad Ali Jinnah—1944

India, the mirror had been a luxury permitted on the days when the family barber gave me a shave. Here I wasted ten minutes every day before a huge mirror, watching myself arranging my tie and parting my hair in the correct fashion. My hair was by no means soft, and every day it meant a regular struggle with the brush to keep it in position.

As if all this were not enough to make me look the thing, I directed my attention to other details that were supposed to go towards the making of an English gentleman. I was told it was necessary for me to take lessons in dancing, French and elocution. French was the *lingua franca* of the Continent over which I had a desire to travel. I decided to take dancing lessons at a class and paid down £ 3 as fees for a term. I must have taken about six lessons in three weeks. But it was beyond me to achieve anything like rhythmic motion. I could not follow the piano and hence found it impossible to keep time. What then was I to do? I thought I should learn to play the violin in order to cultivate an ear for Western music. So I invested £ 3 in a violin and something more in fees. I sought a third teacher to give me lessons in elocution and paid him a preliminary fee of a guinea. He recommended Bell's *Standard Elocutionist* as the text-book, which I purchased. And I began with a speech of Pitt's.

But Mr. Bell rang the bell of alarm in my ear and I awoke.

I had not to spend a lifetime in England, I said to myself. What then was the use of learning elocution? And how could dancing make a gentleman of me ? The violin I could learn even in India. I was a student and ought to go on with my studies. I should qualify myself to join the Inns of Court. If my character made a gentleman of me, so much the better. Otherwise I should forego the ambition.

These and similar thoughts possessed me, and I expressed them in a letter which I addressed to the elocution teacher, requesting him to excuse me from further lessons. I had taken only two or three. I wrote a similar letter to the dancing teacher, and went personally to the violin teacher with a request to dispose of the violin for any price it might fetch. She was rather friendly to me, so I told her how I had discovered that I was pursuing a false idea. She encouraged me in the determination to make a complete change.

This infatuation must have lasted about three months. **The punctiliousness in dress persisted for years. But henceforward I became a student.**

That period of infatuation was not unrelieved by a certain amount of self-introspection on my part. **I kept account of every farthing I spend, and my expenses were carefully calculated.** Every little item, such as omnibus fares or postage or a couple of coppers spent on newspapers, would be entered, and the balance struck every evening before going to bed. That habit has stayed with me ever since, and I know that as a result, though I have had to handle public funds amounting to lakhs, I have succeeded in exercising strict economy in their disbursement, and instead of outstanding debts have had invariably a surplus balance in respect of all the movement I have led.

As I kept strict watch over my way of living, I could see that it was necessary to economize. I therefore decided to reduce my expenses by half. My accounts showed numerous items spent on fares. Again, my living with a family meant the payment of a regular weekly bill. It also included the courtesy of occasionally taking members of the family out to dinner, and likewise attending parties with them. If the friend was a lady, custom required that the man should pay all the expenses.

So I decided to take rooms on my own account. The rooms were so selected as to enable me to reach the place of business on foot in half an hour, and so save fares. The new arrangement combined walks and economy, as it meant a saving of fares and gave me walks of eight or ten miles a day. It was mainly this habit of long walks that kept me practically free from illness throughout my stay in England and gave me a fairly strong body.

London Matriculation

Thus I rented a suite of rooms; one for a sitting room and another for a bedroom. These changes saved me half the expense. But how was I to utilize the time? **I knew that Bar examinations did not require much study, and I therefore did not feel pressed for time.** My weak English was a perpetual worry to me. I should, I thought, not only be called to the Bar, but have some literary degree as well. I inquired about the Oxford and Cambridge University courses, consulted a few friends, and found that, if I elected to go to either of these places, that would mean greater expense and a much longer stay in England. A friend suggested that, if I really wanted to have the satisfaction of taking a difficult examination, I should pass the London Matriculation. I welcomed the suggestion. But the syllabus frightened me. Latin and a modern language were compulsory! How was I to manage Latin? But the friend entered a strong plea for it: 'Latin is very valuable to lawyers. Knowledge of Latin is very useful in understanding law-books. And one paper in Roman Law is entirely in Latin. I decided to learn Latin, no matter how difficult it might be. French I had already begun, so I thought that should be the modern language.

I joined a private Matriculation class. Examinations were held every six months and I had only five months at my disposal. It was an almost impossible task for me. I framed my own time-table to the minute; but neither my intelligence nor memory promised to enable me to tackle Latin and French besides subjects within the given period. The result was that I failed in Latin. I was sorry but did not lose heart. I had acquired a taste for Latin, also I thought my French would be all the better for another trial and I would select a new subject in the science group. Chemistry which was my subject in science had no attraction for want of experiments. This time I chose Heat and Light instead of Chemistry. It was said to be easy and I found it to be so.

I made an effort to simplify my life still further. I felt that my way of living did not yet befit the modest means of my family. I saw that most of those who were spending from eight to fifteen pounds monthly had the advantage of scholarships. I came across a fair number of poor students living more humbly than I. One of them was staying in the slums in a

Gandhi Album–13

Gandhi breaking his fast with a glass of lemon water

Gandhi travelled in the IIIrd class always

room at two shillings a week and living on two pence worth of cocoa and bread per meal from Lockhart's cheap Cocoa Rooms. It was far from me to think of emulating him, but I felt I could surely have one room instead of two and cook some of my meals at home. That would be a saving of four to five pounds each month.

I gave up the suite of rooms and rented one instead, invested in a stove, and began cooking my breakfast at home. The process scarcely took me more than twenty minutes for there was only oatmeal porridge to cook and water to boil for cocoa. I had lunch out and for dinner bread and cocoa at home. Thus I managed to live on a shilling and three pence a day. This was also a period of intensive study. Plain living saved me plenty of time and I passed my examination.

Experiments in Diet

As I searched myself deeper, the necessity for changes both internal and external began to grow on me. I began to make changes in my diet. I saw that the writers on vegetarianism had examined the question very minutely, attacking it in its religious, scientific, practical and medical aspects. Ethically they had arrived at the conclusion that man's supremacy over the lower animals meant not that the former should prey upon the latter, but that the higher should protect the lower. They had also brought out the truth that man eats not for enjoyment but to live. And some of them accordingly suggested and effected in their lives abstention not only from flesh-meat but from eggs and milk. Scientifically some had concluded that man's physical structure showed that he was not meant to be a cooking but a frugivorous animal, that he could take only his mother's milk and, as soon as he had teeth, should begin to take solid foods. Medically they had suggested the rejection of all spices and condiments.

All these considerations had their effect on me, and I came across vegetarians of all these types in vegetarian restaurants. There was a Vegetarian Society in England with a weekly journal of its own. I subscribed to the weekly, joined the Society and very shortly found myself on the Executive Committee. Here

I came in contact with those who were regarded as pillars of vegetarianism, and began my own experiments in dietetics.

I stopped taking the sweets and condiments I had got from home. The mind having taken a different turn, the fondness for condiments wore away, and I now relished the boiled spinach which in Richmond tasted insipid, cooked without condiments. Many such experiments taught me that the real seat of taste was not the tongue but the mind.

There was in those days a body of opinion which regarded tea and coffee as harmful and favoured cocoa. And as I was convinced that one should eat only articles that sustained the body, I gave up tea and coffee as a rule, and substituted cocoa.

There were two divisions in the restaurants I used to visit. One division, which was patronized by fairly well-to-do people, provided any number of courses from which one chose, each dinner thus costing from one to two shillings. The other division provided six-penny dinners of three courses with a slice of bread. I usually dined in the second division.

There were many minor experiments going on along with the main one; as for example, giving up starchy foods at one time, living on bread and fruit alone at another, and once living on cheese, milk and eggs. This last experiment is worth noting. It lasted not even a fortnight. The reformer who advocated starchless food had spoken highly of eggs and held that eggs were not meat. I took eggs in spite of my vow. But the lapse was momentary. The interpretation of my mother included eggs in meat. I gave up eggs and the experiment alike.

My experiments in England were conducted from the point of view of economy and hygiene. The religious aspects of the question was not considered until I went to South Africa. The seed, however, for all of them was sown in England.

Full of the neophyte's zeal for vegetarianism I decided to start a vegetarian club in my locality, Bayswater. I invited Sir Edwin Arnold, who lived there, to be Vice-President. Dr. Oldfield who was Editor of *The Vegetarian* became President. I myself became the Secretary. The Club went well for a while, but came to an end in the course of a few months. For I left the locality, according to my custom of moving from place to place periodically. But this brief and modest experience gave me some little training in organizing and conducting institutions.

Vain Efforts at Making Speeches

I was elected to the Executive Committee of the Vegetarian Society, and made it a point to attend every one of its meetings, but I always felt tongue-tied. Dr. Oldfield once said to me, 'You talk to me quite all right, but why is it that you never open your lips at a committee meeting? You are a drone.' I appreciated the banter. The bees are ever busy, the drone is a thorough idler. And it was not a little curious that while others expressed their opinions at these meetings, **I sat quite silent. Not that I never felt tempted to speak. But I was at a loss now to how to express myself.** All the rest of the members appeared to me to be better informed than I. Then it often happened that just when I had mustered up courage to speak, a fresh subject would be started. This went on for a long time.

Meantime a serious question came up for discussion. I thought it wrong to be absent, and felt it cowardice to register a silent vote. The discussion arose somewhat in this wise. The President of the Society was Mr. Hills, proprietor of the Thames Iron Works. He was a puritan. It may be said that the existence of the Society depended practically on his financial assistance. Many members of the Committee were more or less his proteges. Dr. Allinson of vegetarian fame was also a member of the Committee. He was an advocate of the then new birth control movement, and preached its methods among the working classes. Mr. Hills regarded these methods as cutting at the root of morals. He thought that the Vegetarian Society had for its object not only dietetic but also moral reform, and that a man of Dr. Allinson's anti-puritanic views should not be allowed to remain in the Society. A motion was therefore brought for his removal.

The question deeply interested me. I considered Dr. Allinson's views regarding artificial methods of birth control as dangerous, and I believed that Mr. Hills was entitled, as a puritan, to oppose him. I had also a high regard for Mr. Hills

Gandhi Album–14

Gandhi in his ashram, with Jaya Prakash Narayan

Gandhi in prison

and his generosity. But I thought it was quite improper to exclude a man from a vegetarian society simply because he refused to regard puritan morals as one of the objects of the Society.

There were in the Committee others also who shared my view, but I felt myself personally called upon to express my own. How to do it was the question. I had not the courage to speak and I therefore decided to set down my thought in writing. **I went to the meeting with the document in my pocket. So far as I recollect, I did not find myself equal even to reading it, and the president had it read by someone else.** Dr. Allinson lost the day. Thus in the very first battle of the kind I found myself siding with the losing party. But I had comfort in the thought that the cause was right. I have a faint recollection that, after this incident, I resigned from the Committee.

This shyness I retained throughout my stay in England. Even when I paid a social call the presence of half a dozen or more people would strike me dumb.

I once went to Ventnor with Sjt. Mazmudar. We stayed there with a vegetarian family. Mr. Howard, the author of *The Ethics of Diet,* was also staying at the same watering-place. We met him, and he invited us to speak at a meeting for the promotion of vegetarianism. I had ascertained that it was not considered incorrect to read one's speech. I knew that many did so to express themselves coherently and briefly. To speak *extempore* would have been out of the question for me. **I had therefore written down my speech. I stood up to read it, but could not. My vision became blurred and I trembled,** though the speech hardly covered a sheet of foolscap. Sjt. Mazmudar had to read it for me. His own speech was of course excellent and was received with applause. I was ashamed of myself and sad at heart for my incapacity.

My last effort to make a public speech in England was on the eve of my departure for home. But this time too I only succeeded in making myself ridiculous. I invited my vegetarian friends to dinner in the Holborn Restaurant. 'A vegetarian dinner could be had,' I said to myself, in vegetarian restaurants as a matter of course. But why should it not be possible in a non-vegetarian restaurant too?' And I arranged with the manager of the Holborn Restaurant to provide a strictly vegetarian meal. The vegetarians hailed the new experiment with delight. Speeches there had to be. When my turn for speaking came, **I stood up to make a speech. I had with great care thought out one which would consist of a very few sentences. But I could not proceed beyond the first sentence.** My memory entirely failed me and I made myself ridiculous. 'I thank you, gentlemen, for having kindly responded to my invitation,' I said abruptly, and sat down.

It was only in South Africa that I got over this shyness, though I never completely overcame it. It was impossible for me to speak *impromptu.* I hesitated whenever I had to face strange audiences and avoided making a speech whenever I could. Even today I do not think I could or would even be inclined to keep a meeting of friends engaged in idle talk.

I must say that, beyond occasionally exposing me to laughter, my constitutional shyness has been no disadvantage whatever. Its greatest benefit has been that it has taught me the economy of words. I have naturally formed the habit of restraining my thoughts. And I can now give myself the certificate that a thoughtless word hardly ever escapes my tongue or pen. A man of few words will rarely be thoughtless in his speech; he will measure every word. We find so many people impatient to talk. There is no chairman of a meeting who is not pestered with notes for permission to speak. And whenever the permission is given the speaker generally exceeds the time-limit, asks for more time, and keeps on talking without permission. All this talking can hardly be said to be of any benefit to the world. My shyness has been in reality my shield and buckler. It has allowed me to grow. It has helped me in my discernment of truth.

Trying to Pass Off as a Bachelor

There were comparatively few Indian students in England at that time. It was a practice with them to affect the bachelor even though they might be married. School or college students in England are all bachelors, studies being regarded as incompatible with married life. We had that tradition in the good old days, a student then being invariably known as a *brahmachari.* But in these days we have child-marriages, a thing practically unknown in England. Indian youths in England, therefore, felt ashamed to confess that they were married. There was also another reason, that in the event of the fact being known it would be impossible for the young men to go about or flirt with the young girls of the family in which they lived.

The flirting was more or less innocent. Parents even encouraged it; and that sort of association between young men and young women may even be a necessity there, in view of the fact that every young man has to choose his mate. If, however, Indian youths on arrival in England indulge in these relations, quite natural to English youths, the result is likely to be disastrous, as has often been found. I saw that our youths had succumbed to the temptation and chosen a life of untruth for the sake of companionships which, however innocent in the case of English youths, were for them undesirable. **I too caught the contagion. I did not hesitate to pass myself off as a bachelor though I was married and the father of a son.** But I was none the happier for being a dissembler. Only my reserve and my reticence saved me from going into deeper waters. If I did not talk, no girl would think it worth her while to enter into conversation with me or to go out with me.

My cowardice was on a par with my reserve. It was customary in families like the one in which I was staying at Ventnor for the daughter of the landlady to take out guests for a walk. My landlady's daughter took me one day to the lovely hills round Ventnor. I was no slow walker, but my companion walked even faster, dragging me after her and chattering away all the while. I responded to her chatter sometimes with a whispered 'yes' or 'no', or at the most. 'yes, how beautiful!' She was flying like a bird whilst I was wondering when I should get back home. We thus reached the top of a hill. How to get down again was the question. In spite of her high-heeled boots this sprightly young lady of twenty-five darted down the hill

Gandhi Album–15

Gandhi, with Jawaharlal Nehru

Gandhi with Lord Mountbatten, the last Governer General of India

like an arrow. I was shamefacedly struggling to get down. She stood at the foot smiling and cheering me and offering to come and drag me. How could I be so chickenhearted? With the greatest difficulty, and crawling at intervals, I somehow managed to scramble to the bottom. She loudly laughed 'bravo' and shamed me all the more as well she might.

But I could not escape scathless everywhere. For God wanted to rid me of the canker of untruth. I once went to Brighton, another watering-place like Ventnor. This was before the Ventnor visit. I met there at a hotel an old widow of moderate means. This was my first year in England. The courses on the menu were all described in French, which I did not understand. I sat at the same table as the old lady. She saw that I was a stranger and puzzled, and immediately came to my aid. 'You seem to be a stranger,' she said, "and look perplexed. Why have you not ordered anything?' I was spelling through the menu and preparing to ascertain the ingredients of the courses from the waiter, when the good lady thus intervened. I thanked her, and explaining my difficulty told her that I was at a loss to know which of the courses were vegetarian as I did not understand French.

'Let me help you,' she said. 'I shall explain the card to you and show you what you may eat.' I gratefully availed myself of her help. This was the beginning of an acquaintance that ripened into friendship and was kept up all through my stay in England and long after. She gave me her London address and invited me to dine at her house every Sunday. On special occasions also she would invite me, help me to conquer my bashfulness and introduce me to young ladies and draw me into conversation with them. Particularly marked out for these conversations was a young lady who stayed with her, and often we would be left entirely alone together.

I found all this very trying at first. I could not start a conversation nor could I indulge in any jokes. But she put me in the way. I began to learn; and in course of time looked forward to every Sunday and came to like the conversations with the young friend. The old lady went on spreading her net wider every day. She felt interested in our meetings. Possibly she had her own plans about us.

I was in a quandary. 'How I wished I had told the good lady that I was married!' I said to myself. 'She would then have not thought of an engagement between us. It is, however, never too late to mend. If I declare the truth, I might yet be saved more misery.' With these thoughts in my mind, I wrote a letter to her.

Let the reader know that I could not have written the letter in a moment. I must have drafted and redrafted it many times over. But it lifted a burden that was weighing me down. Almost by return post came her reply:

'I have your frank letter. We were both very glad and had a hearty laugh over it. The untruth you say you have been guilty of is pardonable. But it is well that you have acquainted us with the state of things. My invitation still stands and we shall certainly expect you next Sunday and look forward to hearing all about your child-marriage and to the pleasure of laughing at your expense. Need I assure you that our friendship is not in the least affected by this incident?'

I thus purged myself of the canker of untruth, and I never thence- forward hesitated to talk of my married state wherever necessary.

Acquaintance with Religions

Towards the end of my second year in England I came across two Theosophists, brothers, and both unmarried. They talked to me about the *Gita*. They were reading Sir Edwin Arnold's translation—*The Song Celestial*—and they invited me to read the original with them. I felt ashamed, as I had read the divine poem neither in Sanskrit nor in Gujarati. **I was constrained to tell them that I had not read the Gita,** but that I would gladly read it with them, and that though my knowledge of Sanskrit was meagre, still I hoped to be able to understand the original to the extent of telling where the translation failed to bring out the meaning.

I began reading the *Gita* with them. The verses in the second chapter made a deep impression on my mind, and they still ring in my ears. The book struck me as one of priceless worth. The impression has ever since been growing on me with the result that I regard it today as the book *par excellence* for the knowledge of Truth. It has afforded me invaluable help in my moments of gloom. I have read almost all the English translations of it, and I regard Sir Edwin Arnold's as the best. He has been faithful to the text, and yet it does not read like a translation. Though I read the *Gita* with these friends, I cannot pretend to have studied it then. It was only after some years that it became a book of daily reading.

The brothers also recommended *The Light of Asia* by Sir Edwin Arnold, whom I knew till then as the author only of *The Song Celestial,* and I read it with even greater interest than I did the *Bhagavadgita.* Once I had begun it I could not leave off. They also took me on one occasion to the Blavatsky Lodge and introduced me to Madame Blavatsky and Mrs. Besant. The latter had just then joined the Theosophical Society, and I was following with great interest the controversy about her conversion. The friends advised me to join the Society, but I politely declined saying, 'With my meagre knowledge of my own religion I do not want to belong to any religious body.' I recall having read, at the brothers' instance, Madame Blavatsky's *Key to Theosophy.* This book stimulated in me the desire to read books on Hinduism, and disabused me of the notion fostered by the missionaries that Hinduism was rife with superstition.

About the same time I met a good Christian from Manchester in a vegetarian boarding house. He talked to me about Christianity. I narrated to him my Rajkot recollections. He was pained to hear them. He said, 'I am a vegetarian. I do not drink. Many Christians are meat-eaters and drink, no doubt; but neither meat-eating nor drinking is enjoined by Scripture. Do please read the Bible.' I accepted his advice, and he got me a copy. I have a faint recollection that he himself used to sell copies of the Bible, and I purchased from him an edition containing maps, concordance, and other aids. I began reading it, but I could not possibly read through the Old Testament. I read the book of Genesis, and the chapters that followed invariably sent me to sleep. I disliked reading the book of Numbers.

But the New Testament produced a different impression, especially the Sermon on the Mount which went straight to my heart. I compared it with the *Gita.* The verses, 'But I say unto you, that ye resist not evil: but whosoever shall smite thee on thy right cheek, I turn to him the other also. And if any man take away thy coat let him have thy cloak too,' delighted me beyond measure and put me in mind of Shamal Bhatt's 'For a bowl of water, give a goodly meal... etc. My young mind tried to unify the teaching of the Gita, *The Light of Asia* and the Sermon on the Mount.

This reading whetted my appetite for studying the lives of other religious teachers. A friend recommended Carlyle's *Heroes and Hero-Worship.* I read the chapter on the Hero as a prophet and learnt of the Prophet's greatness and bravery and austere living.

Beyond this acquaintance with religion I could not go at the moment, as reading for the examination left me scarcely any time for outside subjects. But I took mental note of the fact that I should read more religious books and acquaint myself with all the principal religions.

And how could I help knowing something of atheism too? Every Indian knew Bradlaugh's name and his so-called atheism. I read some book about it, the name of which I forget. It had no effect on me, for I had already crossed the Sahara of atheism. Mrs. Besant, who was then very much in the limelight, had turned to theism from atheism, and that fact also strengthened my aversion to atheism. I had read her book *How I Became a Theosophist.*

It was about this time that Bradlaugh died. He was buried in the Woking Cemetery. I attended the funeral, as I believe every Indian residing in London did. A few clergymen also were present to do him the last honours.

During the last year of my stay in England, that is, in 1890, there was a Vegetarian Conference at Portsmouth to which an Indian friend and I were invited. Portsmouth is a sea-port with a large naval population. It has many houses with women of ill fame, women not actually prostitutes, but at the same time, not very scrupulous about their morals. We were put up in one of these houses. Needless to say, the Reception Committee did not know anything about it. It would have been difficult in a town like Portsmouth to find out which were good lodgings and which were bad for occasional travellers like us.

We returned from the Conference in the evening. After dinner we sat down to play a rubber of bridge, in which our landlady joined. Every player indulges in innocent jokes as a matter of course, but here my companion and our hostess began to make indecent ones as well. I did not know that my friend was an adept in the art. It captured me and I also joined in. Just when I was about to go beyond the limit, leaving the cards and the game to themselves, God through the good companion uttered the blessed warning: 'Whence this devil in you, my boy? Be off, quick!'

I was ashamed. I took the warning, and expressed within myself gratefulness to my friend. Remembering the vow I had taken before my mother, I fled from the scene. To my room I went quaking, trembling, and with beating heart, like a quarry escaped from its pursuer.

I recall this as the first occasion on which a woman, other than my wife, moved me to lust. I passed that night sleeplessly, all kinds of thoughts assailing me. Should I leave this house. Should I run away from the place? I left Portsmouth the next evening, my companion staying there some time longer.

I did not then know the essence of religion or of God, and how He works in us. Only vaguely I understood that God had saved me on that occasion. But in all my trials—of a spiritual nature, as a lawyer, in conducting institutions, and in politics—I can say that God saved me. When every hope is gone, 'when helpers fail and comforts flee,' I find that help arrives somehow, from I know not where. Supplication, worship, prayer are no superstition; they are acts more real

Gandhi Album–16

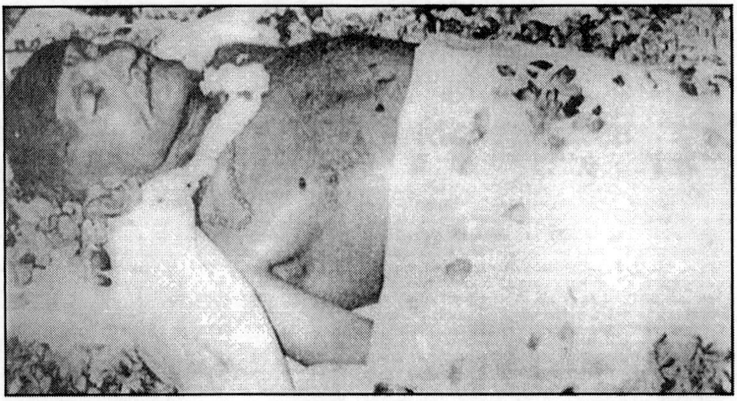

In Peace

than the acts of eating, drinking, sitting or walking. It is no exaggeration to say that they alone are real, all else is unreal.

Visit to Paris

There was a great Exhibition at Paris in 1890. I had read about its elaborate preparations, and I also had a keen desire to see Paris. So I thought I had better combine two things in one and go there at this juncture. A particular attraction of the Exhibition was the Eiffel Tower; constructed entirely of iron, and nearly 1,000 feet high.

I had heard of a vegetarian restaurant in Paris. I engaged a room there and stayed for seven days. I managed everything very economically, both the journey to Paris and the sightseeing there. This I did mostly on foot and with the help of a map of Paris, as also a map of and guide to the Exhibition. I have a fair recollection of the Eiffel Tower as I ascended it twice or thrice. There was a restaurant on the first platform, and just for the satisfaction of being able to say that I had had my lunch at a great height, I threw away seven shillings on it.

The ancient churches of Paris are still in my memory. Their grandeur and their peacefulness are unforgettable. The wonderful construction of Notre Dame and the elaborate decoration of the interior with its beautiful sculptures cannot be forgotten. I felt then that those who expended millions on such divine cathedrals could not but have the love of God in their hearts.

I had read a lot about the fashions and frivolity of Paris. These were in evidence in every street, but the churches stood noticeably apart from these scenes. A man would forget the outside noise and bustle as soon as he entered one of these churches. His manner would change, he would behave with dignity and reverence as he passed someone kneeling before the image of the Virgin. The feeling I had then has since been growing on me, that all this kneeling and prayer could not be mere superstition; the devout souls kneeling before the Virgin could not be worshipping mere marble. They were fired with genuine devotion and they worshipped not stone, but the divinity of which it was symbolic.

I must say a word about the Eiffel Tower. But I then heard it greatly disparaged as well as praised. I remember that Tolstoy was the chief among those who disparaged it. He said that the Eiffel Tower was a monument of man's folly, not of his wisdom. Tobacco, he argued, was the worst of all intoxicants, inasmuch as a man addicted to it was tempted to commit crimes which a drunkard never dared to do. The Eiffel Tower was one of the creations of a man under such influence.

'Called' to the Bar

There were two conditions which had to be fulfilled before a student was formally called to the bar: 'keeping terms', twelve terms equivalent to about three years; and passing examinations. 'Keeping terms' meant eating one's terms, i.e., attending at least six out of about twenty-four dinners in a term. Eating did not mean actually partaking of the dinner, it meant reporting oneself at the fixed hours and remaining present throughout the dinner. Usually of course every one ate and drank the good common, and choice wines provided. A dinner cost from two and six to three and six, that is from two to three rupees. This was considered moderate, inasmuch as one had to pay that same amount for wines alone if one dined at a hotel. To us in India it is a matter for surprise, if we are not 'civilized', that the cost of drink should exceed the cost of food. The first revelation gave me a great shock, and I wondered how people had the heart to throw away so much money on drink. Later I came to understand, I often ate nothing at these dinners, for the things that I might eat were only bread, boiled potato and cabbage. In the beginning I did not eat these, as I did not like them; and later, when I began to relish them, I also gained the courage to ask for other dishes.

The dinner provided for the benchers used to be better than that for the students. A Parsi student, who was also a vegetarian, and I applied, in the interests of vegetarianism, for the vegetarian courses which were served to the benchers. The application was granted, and we began to get fruits and other vegetables from the benchers' table.

Two bottles of wine were allowed to each group of four,

and as I did not touch them, I was ever in demand to form a quarter, so that three might empty two bottles. And there was a 'grand night' in each term when extra wines, like champagne, in addition to port and sherry, were served. I was therefore specially requested to attend and was in great demand on that 'grand night'.

I could not see then, nor have I seen since, how these dinners qualified the students better for the bar. There was once a time when only a few students used to attend these dinners and thus there were opportunities for talks between them and the benchers, and speeches were also made. These occasions helped to give them knowledge of the world with a sort of polish and refinement, and also improved their power of speaking. No such thing was possible in my time, as the benchers had a table all to themselves. The institution had gradually lost all its meaning, but conservative England retained it nevertheless.

The curriculum of study was easy, barristers being humorously known as dinner barrister's. Everyone knew that the examinations had practically no value. In my time there were two, one in Roman Law and the other in Common Law. There were regular text-books prescribed for these examinations which could be taken in compartments, but scarcely any one read them. I have known many to pass the Roman Law examination by scrambling through notes on Roman Law in a couple of weeks, and the Common Law examination by reading notes on the subject in two or three months. Question papers were easy and examiners were generous. The percentage of passes in the Roman Law examination used to be 95 to 99 and of those in the final examination 75 or even more. There was thus little fear of being plucked, and examinations were held not once but four times in the year. They could not be felt as a difficulty.

But I succeeded in turning them into one. I felt that I should read all the text-books. It was a fraud, I thought, not to read these books. I invested much money in them. I decided to read Roman Law in Latin. The Latin which I had acquired in the London Matriculation stood me in good stead. And all this reading was not without its value later on in South Africa, where Roman Dutch is the common law. The reading of Justinian, therefore, helped me a great deal in understanding the South African law.

It took me nine months of fairly hard labour to read through the Common Law of England. For Broom's *Common Law,* a big but interesting volume, took up a good deal of time. Snell's *Equity* was full of interest, but a bit hard to understand. White and Tudor's *Leading Cases,* from which certain cases were prescribed, was full of interest and instruction. I read also with interest Williams' and Edward's *Real Property,* and Goodeve's *Personal Property.* Williams' book read like a novel. The one book I remember to have read on my return to India, with the same unflagging interest, was Mayne's *Hindu Law.*

I passed my examinations, was called to the bar on the 10th of June 1891, and enrolled in the High Court on the 11th. On the 12th I sailed for home.

But notwithstanding my study there was no end to my helplessness and fear. **I did not feel myself qualified to practise law.**

It was easy to be called, but **it was difficult to practise at the bar. I had read the laws, but not learnt how to practise law.** I had read with interest *Legal Maxims,* but did not know how to apply them in my profession. *'Sic utere tuo ut alienum non laedas'* (Use your property in such a way as not to damage that of others) was one of them, but I was at a loss to know how one could employ this maxim for the benefit of one's client. I had read all the leading cases on this maxim, but they gave me no confidence in the application of it in the practice of law.

Besides, **I had learnt nothing at all of Indian law.** I had not the slightest idea of Hindu and Mahomedan law. **I had not even learnt how to draft a plaint,** and felt completely at sea. I had heard of Sir Pherozeshah Mehta as one who roared like a lion in law courts. How, I wondered, could he have learnt the art in England? It was out of the question for me ever to acquire his legal acumen, but **I had serious misgiving as to**

whether I should be able even to earn a living by the profession.

I was torn with these doubts and anxieties whilst I was studying law. I confided my difficulties to some of my friends. One of them suggested that I should seek Dadabhai Naoroji's advice. I possessed a note of introduction to Dadabhai. I thought I had no right to trouble such a great man for an interview. Whenever an address by him was announced, I would attend it, listen to him from a corner of the hall, and go away after having feasted my eyes and ears. In order to come in close touch with the students he had founded an association. I used to attend its meetings, and rejoiced at Dadabhai's solicitude for the students, and the latter's respect for him.

In course of time I mustered up courage to present to him the note of introduction. He said: 'You can come and have my advice whenever you like.' But I never availed myself of his offer. I thought it wrong to trouble him without the most pressing necessity. Therefore I dared not to venture to accept my friend's advice to submit my difficulties to Dadabhai at that time.

I forget now whether it was the same friend or someone else who recommended me to meet Mr. Frederick Pincutt. He was a Conservative, but his affection for Indian students was pure and unselfish. Many students sought his advice and I also applied to him for an appointment, which he granted. I can never forget that interview. He greeted me as a friend. He laughed away my pessimism. 'Do you think,' he said, 'that everyone must be a Pherozeshah Mehta? Pherozeshahs and Badruddins are rare. Rest assured it takes no unusual skill to be an ordinary lawyer. Common honesty and industry are enough to enable him to make a living. All cases are not complicated. Well, let me know the extent of your general reading.'

When I acquainted him with my little stock of reading, he was, as I could see, rather disappointed. But it was only for a moment. Soon his face beamed with a pleasing smile and he said, 'I understand your trouble. Your general reading is meagre.

You have no knowledge of the world, a ***sine qua non*** **for a vakil. You have not even read the history of India. A vakil should know human nature.** He should be able to read a man's character from his face. And every Indian to know ought to have that knowledge. I see that you have not even read Kaye and Malleson's history of the Mutiny of 1857. Get hold of that at once and also read two more books to understand human nature.' These were Lavator's and Shemmelpennick's books on physiognomy.

I was extremely grateful to this venerable friend. In his presence I found all my fear gone, but as soon as I left him I began to worry again. 'To know a man from his face' was the question that haunted me, as I thought of the two books on my way home. The next day I purchased Lavator's book. Shemmelpennick's was not available at the shop. I read Lavator's book and found it more difficult than Snell's *Equity,* and scarcely interesting. I studied Shemmelpennick's physiognomy, but did not acquire the knack of finding out the Shemmelpennick's walking up and down the streets of London.

Lavator's book did not add to my knowledge. Mr. Pincutt's advice did me very little direct service, but his kindness stood me in good stead. His smiling open face stayed in my memory, and I trusted his advice that Pherozeshah Mehta's acumen, memory and ability were not essential to the making of a successful lawyer; honesty and industry were enough. And as I had a fair share of these last I felt somewhat reassured.

I could not read Kaye and Malleson's volumes in England, but I did so in South Africa as I had made a point of reading them at the first opportunity.

Thus with just a little leaven of hope mixed with my despair, I landed at Bombay from S.S. *Assam.* The sea was rough in the harbour, and I had to reach the quay in a launch.

•••

3

FAILURE IN INDIA

The sea was rough in Bombay harbour, not an unusual thing in the Arabian Sea in June and July. It had been choppy all the way from Aden. Almost every passenger was sick; I alone was in perfect form, staying on deck to see the stormy surge, and enjoying the splash of the waves. At breakfast there would be just one or two people besides myself, eating their oatmeal porridge from plates carefully held in their laps, lest the porridge itself find its place there.

The outer storm was to me a symbol of the inner. But even as the former left me unperturbed, I think I can say the same thing about the latter. There was the trouble with the caste that was to confront me. I have already adverted to my helplessness in starting on my profession. And then, as I was a reformer, I was taxing myself as to how best to begin certain reforms. But there was even more in store for me than I knew.

My elder brother had come to meet me at the dock. He had already made the acquaintance of Dr. Mehta and his elder brother, and as Dr. Mehta insisted on putting me up at his house, we went there. Thus the acquaintance begun in England continued in India and ripened into a permanent friendship between the two families.

I was pining to see my mother. I did not know that she was no more in the flesh to receive me back into her bosom. The sad news was now given me, and I underwent the usual ablution. My brother had kept me ignorant of her death, which took place whilst I was still in England. He wanted to spare me the blow in a foreign land. The news, however, was none the less a severe shock to me. My grief was even greater than over my father's death. Most of my cherished hopes were shattered. But I remember that I did not give myself up to any wild expression of grief.

Dr. Mehta introduced me to several friends, one of them being his brother Shri Revashankar Jagjivan, with whom there grew up a lifelong friendship. But the introduction that I need particularly take note of was the one to the poet Raychand or Rajchandra, the son-in-law of an elder brother of Dr. Mehta, and partner of the firm of jewellers conducted in the name of Revashankar Jagjivan. He was not above twenty-five then, but my first meeting with him convinced me that he was a man of great character and learning. He was also known as *Shatavadhani* (one having the faculty of remembering or attending to a hundred things simultaneously), and Dr. Mehta recommended me to see some of his memory feats. I exhausted my vocabulary of all the European tongues I knew, and asked the poet to repeat the words. He did so in the precise order in which I had given them. I envied his gift without, however, coming under its spell. The thing that did cast its spell over me I came to know afterwards. This was his wide knowledge of the scriptures, his spotless character, and his burning passion for self-realization. I saw later that this last was the only thing for which he lived.

Raychandbhai's commercial transactions covered hundreds of thousands. He was a connoisseur of pearls and diamonds. No knotty business problem was too difficult for him. But all these things were not the centre round which his life revolved. That centre was the passion to see God face to face. I was but a briefless barrister then, and yet whenever I saw him he would engage me in conversation of a seriously religious nature. Though I was then groping and could not be said to have any serious interest in religious discussion, still I found his talk of absorbing interest. I have since met many a religious leader or teacher. I have tried to meet the heads of various faiths, and I must say that no one else has ever made on me the impression that Raychandbhai did.

And yet in spite of this regard for him I could not

enthrone him in my heart as my Guru. I believe in the Hindu theory of Guru and his importance in spiritual realization. I think there is a great deal of truth in the doctrine that true knowledge is impossible without a Guru.

Three moderns have left a deep impression my life, and captivated me: Raychandbhai by his living contact; Tolstoy by his book, *The Kingdom of God is Within You*; and Ruskin by his *Unto This Last*.

The Caste Problem

My elder brother had built high hopes on me. The desire for wealth and name and fame was great in him. He had a big heart, generous to a fault. This, combined with his simple nature, had attracted to him many friends, and through them he expected to get me briefs. He had also assumed that I should have a swinging practice and had, in that expectation, allowed the household expenses to become top-heavy. He had also left no stone unturned in preparing the field for my practice.

The storm in my caste over my foreign voyage was still brewing. It had divided the caste into two camps, one of which immediately readmitted me, while the other was bent on keeping me out. To please the former my brother took me to Nasik before going to Rajkot, gave me a bath in the sacred river and, on reaching Rajkot, gave a caste dinner. The trouble about readmission to the caste was thus practically over.

I never tried to seek admission to the section that had refused it. Nor did I feel even mental resentment against any of the headmen of that section. Some of these regarded me with dislike, but I scrupulously avoided hurting their feelings. I fully respected the caste regulations about excommunication. According to these, none of my relations, including my father-in-law and mother-in-law, and even my sister and brother-in-law, could entertain me; and I would not drink water at their houses. They were prepared secretly to evade the prohibition, but it went against the grain with me to do a thing in secret that I would not do in public.

The result of my scrupulous conduct was that I never

had occasion to be troubled by the caste; nay, I have experienced nothing but affection and generosity from the general body of the section that still regards me as excommunicated. They have even helped me in my work, without ever expecting me to do anything for the caste. **It is my conviction that all these good things are due to my non-resistance. Had I agitated for being admitted to the caste,** they would surely have retaliated, and instead of steering clear of the storm, I should have found myself in a whirlpool of agitation, and perhaps a party to dissimulation.

My relations with my wife were still not as I desired. Even my stay in England had not cured me of jealousy. I continued my squeamishness and suspiciousness in respect of every little thing, and hence all my cherished desires remained unfulfilled. I had decided that my wife should learn reading and writing and that I should help her in her studies, but **my lust came in the way and she had to suffer for my own shortcoming. Once I went the length of sending her away to her father's house, and consented to receive her back only after I had made her thoroughly miserable.** I saw later that all this was pure folly on my part.

I had planned reform in the education of children. My brother had children, and my own child which I had left at home when I went to England was now a boy of nearly four. It was my desire to teach these little ones physical exercise and make them hardy, and also to give them the benefit of my personal guidance. In this I had my brother's support and I succeeded in my efforts more or less. I very much liked the company of children, and the habit of playing and joking with them has stayed with me till today. I have ever since thought that I should make a good teacher of children.

The necessity for food reform was obvious. Tea and coffee had already found their place in the house. My brother had thought it fit to keep some sort of English atmosphere ready for me on my return and to that end, crockery and such other things, which used to be kept in the house only for special occasions, were now in general use. My 'reforms' put the finishing touch. I introduced oatmeal porridge, and cocoa was to replace tea and coffee. But in truth it became an addition to tea and coffee. Boots and shoes were already there. I completed the Europeanization by adding the European dress.

Expenses thus went up. New things were added every day. We had succeeded in tying a white elephant at our door. But how was the wherewithal to be found? To start practice in Rajkot would have meant sure ridicule. **I had hardly the knowledge of a qualified vakil and yet I expected to be paid ten times his fee! No client would be fool enough to engage me.** And even if such a one was to be found, should I add arrogance and fraud to my ignorance, and increase the burden of debt to the world?

Friends advised me to go to Bombay for some time in order to gain experience of the High Court, to study Indian law and to try and get what briefs I could. I took up the suggestion and went.

Life in Bombay

In Bombay I started a household with a cook as incompetent as myself. He was a Brahmin. I did not treat him as a servant but as a member of the household. He would pour water over himself but never wash. His *dhoti* was dirty, as also his sacred thread, and he was completely innocent of the scriptures. But how was I to get a better cook?

'Well, Ravishankar,' I would ask him, 'you may not know cooking, but surely you must know your *sandhya* etc.'

'*Sandhya,* sir! The plough is our *sandhya* and the spade our daily ritual. That is the type of Brahmin I am. I must live on your mercy. Otherwise agriculture is of course there for me.'

So I had to be Ravishankar's teacher. Time I had enough. I began to do half the cooking myself and introduced the English experiments in vegetarian cookery. I invested in a stove, and with Ravishankar began to run the kitchen. I had no scruples about interdining, Ravishankar too came to have none, and so we went on merrily together. There was only one obstacle. Ravishankar had sworn to remain dirty.

But it was impossible for me to get along in Bombay for more than four or five months, there being no income to square with the ever-increasing expenditure. This was how I began life. I found the barrister's profession a bad job—much show and little knowledge. I felt a crushing sense of my responsibility.

Whilst in Bombay, I began, on the one hand, my study of Indian law and, on the other, my experiments in dietetics in which Virchand Gandhi, a friend, joined me. My brother, for his part, was trying his best to get me briefs. The study of Indian law was a tedious business. The Civil Procedure Code I could in no way get on with. Not so, however, with the Evidence Act. Virchand Gandhi was reading for the Solicitor's Examination and would tell me all sorts of stories about barristers and vakils. 'Sir Pherozeshah's ability,' he would say, 'lies in his profound knowledge of law. He has the Evidence Act by heart and knows all the cases on the thirty-second section. Badruddin Tyabji's wonderful power of argument inspires the judge with awe.'

The stories of stalwarts such as these would unnerve me. 'It is not unusual,' he would add, 'for a barrister to vegetate for five or seven years. That's why I have signed the articles for solicitorship. You should count yourself lucky if you can paddle your own canoe in three years' time.'

Expenses were mounting up every month. To have a barrister's board outside the house, whilst still preparing for the barrister's profession inside, was a thing to which I could not reconcile myself. Hence I could not give undivided attention to my studies. I developed some liking for the Evidence Act and read Mayne's *Hindu Law* with deep interest, but I had not the courage to conduct a case. I was helpless beyond words, even as the bride come fresh to her father-in-law's house.

My First Case a Failure

About this time, I took up the case of one Mamibai. It was a 'small cause'. 'You will have to pay some commission to the tout,' I was told. I emphatically declined.

'But even that great criminal lawyer Mr. So-and-So, who makes three to four thousand a month, pays commission!'

'I do not need to emulate him,' I rejoined. 'I should be content with Rs. 300 a month. Father did not get more.'

'But those days are gone. Expenses in Bombay have gone up frightfully. You must be businesslike.'

I was adamant. I gave no commission, but got Mamibai's case all the same. It was an easy case. I charged Rs. 30 for my fees. The case was not likely to last longer than a day. This was my *debut* in the Small Causes Court. I appeared for the defendant and had thus to cross-examine the plaintiff's witnesses. **I stood up, but my heart sank into my boots. My head was reeling.** I could think of no question to ask. The judge must have laughed, and the vakils no doubt enjoyed the spectacle. But I was past seeing anything. **I sat down and told the agent that I could not conduct the case,** that he has better engage Patel and have the fee from me. Mr. Patel was duly engaged for Rs. 51. To him, of course, the case was child's play.

I hastened from the Court, not knowing whether my client won or lost her case, but I was ashamed of myself, and decided not to take up any more cases until I had courage enough to conduct them. Indeed **I did not go to Court again until I went to South Africa.** There was no virtue in my decision. I had simply made a virtue of necessity. There would be no one so foolish as to entrust his case to me, only to lose it!

But there *was* another case in store for me at Bombay. It was a memorial to be drafted. A poor Musalman's land was confiscated in Porbandar. He approached me as the worthy son of a worthy father. His case appeared to be weak, but I consented to draft a memorial for him, the cost of printing to be borne by him. I drafted it and read it out to friends. They approved of it, and that to some extent made me feel confident that I was qualified enough to draft a memorial.

For a Teacher's Job

My business could flourish if I drafted memorials without any fees. But that would bring no grist to the mill. So I thought I might take up a teacher's job. My knowledge of English was good enough, and I should have loved to teach English to Matriculation boys in some school. In this way I could have met part at least of the expenses. I came across an advertisement in the papers: 'Wanted, an English teacher to teach one hour daily. Salary Rs. 75.' The advertisement was from a famous high school. I applied for the post and was called for an interview. I went there in high spirits, but **when the principal found that I was not a graduate, he regretfully refused me.**

'But I have passed the London Matriculation with Latin as my second language.'

'True, but we want a graduate.'

There was no help for it. I wrung my hands in despair. My brother also felt much worried. We both came to the conclusion that it was no use spending more time in Bombay. I should settle in Rajkot where my brother, himself a petty pleader, could give me some work in the shape of drafting applications and memorials. And then as there was already a household at Rajkot, the breaking up of the one at Bombay meant a considerable saving, I liked the suggestion. My little establishment was thus closed after a stay of six months in Bombay.

I used to attend High Court daily whilst in Bombay, but I cannot say that I learnt anything there. I had not sufficient knowledge to learn much. Often I could not follow the cases and dozed off. There were others also who kept me company in this, and thus lightened my load of shame. After a time, I even lost the sense of shame, as I learnt to think that it was fashionable to doze in the High Court.

If the present generation has also its briefless barristers like me in Bombay, I would commend them a little practical precept about living. **Although I lived in Girgaum I hardly ever took a carriage or a tramcar. I had made it a rule to walk to the High Court.** It took me quite forty-five minutes, and of course I invariably returned home on foot. I had inured myself to the heat of the sun. This walk to and from the Court saved a fair amount of money, and when many of my friends in Bombay used to fall ill, I do not remember having once had an illness. Even when I began to earn money, I kept up the practice of walking to and from the office, and I am still reaping the benefits of that practice.

Back to Rajkot

Disappointed, I left Bombay and went to Rajkot where I set up my own office. **Here I got along moderately well. Drafting applications and memorials brought me in, on an average, Rs. 300 a month.** For this work I had to thank influence rather than my own ability, for my brother's partner had a settled practice. All applications etc. which were, really or to his mind, of an important character, he sent to big barristers. To my lot fell the applications to be drafted on behalf of his poor clients.

I must confess that here I had to compromise the principle of giving no commission, which in Bombay I had so scrupulously observed. I was told that conditions in the two cases were different; that whilst in Bombay commissions had to be paid to touts, here they had to be paid to vakils who briefed you; and that here as in Bombay all barristers, without exception, paid a percentage of their fees as commission.

Though I thus began to make both ends meet, I got the first shock of my life about this time. I had heard what a British officer was like, but up to now had never been face to face with one.

A Great Shock

My brother had been secretary and adviser to the late Ranasaheb of Porbandar before he was installed on his *gadi,* and hanging over his head at this time was the charge of having given wrong advice when in that office. The matter had gone to the Political Agent who was prejudiced against my brother. Now I had known this officer when in England, and he may be said to have been fairly friendly to me. My brother thought that I should avail myself of the friendship and, putting in a good word on his behalf, try to disabuse the Political Agent of his prejudice.

I did not at all like this idea. I should not, I thought, try to take advantage of a trifling acquaintance in England. If my brother was really at fault, what use was my recommendation? If he was innocent, he should submit a petition in the proper course and, confident of his innocence, face the result.

My brother did not relish this advice. 'You do not know Kathiawad,' he said, 'and you have yet to know the world. Only influence counts here. It is not proper for you, a brother, to shirk your duty, when you can clearly put in a good word about me to an officer you know.'

I could not refuse him, so I went to the officer much against my will. I knew I had no right to approach him and was fully conscious that I was compromising my self-respect. But I sought an appointment and got it. I reminded him of the old acquaintance, but I immediately saw that Kathiawad was different from England; that an officer on leave was not the same as an officer on duty. The Political Agent owned the acquaintance, but the reminder seemed to stiffen him. Surely you have not come here to abuse that acquaintance, have you?' appeared to be the meaning of that stiffness, and seemed to be written on his brow.

Nevertheless I opened my case. The *sahib* was impatient. 'Your brother is an intriguer. I want to hear nothing more from you. I have no time. If your brother has anything to say, let him apply through the proper channel.' The answer was enough, was perhaps deserved. But selfishness is blind. I went on with my story. The *sahib* said: 'You must go now.'

'But please hear me out,' said I. That made him more angry. He called his peon and ordered him to show me the door. I was still hesitating when the peon came in, placed his hands on my shoulders and put me out of the room.

The *sahib* went away as also the peon, and I departed, fretting and fuming. I at once wrote out and sent over a note to this effect: 'You have insulted me. You have assaulted me through your peon. If you make no amends, I shall have to proceed against you.'

Quick came the answer through his *sowar:* 'You were rude to me. I asked you to go and you would not. I had no option but to order my peon to show you the door. Even after he asked you to leave the office, you did not do so. He therefore had to use just enough force to send you out. You are at liberty to proceed as you wish.'

With this answer in my pocket, I came home crestfallen, and told my brother all that had happened. He was grieved, but was at a loss as to how to console me. He spoke to his vakil friends. For I did not know how to proceed against the *sahib.* Sir Pherozeshah Mehta happened to be in Rajkot at this time, having come down from Bombay for some case. But how could a junior barrister like me dare to see him? So I sent him the papers of my case, through the vakil who had engaged him, and begged for his advice.

'Tell Gandhi,' he said, 'such things are the common experience of many vakils and barristers. He is still fresh from England, and hot-blooded. He does not know British officers. If he would learn something and have an easy time here, let him tear up the note and pocket the insult. He will gain nothing by proceeding against the *sahib,* and on the contrary, will very likely ruin himself. 'Tell him he has yet to know life.'

The advice was as bitter as poison to me, but I had to swallow it. I pocketed the insult, but also profited by it. 'Never again shall I place myself in such a false position, never again shall I try to exploit, plot friendship in this way,' said I to myself, and since then I have never been guilty of a breach of that determination. This shock changed the course of my life.

Now most of my work would naturally be in his court. It was beyond me to conciliate him. I had no desire to curry favour with him. Indeed, having once threatened to proceed against him, I did not like to remain silent.

Meanwhile I began to learn something of the petty politics

of the country. Kathiawad, being a conglomeration of small States, naturally had its rich crop of politics. Petty intrigues between states, and intrigues of officers for power were the order of the day. Princes were always at the mercy of others and ready to lend their ears to sycophants. Even the *sahib's* peon had to be cajoled, and the *sahib's shirestedar* was more than his master, as he was his eyes, his ears and his interpreter. The *shirestedar's* will was law, and his income was always reputed to be more than the *sahib's*. This may have been an exaggeration, but he certainly lived beyond his salary. This atmosphere appeared to me to be poisonous, and how to remain unscathed was a perpetual problem for me.

I was thoroughly depressed and my brother dearly saw it. We both felt that, if I could secure some job, I should be free from this atmosphere of intrigue. But without intrigue a ministership or judgeship was out of the question. And the quarrel with the *sahib* stood in the way of my practice.

Porbandar was then under administration, and I had some work there in the shape of securing more powers for the Prince. Also I had to see the Administrator in respect of the heavy *vighoti* (land rent) exacted from the Mers. This officer, though an Indian, was, I found, one better than the *sahib* in arrogance. He was able, but the ryots appeared to me to be none the better off for his ability. I succeeded in securing a few more powers for the Rana, but hardly any relief for the Mers. It struck me that their cause was not even carefully gone into.

So even in this mission I was comparatively disappointed. I thought justice was not done to my clients, but I had not the means to secure it. At the most I could have appealed to the Political Agent or to the Governor who would have dismissed the appeal saying, 'we decline to interfere.' If there had been any rule or regulation governing such decisions, it would have been something, but here the *sahib's* will was law. I was exasperated.

Opportunity in Africa

In the meantime a Meman firm from Porbandar wrote

to my brother making the following offer: 'We have business in South Africa. Ours is a big firm, and we have a big case there in the Court, our claim being £ 40,000. It has been going on for a long time. We have engaged the services of the best vakils and barristers. If you sent your brother there, he would be useful to us and also to himself. He would be able to instruct our counsel better than ourselves. And he would have the advantage of seeing a new part of the world, and of making new acquaintances.'

My brother discussed the proposition with me. I could not clearly make out whether I had simply to instruct the counsel or to appear in court. But I was tempted.

My brother introduced me to Sheth Abdul Karim Jhaveri, a partner of Dada Abdulla and Co., the firm in question. 'It won't be a difficult job,' the Sheth assured me. 'We have big Europeans as our friends, whose acquaintance you will make. You can be useful to us in our shop. Much of our correspondence is in English and you can help us with that too. You will be our guest and will have no expense whatever.'

'How long do you require my services?' I asked. 'And what will be the payment?'

'Not more than a year. We will pay you a first class return fare and a sum of £ 105, all found.'

This was hardly going there as a barrister. It was going as a servant of the firm. But I wanted somehow to leave India. There was also the tempting opportunity of seeing a new country, and of having new experience. Also I could send £ 105 to my brother and help in the expenses of the household. I closed with the offer without any higgling, and got ready to go to South Africa.

•••

4

THREE TURBULENT YEARS IN S. AFRICA

(AGE 23-26)

When starting for South Africa I did not feel the wrench of separation which I had experienced when leaving for England. This time I only felt the pang of parting with my wife. Another baby had been born to us since my return from England. Our love I could not yet be called free from lust, but it was getting gradually purer. Since my return from Europe, we had lived very little together; and as I had now become her teacher, however indifferent, and helped her to make certain reforms, we both felt the necessity of being more together, if only to continue the reforms. But the attraction of South Africa rendered the separation bearable. 'We are bound to meet again in a year,' I said to her, by way of consolation, and left Rajkot for Bombay.

Here I was to get my passage through the agent of Dada Abdulla and Company. But no berth was available on the boat, and if I did not sail then, I should be stranded in Bombay. 'We have tried our best,' said the agent, 'to secure a first class passage, but in vain—unless you are prepared to go on deck. Your meals can be arranged for in the saloon.' Those were the days of my first class travelling, and how could a barrister travel as a deck passenger? So I refused the offer. I suspected the agent's veracity, for I could not believe that a first class passage was not available. With the agent's consent I set about securing it myself. I went on board the boat and met the chief officer.

He said to me quite frankly, 'We do not usually have such a rush. But as the Governor-General of Mozambique is going by this boat, all the berths are engaged.'

'Could you not possibly squeeze me in?' I asked.

He surveyed me from top to toe and smiled. 'There is just one way,' he said. 'There is an extra berth in my cabin, which is usually not available for passengers. But I am prepared to give it to you.' I thanked him and got the agent to purchase the passage. In April 1893 I set forth full of zest to try my luck in South Africa.

The first port of call was Lamu which we reached in about thirteen days. The Captain and I had become great friends by this time. After Lamu the next port was Mombasa and then Zanzibar. The halt here was a long one—eight or ten days—and we then changed to another boat.

The Captain invited an English friend and me to accompany him on an outing, and we all went ashore in his boat. I had not the least notion of what the outing meant. And little did the Captain know what an ignoramus I was in such matters. We were taken to some Negro women's quarters by a tout. We were each shown into a room. I simply stood there dumb with shame. Heaven only knows what the poor woman must have thought of me. When the Captain called me I came out just as I had gone in. He saw my innocence. At first I felt very much ashamed, but as I could not think of the thing except with horror, the sense of shame wore away, and I thanked God that the sight of the woman had not moved me in the least. I was disgusted at my weakness and pitied myself for not having had the courage to refuse to go into the room.

This in my life was the third trial of its kind. Many a youth, innocent at first, must have been drawn into sin by a false sense of shame. I could claim no credit for having come out unscathed. I could have credit if I had refused to enter that room. I must entirely thank the All-merciful for having saved me. The incident increased my faith in God and taught me, to a certain extent, to cast off false shame.

The next call was at Mozambique and thence we reached

Natal towards the close of May. The port of Natal is Durban, also known as Port Natal. Abdulla Sheth was there to receive me.

As the ship arrived at the quay and I watched the people on board to meet their friends, I observed that the Indians were not held in much respect. I could not fail to notice a sort of snobbishness about the manner in which those who knew Abdulla Sheth behaved towards him, and it stung me. Abdulla Sheth had got used to it. Those who looked at me did so with a certain amount of curiosity. My dress marked me out from other Indians. I had a frock-coat and a turban.

I was taken to the firm's quarters and shown into the room set apart for me, next to Abdulla Sheth's. He did not understand me. I could not understand him. He read the papers his brother had sent through me, and felt more puzzled. He thought his brother had sent him a white elephant. My style of dress and living struck him as being expensive like that of the Europeans.

There was no particular work then which could be given me. Their case was going on in the Transvaal. There was no meaning in sending me there immediately. And how far could he trust my ability and honesty? He would not be in Pretoria to watch me. The defendants were in Pretoria, and for aught he knew they might bring undue influence to bear on me. And if work in connection with the case in question was not to be entrusted to me, what work would I be given to do, as all other work could be done much better by his clerks? The clerks could be brought to book, if they did wrong. Could I be, if I also happened to err? So if no work in connection with the case could be given me, I should have to be kept for nothing.

Abdulla Sheth was practically unlettered, but he had a rich fund of experience. He had an acute intellect and was conscious of it. By practice he had picked up just sufficient English for conversational purposes, but that served him for carrying on all his business, whether it was dealing with Bank Managers and European merchants or explaining his case to his counsel. The Indians held him in very high esteem. His firm was then the biggest, or at any rate one of the biggest, of the Indian firms. With all these advantages he had one disadvantage—he was by nature suspicious.

He was proud of Islam and loved to discourse on Islamic philosophy. Though he did not know Arabic, his acquaintance with the Holy Koran and Islamic literature in general was fairly good. Illustrations he had in plenty, always ready at hand. Contact with him gave me a fair amount of practical knowledge of practical knowledge of Islam.

Take off your Turban

On the second or third day of my arrival, he took me to see the Durban court. There he introduced me to several people and seated me next to his attorney. The Magistrate kept staring at me and finally asked me to take off my turban. This I refused to do and left the court.

So here too there was fighting in store for me.

Abdulla Sheth explained to me why some Indians were required to take off their turbans. Those wearing the Musalman costume might, he said, keep their turbans on, but the other Indians on entering a court had to take theirs off as a rule.

In the course of these two or three days I could see that the Indians were divided into different groups. One was that of Musalman merchants, who would call themselves 'Arabs'. Another was that of Hindu, and yet another of Parsi clerks. The Hindu clerks were neither here nor there, unless they cast in their lot with the 'Arabs'. The Parsi clerks would call themselves Persians. These three classes had some social relations with one another. But by far the classes was that composed of Tamil, Telugu and North Indian indentured and freed labourers. The indentured labourers were those who went to Natal on an agreement to serve for five years, and came to be known there as *girmitiyas* from *girmit,* which was the corrupt form of the English word 'agreement'. The other three classes had none but business relations with this class.

Englishmen called them 'coolies', and as the majority of Indians belonged to the labouring class, all Indians were called 'coolies', or *'samis'*. *'Sami'* is a Tamil suffix occurring after many Tamil names, and it is nothing else than the Samskrit *Swami,* meaning a master. Whenever, therefore, an Indian resented being addressed as a *'sami'* and had enough wit in him, he would try to return the compliment in this wise: 'You may call me *sami,* but you forget that *sami* means a master. I am not your master!' Some Englishmen would wince at this, while others would get angry, swear at the Indian and, if there was a chance, would even belabour him; for *'sami'* to him was nothing better than a term of contempt. To interpret it to mean a master amounted to an insult!

I was hence known as a 'coolie barrister'. The merchants were known as 'coolie merchants'. The original meaning of the word 'coolie' was thus forgotten, and it became a common appellation for all Indians. The Musalman merchant would resent this and say: 'I am not a coolie, I am an Arab,' or 'I am a merchant,' and the Englishman, if courteous, would apologize to him.

The question of wearing the turban had a great importance in this state of things. Being obliged to take off one's Indian turban would be pocketing an insult. **So I thought I had better bid good-bye to the Indian turban and begin wearing an English hat** which would save me from the insult and the unpleasant controversy.

But Abdulla Sheth disapproved of the idea. He said, 'If you do anything of the kind, it will have a very bad effect. You will compromise those insisting on wearing Indian turbans. And an Indian turban sits well on your head. If you wear an English hat, you will pass for a waiter.'

There was practical wisdom, patriotism and a little bit of narrowness in this advice. Amongst the indentured Indians there were three classes—Hindus, Musalmans and Christians. The last were the children of indentured Indians who became converts to Christianity. Even in 1893 their number was large. They wore the English costume, and the majority of them earned their living by service as waiters in hotels. Abdulla

Sheth's criticism of the English hat was with reference to this class.

On the whole I liked Abdulla Sheth's advice. I wrote to the press about the incident and defended the wearing of my turban in the court. The question was very much discussed in the papers, which described me as an 'unwelcome visitor'. Thus **the incident gave me an unexpected advertisement in South Africa within a few days of my arrival there.** My turban stayed with me practically until the end of my stay in South Africa.

I soon came in contact with the Christian Indians living in Durban. The Court Interpreter, Mr. Paul, was a Roman Catholic. I made his acquaintance, as also that of the late Mr. Subhan Godfrey, then a teacher under the Protestant Mission, and father of Mr. James Godfrey, who as a member of the South African Deputation, visited India in 1924. I likewise met the late Parsi Rustomji and the late Adamji Miyakhan about the same time. All these friends, who up to then had never met one another except on business, came ultimately into close contact.

Whilst I was thus widening the circle of my acquaintance, the firm received a letter from their lawyer saying that preparations should be made for the case, and that Abdulla Sheth should go to Pretoria himself or send a representative.

Abdulla Sheth gave me this letter to read, and asked me if I would go to Pretoria. 'I can only say after I have understood the case from you,' said I. 'At present I am at a loss to know what I have to do there.' He thereupon asked his clerks to explain the case to me.

As I began to study the case, I felt as though I ought to begin from the ABC of the subject. During the few days I had had at Zanzibar, I had been to the court to see the work there. A Parsi lawyer was examining a witness and asking him questions regarding credit and debit entries in account books. It was all Greek to me. Book-keeping I had learnt neither at school nor during my stay in England. And the case for which I had come to South Africa was mainly about accounts. Only one who knew accounts could understand and explain it. The clerk went on talking- about this debited and that credited, and I felt more and more confused, I did not know what a P. Note meant. I failed to find the word in the dictionary. I revealed my ignorance to the clerk, and learnt from him that a P. Note meant a promissory note. I purchased a book on book-keeping and studied it. That gave me some confidence. I understood the case. I saw that Abdulla Sheth, who did not know how to keep accounts, had so much practical knowledge that he could quickly solve intricacies of book-keeping. I told him that I was prepared to go to Pretoria.

'Where will you put up?' asked the Sheth.

'Wherever you want me to,' said I.

'Then I shall write to our lawyer. He will arrange for your lodgings. I shall also write to my Meman friends there, but I would not advise you to stay with them. The other party has great influence in Pretoria. Should anyone of them manage to read our private correspondence, it might do us much harm. The more you avoid familiarity with them, the better for us.'

'I shall stay where your lawyer puts me up, or I shall find out independent lodgings. Pray don't worry. Not a soul shall know anything that is confident between us. But I do intend cultivating the acquaintance of the other party. I should like to be friends with them. I would try, if possible, to settle the case out of court. After all Tyeb Sheth is a relative of yours.'

Sheth Tyeb Haji Khan Muhammad was a near relative of Abdulla Sheth.

The mention of a probable settlement somewhat startled the Sheth, I could see. But I had already been six or seven days in Durban, and we now knew and understood each other. I was no longer a 'white elephant'. So he said:

'Y....es, I see. There would be nothing better than a settlement out of court. But we are all relatives and know one another very well indeed. Tyeb Sheth is not a man to consent to a settlement easily. With the slightest unwariness on our part, he would screw all sorts of things out of us, and do us down in the end. So please think twice before you do anything.'

'Don't be anxious about that,' said I. 'I need not talk to Tyeb Sheth, or for that matter to anyone else, about the case. I would only suggest to him to come to an understanding, and so save a lot necessary litigation.'

'Get Out of the Compartment'

On the seventh or eighth day after my arrival, I left Durban. A first class seat was booked for me. It was usual there to pay five shillings extra, if one needed a bedding. Abdulla Sheth insisted that I should book one bedding but, out of obstinacy and pride and with a view to saving five shillings, I declined. Abdulla Sheth warned me: 'Look, now,' said he, this is a different country from India. Thank God, we have enough and to spare. Please do not stint yourself in anything that you may need.'

I thanked him and asked him not to be anxious.

The train reached Maritzburg, the capital of Natal, at about 9 p.m. Beddings used to be provided at this station. A railway servant came and asked me if I wanted one. 'No,' said I, 'I have one with me.' He went away. But a passenger came next, and looked me up and down. He saw that I was a 'coloured' man. This disturbed him. Out he went and came in again with one or two officials. They all kept quiet, when another official came to me and said, 'Come along, you must go to the van compartment.'

'But I have a first class ticket,' said I.

'That doesn't matter,' rejoined the other. 'I tell you, you must go to the van compartment.'

'I tell you, I was permitted to travel in this compartment at Durban, and I insist on going on in it.'

'No, you won't,' said the official. 'You must leave this compartment, or else I shall have to call a police constable to push you out.'

'Yes, you may. I refuse to get out voluntarily.'

The constable came. He took me by the hand and

pushed me out. My luggage was also taken out. I refused to go to the other compartment and the train steamed away. I went and sat in the waiting room, keeping my handbag with me, and leaving the other luggage where it was. The railway authorities had taken charge of it.

It was winter, and winter in the higher regions of South Africa is severely cold. Maritzburg being at a high altitude, the cold was extremely bitter. My overcoat was in my luggage, but I did not dare to ask for it lest I should be insulted again, so I sat and shivered. There was no light in the room. A passenger came in at about midnight and possibly wanted to talk to me. But I was in no mood to talk.

I began to think of my duty. Should I fight for my rights or go back to India, or should I go on to Pretoria without minding the insults, and return to India after finishing the case? It would be cowardice to run back to India without fulfilling my obligation. The hardship to which I was subjected was superficial—only a symptom of the deep disease of colour prejudice. **I should try, if possible, to root out the disease and suffer hardships in the process.** Redress for wrongs I should seek only to the extent that would be necessary for the removal of the colour prejudice.

So I decided to take the next available train to Pretoria.

The following morning I sent a long telegram to the General Manager of the Railway and also informed Abdulla Sheth, who immediately met the General Manager. The Manager justified the conduct of the railway authorities, but informed him that he had already instructed the Station Master to see that I reached my destination safely. Abdulla Sheth wired to the Indian merchants in Maritzburg and to friends in other places to meet me and look after me. The merchants came to see me at the station and tried to comfort me by narrating their own hardships and explaining that what had happened to me was nothing unusual. They also said that Indians travelling first or second class had to expect trouble from railway officials and white passengers. The day was thus spent in listening to these tales of woe. The evening train arrived.

There was a reserved berth for me. I now purchased at Maritzburg the bedding ticket I had refused to book at Durban.

The train took me to Charlestown. It reached Charlestown in the morning. There was no railway, in those days, between Charlestown and Johannesburg, but only a stage-coach, which halted at Standerton for the night *en route.* I possessed a ticket for the coach, which was not cancelled by the break of the journey at Maritzburg for a day; besides, Abdulla Sheth had sent a wire to the coach agent at Charlestown.

Physical Assault

But the agent only needed a pretext for putting me off, and so, when he discovered me to be a stranger, he said, 'Your ticket is cancelled.' I gave him the proper reply. The reason at the back of his mind was not want of accommodation, but quite another. Passengers had to be accommodated inside the coach, but as I was regarded as a 'coolie' and looked a stranger, it would be proper, thought the 'leader', as the white man in charge of the coach was called, not to seat me with the white passengers. There were seats on either side of the coachbox. The leader sat on one of these as a rule. Today he sat inside and gave me his seat. I knew it was sheer injustice and an insult, but I thought it better to pocket it. I could not have forced myself inside, and if I had raised a protest, the coach would have gone off without me. This would have meant the loss of another day, and Heaven only knows what would have happened the next day. So, much as I fretted within myself, I prudently sat next to the coachman.

At about three o'clock the coach reached Pardekoph. Now the leader desired to sit where I was seated, as he wanted to smoke and possibly to have some fresh air. So he took a piece of dirty sackcloth from the driver, spread it on the footboard and, addressing me said, '*Sami*, you sit on this, I want to sit near the driver.' The insult was more than I could bear. In fear and trembling I said to him, 'It was you who seated me here, though I should have been accommodated inside. I put up with the insult. Now that you want to sit outside and smoke, you would have me sit at your feet. I will not do so, but I am prepared to sit inside.'

As I was struggling through these sentences, **the man came down upon me and began to heavily box my ears. He seized me by the arm and tried to drag me down.** I clung to the brass rails of the coachbox and was determined to keep my hold even at the risk of breaking my wristbones. The passengers were witnessing the scene—the man swearing at me, dragging and belabouring me, and I remaining still. He was strong and I was weak. Some of the passengers were moved to pity and exclaimed: 'Man, let him alone. Don't beat him. He is not to blame. He is right. If he can't stay there, let him come and sit with us.' 'No fear,' cried the man, but he seemed somewhat crestfallen and stopped beating me. He let go my arm, swore at me a little more, and asking the Hottentot servant who was sitting on the other side of the coachbox to sit on the footboard, took the seat so vacated.

The passengers took their seats and, the whistle given, the coach rattled away. My heart was beating fast within my breast, and I was wondering whether I should ever reach my destination alive. The man cast an angry look at me now and then and, pointing his finger at me, growled: 'Take care, let me once get to Standerton and I shall show you what I do.' I sat speechless and prayed to God to help me.

After dark we reached Standerton and I heaved a sigh of relief on seeing some Indian faces. As soon as I got down, these friends said: 'We are here to receive you and take you to Isa Sheth's shop. We have had a telegram from Dada Abdulla.' I was very glad, and we went to Sheth Isa Haji Sumar's shop. The Sheth and his clerks gathered round me. I told them all that I had gone through. They were very sorry to hear it and comforted me by relating to me their own bitter experiences.

I wanted to inform the agent of the Coach Company of the whole affair. So I wrote him a letter, narrating everything that had happened, and drawing his attention to the threat his man had held out. I also asked for an assurance that he would accommodate me with the other passengers inside the coach when we started the next morning. To which the agent replied to this effect: 'From Standerton we have a bigger coach with different men in charge. The man complained of will not be there tomorrow, and you will have a seat with the other passengers.' This somewhat relieved me. I had, of course, no intention of proceeding against the man who had assaulted me, and so the chapter of the assault closed there.

In the morning Isa Sheth's man took me to the coach, I got a good seat and reached Johannesburg quite safely that night.

No Room in the Hotel

Standerton is a small village and Johannesburg a big city. Abdulla Sheth had wired to Johannesburg also, and given me the name and address of Muhammad Kasam Kamruddin's firm there. Their man had come to receive me at the stage, but neither did I see him nor did he recognize me. So I decided to go to a hotel. I knew the names of several. Taking a cab I asked to be driven to the Grand National Hotel. I saw the Manager and asked for a room. He eyed me for a moment, and politely saying, 'I am very sorry, we are full up,' bade me good-bye. So I asked the cabman to drive to Muhammad Kasam Kamruddin's shop. Here I found Abdul Gani Sheth expecting me, and he gave me a cordial greeting. He had a hearty laugh over the story of my experience at the hotel. 'However did you expect to be admitted to a hotel?' he said.

'Why not?' I asked.

'You will come to know after you have stayed here a few days,' said he. 'Only *we* can live in a land like this, because, for making money, we do not mind pocketing insults, and here we are.' With this he narrated to me the story of the hardships of Indians in South Africa.

He said: 'This country is not for men like you. Look now, you have to go to Pretoria tomorrow. You will *have* to travel third class. Conditions in the Transvaal are worse than in Natal. First and second class tickets are never issued to Indians.'

'You cannot have made persistent efforts in this direction.'

'We have sent representations, but I confess our own men

too do not want as a rule to travel first or second.'

I sent for the railway regulations and read them. There was a loophole. The language of the old Transvaal enactments was not very exact or precise; that of the railway regulations was even less so.

I said to the Sheth: 'I wish to go first class, and if I cannot, I shall prefer to take a cab to Pretoria, a matter of only thirty-seven miles.'

Ticket on a Condition

Sheth Abdul Gani drew my attention to the extra time and money this would mean, but agreed to my proposal to travel first, and accordingly we sent a note to the Station Master. I mentioned in my note that I was a barrister and that I always travelled first. I also stated in the letter that I needed to reach Pretoria as early as possible, that as there was no time to await his reply I would receive it in person at the station, and that I should expect to get a first class ticket. There was of course a purpose behind asking for the reply in person. I thought that, if the Station Master gave a written reply, he would certainly say 'no', especially because he would have his own notion of a 'coolie' barrister. I would therefore appear before him in faultless English dress, talk to him and possibly persuade him to issue a first class ticket. So I went to the station in a frock-coat and necktie, placed a sovereign for my fare on the counter and asked for a first class ticket.

'You sent me that note?' he asked.

'That is so. I shall be much obliged if you will give me a ticket. I must reach Pretoria today.'

He smiled and, moved to pity, said: 'I am not a Transvaaler. I am a Hollander. I appreciate your feelings, and you have my sympathy. I do want to give you a ticket—on one condition, however, that, **if the guard should ask you to shift to the third class, you will not involve me in the affair by which I mean that you should proceed against the Railway Company.** I wish you a safe journey. I can see you are a gentleman.'

With these words he booked the ticket. I thanked him and gave him the necessary assurance.

Sheth Abdul Gani had come to see me off at the station. The incident gave him an agreeable surprise, but he warned me saying: 'I shall be thankful if you reach Pretoria all right. I am afraid the guard will not leave you in peace in the first class, and even if he does, the passengers will not.'

I took my seat in a first class compartment and the train started. At Germiston the guard came to examine the tickets. He was angry to find me there, and signalled to me with his finger to go to the third class. I showed him my first class ticket. 'That doesn't matter,' said he, 'remove to the third class.'

There was only one English passenger in the compartment. He took the guard to task. 'What do you mean by troubling the gentleman?' he said. 'Don't you see he has a first class ticket? I do not mind in the least his travelling with me.' Addressing me, he said, 'You should make yourself comfortable where you are.'

The guard muttered: 'If you want to travel with a coolie, do I care?' and went away.

At about 8 o'clock in the evening the train reached Pretoria.

I had expected someone on behalf of Dada Abdulla's attorney to meet me at Pretoria station. I knew that no Indian would be there to receive me, since I had particularly promised not to put up at an Indian house. But the attorney had sent no one. I understood later that, as I had arrived on a Sunday, he could not have sent anyone without inconvenience. I was perplexed, and wondered where to go, as I feared that no hotel would accept me.

Pretoria station in 1893 was quite different from what it was in 1914. The lights were burning dimly. The travellers were few. I let all the other passengers go and thought that, as soon as the ticket collector was fairly free, I would hand him my ticket and ask him if he could direct me to some small hotel or any other such place where I might go; otherwise I would spend the night at the station. I must confess I shrank from asking him even this, for I was afraid of being insulted.

'Stay if you won't eat in the Dining Room'

The station became clear of all passengers. I gave my ticket to the ticket collector and began my inquiries. He replied to me courteously, but I saw that he could not be of any considerable help. But an American Negro who was standing nearby broke into the conversation.

'I see,' said he, 'that you are an utter stranger here, without any friends. If you will come with me, I will take you to a small hotel, of which the proprietor is an American who is very well known to me. I think he will accept you.'

I had my own doubts about the offer, but I thanked him and accepted his suggestion. He took me to Johnston's Family Hotel. He drew Mr. Johnston aside to speak to him, and the latter agreed to accommodate me for the night, on condition that I should have my dinner served in my room.

'I assure you,' said he, 'that I have no colour prejudice. But I have only European customers, and, if I allowed you to eat in the dining-room, my guests might be offended and even go away.'

'Thank you,' said I, 'even for accommodating me for the night. I am now more or less acquainted with the conditions here, and I understand your difficulty. I do not mind your serving the dinner in my room. I hope to be able to make some other arrangement tomorrow.'

I was shown into a room, where I now sat waiting for the dinner and musing, as I was quite alone. There were not many guests in the hotel, and I had expected the waiter to come very shortly with the dinner. Instead Mr. Johnston appeared. He said: 'I was ashamed of having asked you to have your dinner here. So I spoke to the other guests about you, and asked them if they would mind your having your dinner in the dining-room. They said they had no objection, and that they did not mind your staying here as long as you liked. Please, therefore, come to the dining-room, if you will, and stay here as long as you wish.'

I thanked him again, went to the dining-room and had a hearty dinner.

Stay With a Poor Baker

Next morning called on the attorney, Mr. A. W. Baker. Abdulla Sheth had given me some description of him, so his cordial reception did not surprise me. He received me very warmly and made kind inquiries. I explained all about myself. Thereupon he said: 'We have no work for you here as barrister, for we have engaged the best counsel. The case is a prolonged and complicated one, so I shall take your assistance only to the extent of getting necessary information. And of course you will make communication with my client easy for me, as I shall now ask for all the information I want from him through you. That is certainly an advantage. I have not yet found rooms for you. I thought I had better do so after having seen you. There is a fearful amount of colour prejudice here, and therefore it is not easy to find lodgings for such as you. But I know a poor woman. She is the wife of a baker. I think she will take you and thus add to her income at the same time. Come, let us go to her place.'

So he took me to her house. He spoke with her privately about me, and she agreed to accept me as a boarder at 35 shillings a week.

Mr. Baker, besides being an attorney, was a staunch lay preacher. He is still alive and now engaged purely in missionary work, having given up the legal profession.

During the very first interview Mr. Baker ascertained my religious views. I said to him: 'I am a Hindu by birth. And yet I do not know much of Hinduism, and I know less of other religions. In fact I do not know where I am, and what is and what should be my belief. I intend to make a careful study of my own religion and, as far as I can, of other religions as well.'

Mr. Baker was glad to hear all this, and said: 'I am one of the Directors of the South Africa General Mission. I have built a church at my own expense, and deliver sermons in it regularly. I am free from colour prejudice. I have some co-workers, and we meet at one o'clock every day for a few minutes and pray for peace and light. I shall be glad if you will join us there. I shall introduce you to my co-workers who will be happy to meet you, and I dare say you will also like their company. I shall give you, besides, some religious books to read, though of course the book of books is the Holy Bible, which I would specially recommend to you.'

I thanked Mr. Baker and agreed to attend the one o'clock prayers as regularly as possible.

It was now dark. I returned home, had my dinner, went to my room and lay there absorbed in deep thought. What can be the meaning of Mr. Baker's interest in me? How far should I undertake the study of Christianity? How was I to obtain literature about Hinduism? I could come to only one conclusion: I should make a dispassionate study of all that came to me, and deal with Mr. Baker's group as God might guide me; I should not think of embracing another religion before I had fully understood my own.

Conversion Efforts

The next day at one o'clock I went to Mr. Baker's prayer-meeting. There I was introduced to Miss Harris, Miss Gabb, Mr. Coates and others. Everyone kneeled down to pray, and I followed suit. The prayers were supplications to God for various things, according to each person's desire.

A prayer was now added for my welfare: 'Lord, show the path to the new brother who has come amongst us. Give him, Lord, the peace that Thou hast given us. May the Lord Jesus who has saved us save him too. We ask all this in the name of Jesus.' There was no singing of hymns or other music at these meetings. After the supplication for something special every day, we dispersed, each going to his lunch, that being the hour for it. The prayer did not take more than five minutes.

The Misses Harris and Gabb were both elderly maiden ladies. Mr. Coates was a Quaker. The two ladies lived together, and they gave me a standing invitation to four o'clock tea at their house every Sunday.

When we met on Sunday, I used to give Mr. Coates my religious diary for the week, and discuss with him the books I had read and the impression they had left on me. The ladies used to narrate their sweet experiences and talk about the peace they had found.

Mr. Coates was a frank-hearted staunch young man. We went out for walks together, and he also took me to other Christian friends. As we came closer to each other, he began to give me books of his own choice, until my shelf was filled with them. He loaded me with books, as it were. In pure faith I consented to read all those books, and as I went on reading them we discussed them.

I read a number of such books in 1893. I do not remember the names of them all, but they included the *Commentary* of Dr. Parker of the City Temple, Pearson's *Many Infallible Proofs* and Butler's *Analogy.* Parts of these were unintelligible to me. I liked some things in them, while I did not like others. *Many Infallible Proofs* were proofs in support of the religion of the Bible, as the author understood it. The book had no effect on me. Parker's *Commentary* was morally stimulating but it could not be of any help to one who had no faith in the prevalent Christian beliefs. Butler's *Analogy* struck me to be a very profound and difficult book, which should be read four or five times to be understood properly. It seemed to me to be written with a view to converting atheists to theism. The arguments advanced in it regarding the existence of God were unnecessary for me, as I had then passed the stage of unbelief; but the arguments in proof of Jesus being the only incarnation of God and the Mediator between God and man left me unmoved.

But Mr. Coates was not the man easily to accept defeat. He had great affection for me. He saw, round my neck, the *Vaishnava* necklace of Tulsi-beads. He thought it to be superstition, and was pained by it. 'This superstition does not become you. Come, let me break the necklace.'

'No, you will not. It is a sacred gift from my mother.'

'But do you believe in it?'

'I do not know its mysterious significance. I do not think I should come to harm if I did not wear it. But I cannot, without sufficient reason, give up a necklace that she put round my neck out of love and in the conviction that it would be conducive to my welfare. When, with the passage of time, it wears away and breaks of its own accord, I shall have no desire to get a new one. But this necklace cannot be broken.'

Mr. Coates could not appreciate my argument, as he had no regard for my religion. He was looking forward to delivering me from the abyss of ignorance. He wanted to convince me that, no matter whether there was some truth in other religions, salvation was impossible for me unless I accepted Christianity which represented the truth, and that my sins would not be washed away except by the intercession of Jesus, and that all good works were useless.

Just as he introduced me to several books, he introduced me to 'several friends whom he regarded as staunch Christians. One of these introductions was to a family which belonged to the Plymouth Brethren, a Christian sect.

Many of the contacts for which Mr. Coates was responsible were good. Most struck me as being God-fearing. But during my contact with this family, one of the Plymouth Brethren confronted me with an argument for which I was not prepared:

'You cannot understand the beauty of our religion. From what you say it appears that you must be brooding over your transgressions every moment of your life, always wending them and atoning for them. How can this ceaseless cycle of action bring you redemption? You can never have peace. You admit that we are all sinners. Now look at the perfection of our belief. Our attempts at improvement and atonement are futile. And yet redemption we must have. How can we bear the burden of sin? We can but throw it on Jesus. He is the only sinless Son of God. It is His word that those who believe in Him shall have everlasting life. Therein lies God's infinite mercy. And as we believe in the atonement of Jesus, our own sins do not bind us. Sin we must. It is impossible to live in this world sinless. And therefore Jesus suffered and atoned for all the sins of mankind. Only he who accepts His great redemption can have eternal peace. Think what a life of restlessness is yours, and what a promise of peace we have.'

The argument utterly failed to convince me. I humbly replied:

'If this be the Christianity acknowledged by all Christians, I cannot accept it. I do not seek redemption from the consequences of my sin. I seek to be redeemed from sin itself, or rather from the very thought of sin. Until I have attained that end, I shall be content to be restless.'

To which the Plymouth Brother rejoined: 'I assure you, your attempt is fruitless. Think again over what I have said.'

And the Brother proved as good as his word. He knowingly committed transgressions, and showed me that he was undisturbed by the thought of them.

But I already knew before meeting with these friends that all Christians did not believe in such a theory of atonement. Mr. Coates himself walked in the fear of God. His heart was pure, and he believed in the possibility of self-purification. The two ladies also shared this belief. Some of the books that came into my hands were full of devotion. So, although Mr. Coates was very much disturbed by this latest experience of mine, I was able to reassure him and tell him that the distorted belief of a Plymouth Brother could not prejudice me against Christianity.

My difficulties lay elsewhere. They were with regard to the Bible and its accepted interpretation. (It is noteworthy that in 1893 Swami Vivekananda was winning over the Americans with his addresses at the Parliament of Religions in Chicago.—*Ed.*)

Truthfulness in Business: Launching a New Idea

Sheth Tyeb Haji Khan Muhammad had in Pretoria the same position as was enjoyed by Dada Abdulla in Natal. There was no public movement that could be conducted without him. I made his acquaintance the very first week and told him of my intention to get in touch with every Indian in Pretoria. I expressed a desire to study the conditions of Indians there, and asked for his help in my work, which he gladly agreed to give.

My first step was to call a meeting of all the Indians in Pretoria and to present to them a picture of their condition in the Transvaal. The meeting was held at the house of Sheth Haji Muhammad Haji Joosab, to whom I had a letter of introduction. It was principally attended by Meman merchants, though there was a sprinkling of Hindus as well. The Hindu population in Pretoria was, as a matter of fact, very small.

My speech at this meeting may be said to have been the first public speech in my life. I went fairly prepared with my **subject, which was about observing truthfulness in business.** I had always heard the merchants say that truth was not possible in business. I did not think so then, nor do I now. Even today there are merchant friends who contend that truth is inconsistent with business. Business, they say, is a very practical affair, and truth a matter of religion; and they argue that practical affairs are one thing, while religion is quite another. Pure truth, they hold, is out of the question in business, one can speak it only so far as is suitable. **I strongly contested the position in my speech and awakened the merchants to a sense of their duty, which was twofold. Their responsibility to be truthful was all the greater in a foreign land, because the conduct of a few Indians was the measure of that of the millions of their fellow-countrymen.**

I had found our people's habits to be insanitary, as compared with those of the Englishmen around them, and drew their attention to it. I laid stress on the necessity of forgetting all distinctions such as Hindus, Musalmans, Parsis, Christians, Gujaratis, Madrasis, Punjabis, Sindhis, Kachchhis, Surtis and so on. **I suggested, in conclusion the formation of an association to make representations to the authorities** concerned in respect of the hardships of the Indian settlers, and offered to place at its disposal as much of my time and service as was possible.

I saw that I made a considerable impression on the meeting.

My speech was followed by discussion. Some offered to supply me with facts. I felt encouraged. I saw that very few amongst my audience knew English. As I felt that knowledge of English would be useful in that country, **I advised those who had leisure to learn English.** I told them that it was possible to learn a language even at an advanced age, and cited cases of people who had done so. I undertook, besides, to teach a class, if one was started, or personally to instruct individuals desiring to learn the language.

The class was not started, but three young men expressed their readiness to learn at their convenience, and on condition that I went to their places to teach them. Of these, two were Musalmans—one of them a barber and the other a clerk—and the third was a Hindu, a petty shopkeeper. I agreed to suit them all. I had no misgivings regarding my capacity to teach. My pupils might become tired, but not I. Sometimes it happened that I would go to their places only to find them engaged in their business. But I did not lose patience. None of the three desired a deep study of English, but two may be said to have made fairly good progress in about eight months. Two learnt enough to keep accounts and write ordinary business letters. The barber's ambition was confined to acquiring just enough English for dealing with his customers. As a result of their studies, two of the pupils were equipped for making a fair income.

Starting a Movement

I was satisfied with the result of the meeting. It was decided to hold such meetings, as far as I remember, once a week or, may be, once a month. These were held more or less regularly, and on these occasions there was a free exchange of ideas. **The result was that there was now in Pretoria no Indian I did not know,** or whose condition I was not acquainted with. **This prompted me in turn to make the**

acquaintance of the British Agent in Pretoria, Mr. Jacobus de Web. He had sympathy for the Indians, but he had very little influence. However, **he agreed to help us as best he could and invited me to meet him whenever I wished.**

I now communicated with the railway authorities and told them that, even under their own regulations, the disabilities about travelling under which the Indians laboured could not be justified. **I got letter in reply to the effect that first and second class tickets would be issued to Indians who were properly dressed.** This was far from giving adequate relief, as it rested with the Station Master to decide who was 'properly dressed.'

The British Agent showed me some papers dealing with Indian affairs. Tyeb Sheth had also given me similar papers. I learnt from them how cruelly the Indians were hounded out from the Orange Free State.

In short, my stay in Pretoria enabled me to make a deep study of the social, economic and political condition of the Indians in the Transvaal and the Orange Free State. I had no idea that this study was to be of invaluable service to me in the future. For I had thought of returning home by the end of the year, or even earlier, if the case was finished before the year was out. But God disposed otherwise.

Laws against Indians

In the Orange Free State the Indians were deprived of all their rights by a special law enacted in 1888 or even earlier. If they chose to stay there, they could do so only to serve as waiters in hotels or to pursue some other such menial calling. The traders were driven away with a nominal compensation. They made representations and petitions, but in vain.

A very stringent enactment was passed in the Transvaal in 1885. It was slightly amended in 1886, and it was provided under the amended law that all Indians should pay a poll tax of £ 3 as fee for entry into the Transvaal. They might not own land except in locations set apart for them, and in practice even that was not to be ownership. They had no franchise. All this was under the special law for Asiatics, to whom the laws for the coloured people were also applied. Under these latter, **Indians might not walk on pubic footpaths and might not move out of doors after 9 p.m. without a permit.** The enforcement of this last regulation was elastic so far as the Indians were concerned. Those who passed as 'Arabs' were, as a matter of favour, exempted from it. The exemption thus naturally depended on the sweet will of the police.

I had to experience the effect of both these regulations. I often went out at night for a walk with Mr. Coates, and we rarely got back home much before ten o'clock. What if the police arrested me? Mr. Coates was more concerned about this than I. He had to issue passes to his Negro servants. But how could he give one to me? Only a master might issue a permit to a servant.

So Mr. Coates or some friend of his took me to the State Attorney, Dr. Krause. We turned out to be barristers of the same Inn. The fact that I needed a pass to enable me to be out of doors after 9 p.m. was too much for him. He expressed sympathy for me. Instead of ordering for me a pass, **he gave me a letter authorizing me to be out of doors at all hours without police interference.** I always kept this letter on me whenever I went out. The fact that I never had to make use of it was a mere accident.

Dr. Krause invited me to his place, and we may be said to have become friends. I occasionally called on him, and it was through him that I was introduced to his more famous brother, who was Public Prosecutor in Johannesburg. During the Boer War he was court-martialled for conspiring to murder an English officer, and was sentenced to imprisonment for seven years. He was also debarred by the Benchers. On the termination of hostilities he was released and, being honourably readmitted to the Transvaal bar, resumed practice.

These connections were useful to me later on in my public life, and simplified much of my work.

Kicked from a Footpath

The consequences of the regulation regarding the use of footpaths were rather serious for me. I always went out for a walk through President Street to an open plain. President Kruger's house was in this street—a very modest, unostentatious building, without a garden, and not distinguishable from other houses in its neighbourhood. The houses of many of the millionaires in Pretoria were far more pretentious, and were surrounded by gardens. Indeed President Kruger's simplicity was proverbial. Only the presence of a police patrol before the house indicated that it belonged to some official. I nearly always went along the footpaths past this patrol without the slightest hitch or hindrance.

Now the man on duty used to be changed from time to time. Once one of these men, **without giving me the slighest warning, without even asking me to leave the footpath, pushed and kicked me into the street.** I was dismayed. Before I could question him as to his behaviour, Mr. Coates, who happened to be passing the spot on horseback, hailed me and said: 'Gandhi, I have seen everything. I shall gladly be your witness in court if you proceed against the man. I am very sorry you have been so rudely assaulted.'

'You need not be sorry,' I said. 'What does the poor man know? All coloured people are the same to him. He no doubt treats Negroes just as he has treated me. I have made it a rule not to go to court in respect of any personal grievance. So I do not intend to proceed against him.'

'That is just like you,' said Mr. Coates, 'but do think it over again. We must teach such men a lesson.' He then spoke to the policeman and reprimanded him. I could not follow their talk, as it was in Dutch, the policemen being a Boer. **But he apologized to me**, for which there was no need. I had already forgiven him. But I never again went through this street. There would be other men coming in this man's place and, ignorant of the incident, they would behave likewise. Why should I unnecessarily court another kick? I therefore selected a different walk.

The incident deepened my feeling for the Indian settlers. I discussed with them the advisability of making a test case, if it were found necessary to do so, after having seen the British

Agent in the matter of these regulations.

I thus made an intimate study of the hard condition of the Indian setters, not only by reading and hearing about it, but by personal experience. **I saw that South Africa was no country for self-respecting Indians, and my mind became more and more occupied with the question as to how this state of things might be improved.**

Devises the True Practice of Law

The year's stay in Pretoria was a most valuable experience in my life. **Here it was that I had opportunities of learning public work and acquired some measure of my capacity for it. Here it was that the religious spirit within me became a living force,** and here too I acquired a true knowledge of legal practice. Here I learnt the things that a junior barrister learns in a senior barrister's chamber, and **here I also gained confidence that I should not after all fail as a lawyer.** It was likewise here that I learnt the secret of success as a lawyer.

Dada Abdulla's was no small case. The suit was for £ 40,000. Arising out of business transactions, it was full of intricacies of accounts. Part of the claim was based on promissory notes, and part on the specific performance of promise to deliver promissory notes. The defence was that the promissory notes were fraudulently taken and lacked sufficient consideration. There were numerous points of fact and law in this intricate case.

Both parties had engaged the best attorneys and counsel. I thus had a fine opportunity of studying their work. The preparation of the plaintiff's case for the attorney and the sifting of facts in support of his case had been entrusted to me. It was an education to see how much the attorney accepted, and how much he rejected from my preparation, as also to see how much use the counsel made of the brief prepared by the attorney.

I took the keenest interest in the case. Indeed I threw myself into it. I read all the papers pertaining to the transactions. My client was a man of great ability and reposed absolute confidence in me, and this rendered my work easy. I made a fair study of book-keeping. My capacity for translation was improved by having to translate the correspondence, which was for the most part in Gujarati.

Although, as I have said before, I took a keen interest in religious communion and in public work and always gave some of my time to them, **they were not then my primary interest. The preparation of the case was my primary interest.** As a result, I acquired such a grasp of the facts of the case as perhaps was not possessed even by the parties themselves, inasmuch as I had with me the papers of both the parties.

When I was making preparation for Dada Abdulla's case, I had not fully realized the paramount importance of facts. **Facts mean truth, and once we adhere to truth, the law comes to our aid naturally.** I saw that the facts of Dada Abdulla's case made it very strong indeed, and that the law was bound to be on his side. But I also saw that the litigation, if it were persisted in, would ruin the plaintiff and the defendant, who were relatives and both belonged to the same city. No one knew how long the case might go on. Both, therefore, desired an immediate termination of the case, if possible.

I approached Tyeb Sheth and requested and advised him to go to arbitration. I recommended him to see his counsel. I suggested to him that, if an arbitrator commanding the confidence of both parties could be appointed, the case would be quickly finished. The lawyers' fees were so rapidly mounting up that they were enough to devour all the resources of the clients, big merchants as they were. The case occupied so much of their attention that they had no time left for any other work. In the meantime mutual ill-will was steadily increasing. I became disgusted with the profession. As lawyers the counsel on both sides were bound to rake up points of law in support of their own clients. I also saw for the first time that the winning party never recovers all the costs incurred. Under the Court Fees Regulation there was a fixed scale of costs to be allowed as between party and party, the actual costs as between attorney and client being very much higher. This was more than I could bear. **I felt that my duty was to befriend both parties and**

bring them together. I strained everÛ nerve to bring about a compromise. At last Tyeb Sheth agreed. An arbitrator was appointed, the case was argued before him, and Dada Abdulla won.

But that did not satisfy me. If my client were to seek immediate execution of the award, it would be impossible for Tyeb Sheth to meet the whole of the awarded amount, and there was an unwritten law among the Porbandar Memans living in South Africa that death should be preferred to bankruptcy. It was impossible for Tyeb Sheth to pay down the whole sum of about £37,000 and costs. He meant to pay not a pie less than the amount, and he did not want to be declared bankrupt. There was only one way. Dada Abdulla should allow him to pay in moderate instalments. He was equal to the occasion, and granted Tyeb Sheth instalments spread over a very long period. **Both were happy over the result, and both rose in the public estimation. My joy was boundless I had learnt the true practice of law. I had learnt to find out the better side of human nature and to enter men's hearts.** I realized that the true function of a lawyer was to unite parties riven asunder. The lesson was so indelibly burnt into me that large part of my time during the twenty years of my practice as a lawyer was occupied in **bringing about private compromises of hundreds of cases.** I lost nothing thereby—not even money, certainly not my soul.

Conversion Efforts Fail

Mr. Baker was getting anxious about my future. He took me to the Wellington Convention. The Protestant Christians organize such gatherings every few years for religious enlightenment or, in other words, self-purification. One may call this religious restoration or revival. The Wellington Convention was of this type. The chairman was the famous divine of the place, the Rev. Andrew Murray. Mr. Baker had hoped that the atmosphere of religious exaltation at the Convention, and the enthusiasm and earnestness of the people attending it, would inevitably lead me to embrace Christianity.

But his final hope was the efficacy of prayer. He had an

abiding faith in prayer. It was his firm conviction that God could not but listen to prayer fervently offered. He would cite the instances of men like George Muller of Bristol, who depended entirely on prayer even for his temporal needs. I listened to his discourse on the efficacy of prayer with unbiased attention, and **assured him that nothing could prevent me from embracing Christianity, should I feel the call. I had no hesitation in giving him this assurance, as I had long since taught myself to follow the inner voice.** I delighted in submitting to it.

This Convention was an assemblage of devout Christians. I was delighted at their faith. I met the Rev. Murray. I saw that many were praying for me. I liked some of their hymns, they were very sweet.

The Convention lasted for three days. I could understand and appreciate the devoutness of those who attended it. But I saw no reason for changing my belief—my religion. **It was impossible for me to believe that I could go to heaven or attain salvation only by becoming a Christian.** When I frankly said so to some of the good Christian friends, they were shocked. But there was no help for it.

My difficulties lay deeper. It was more than I could believe that Jesus was the only incarnate son of God, and that only he who believed in him would have everlasting life. If God could have sons, all of us were His sons. If Jesus was like God, or God Himself, then all men were like God and could be God Himself. My reason was not ready to believe literally that Jesus by his death and by his blood redeemed the sins of the world. Metaphorically there might be some truth in it. Again, according to Christianity only human beings had souls, and not other living beings, for whom death meant complete extinction; while I held a contrary belief. Jesus's death on the Cross was a great example to the world, but that there was anything like a mysterious or miraculous virtue in it my heart could not accept. The pious lives of Christians did not give me anything that the lives of men of other faiths had failed to give. Philosophically there was nothing extraordinary in Christian principles. From the point of view of sacrifice, it seemed to me that the Hindus greatly surpassed the Christians.

Thus if I could not accept Christianity either as a perfect, or the greatest religion, neither was I then convinced of Hinduism being such. **Hindu defects were pressingly visible to me. If untouchability could be a part of Hinduism, it could but be a rotten part or an excrescence.** I could not understand the *raison d'etre* of a multitude of sects and castes. What was the meaning of saying that the Vedas were the inspired Word of God? If they were inspired, why not also the Bible and the Koran?

As Christian friends were endeavouring to convert me, even so were Musalman friends. Abdulla Sheth had kept on inducing me to study Islam, and of course he had always something to say regarding its beauty.

I purchased Sale's translation of the Koran and began reading it. I also obtained other books on Islam. I communicated with Christian friends in England. One of them introduced me to Edward Maitland, with whom I opened correspondence. He sent me *The Perfect Way,* a book he had written in collaboration with Anna Kingsford. The book was a repudiation of the current Christian belief. He also sent me another book, *The New Interpretation of the Bible.* I liked both. **They seemed to support Hinduism. Tolstoy's *The Kingdom of God is Within You* overwhelmed me.** It left an abiding impression on me.

My studies thus carried me in a direction unthought of by the Christian friends. My correspondence with Edward Maitland was fairly prolonged, and that with Raychandbhai continued until his death. I read some of the books he sent me. These included *Panchikaran, Maniratnamala, Mumukshu Prakaran of Yogavasishtha,* Haribhadra Suri's *Shaddarshana Samuchchaya* and others.

Though I took a path my Christian friends had not intended for me, I have remained for ever indebted to them for the religious quest that they awakened in me.

Starting a Campaign

The case having been concluded, I had no reason for staying in Pretoria. So I went back to Durban and began to make preparations for my return home. But Abdulla Sheth was not the man to let me sail without a send-off. He gave a farewell party in my honour at Sydenham.

It was proposed to spend the whole day there. Whilst I was turning over the sheets of some of the newspapers I found there, I chanced to see a paragraph in a corner of one of them under the caption 'Indian Franchise'. It was with reference to the Bill then before the House of Legislature, which sought to deprive the Indians of their right to elect members of the Natal Legislative Assembly. I was ignorant of the Bill, and so were the rest of the guests who had assembled there.

I inquired of Abdulla Sheth about it. He said: 'What can we understand in these matters? We can only understand things that affect our trade. As you know all our trade in the Orange Free State has been swept away. We agitated about it, but in vain. We are after all lame men, being unlettered. We generally take in newspapers simply to ascertain the daily market rates, etc. What can we know of legislation? Our eyes and ears are the European attorneys here.'

'But,' said I, 'there are so many young Indians born and educated here. Do not they help you?'

'They!' exclaimed Abdulla Sheth in despair, 'They never care to come to us, and to tell you the truth, we care less to recognize them. Being Christians, they are under the thumb of the white clergymen, who in their turn are subject to the Government.'

This opened my eyes. I felt that this class should be claimed as our own. Was this the meaning of Christianity? Did they cease to be Indians because they had become Christians?

But I was on the point of returning home—and hesitated to express What was passing through my mind in this matter. I simply said to Abdulla Sheth: 'This Bill, if it passes into law, will make our lot extremely difficult. It is the first nail into our coffin. It strikes as the root of our self-respect.'

'It may,' echoed Sheth Abdulla. 'I will tell you the genesis of the franchise question. We knew nothing about it. But Mr. Escombe, one of our best attorneys, whom you know, put the idea into our heads. It happened thus. He is a great fighter, and there being no love lost between him and the Wharf Engineer, he feared that the Engineer might deprive him of his votes and defeat him at the election. So he acquainted us with our position, and at his instance we all registered ourselves as voters, and voted for him. You will now see how the franchise has not for us the value that you attach to it. But we understand what you say. Well, then, what is your advice?'

The other guests were listening to this conversation with attention. One of them said: 'Shall I tell you what should be done? **You cancel your passage by this boat, stay here a month longer, and we will fight as you direct us.'**

All the others chimed in: 'Indeed! indeed. Abdulla Sheth, you must detain Gandhibhai.'

The Sheth was a shrewd man. He said: 'I may not detain him now. Or rather, you have as much right as I to do so. But you are quite right. Let us *all* persuade him to stay on. But you should remember that he is a barrister. What about his fees?'

The mention of fees pained me, and I broke in: 'Abdulla Sheth, fees are out of the question. There can be no fees for public work. I can stay, if at all, as a servant. And as you know, I am not acquainted with all these friends. But if you believe that they will co-operate, I am prepared to stay a month longer. There is one thing, however. Though you need not pay me anything, work of the nature we contemplate cannot be done without some funds to start with. Thus we may have to send telegrams, we may have to print some literature, some touring may have to be done, the local attorneys may have to be consulted, and as I am ignorant of your laws, I may need some law-books for reference. All this cannot be done without money. And it is clear that one man is not enough for this work. Many must come forward to help him.'

And a chorus of voices was heard: 'Allah is great and merciful. Money will come in. Men there are, as many as you may need. You please consent to stay, and all will be well.'

The farewell party was thus turned into a working committee. I suggested finishing dinner etc. quickly and getting back home. **I worked out in my own mind an outline of the campaign.** I ascertained the names of those who were on the list of voters, and made up my mind to stay on for a month. Thus God laid the foundations of my life in South Africa and sowed the seed of the fight for national self-respect.

Opposing the Franchise Bill

Sheth Haji Muhammad Haji Dada was regarded as the foremost leader of the Indian community in Natal in 1893. Financially Sheth Abdulla Haji Adam was the chief among them, but he and others always gave the first place to Sheth Haji Muhammad in public affairs. A meeting was, therefore, held under his presidentship at the house of Abdulla Sheth, at which **it was resolved to offer opposition to the Franchise Bill.**

Volunteers were enrolled. Natal-born Indians, that is, mostly Christian Indian youths, had been invited to attend this meeting. Mr. Paul, the Durban Court Interpreter, and Mr. Subhan Godfrey, Headmaster of a mission school, were present, and it was they who were responsible for bringing together at the meeting a good number of Christian youths. All these enrolled themselves as volunteers.

Many of the local merchants were of course enrolled, noteworthy among them being Sheths Dawud Muhammad, Muhammad Kasam Kamruddin, Adamji Miyakhan, A. Kolandavellu Pillai, C. Lachhiram, Rangaswami Padiachi, and Amad Jiva. Parsi Rustomji was of course there. From among the clerks were Messrs. Manekji, Toshi, Narsinham and others, employees of Dada Abdulla and Co. and other big firms. They were all agreeably surprised to find themselves taking a share in public work. To be invited thus to take part was a new experience in their lives. In face of the calamity that had overtaken the community, all distinctions such as high and low, small and great, master and servant, Hindus, Musalmans, Parsis, Christians, Gujaratis, Madrasis, Sindhis, etc., were forgotten. All were alike the children and servants of the motherland.

The Bill had already passed, or was about to pass, its second reading. In the speeches on the occasion **the fact that Indians had expressed no opposition to the stringent Bill was urged as proof of their unfitness for the franchise.**

I explained the situation to the meeting. The first thing we did was to despatch a telegram to the Speaker of the Assembly requesting him to postpone further discussion of the Bill. A similar telegram was sent to the Premier, Sir John Robinson, and another to Mr. Escombe as a friend of Dada Abdulla's. The speaker promptly replied that discussion of the Bill would be postponed for two days. This gladdened our hearts.

The petition to be presented to the Legislative Assembly was drawn up. Three copies had to be prepared and one extra was needed for the press. It was also proposed to obtain as many signatures to it as possible, and **all this work had to be done in the course of a night.** The volunteers with a knowledge of English and several others sat up the whole night. Mr. Arthur, an old man, who was known for his calligraphy, wrote the principal copy. The rest were written by others to someone's dictation. Five copies were thus got ready simultaneously. Merchant volunteers went out in their own carriages, or carriages whose hire they had paid, to obtain signatures to the petition. This was accomplished in quick time and the petition was despatched. The newspapers published it with favourable comments. **It likewise created an impression on the Assembly.** It was discussed in the House. Partisans of the Bill offered a defence, an admittedly lame one, in reply to the arguments advanced in the petition. The Bill, however, was passed.

We all knew that this was a foregone conclusion, but **the agitation had infused new life into the community and had brought home to them the conviction that the**

community was one and indivisible, and that it was as much their duty to fight for its political rights as for its trading rights.

Lord Ripon was at this time Secretary of State for the Colonies. It was decided to submit to him a monster petition. This was no small task and could not be done in a day. Volunteers were enlisted, and all did their due share of the work.

I took considerable pains over drawing up this petition. I read all the literature available on the subject. My argument centred round a principle and an expedience. **I argued that we had a right to the franchise in Natal, as we had a kind of franchise in India.** I urged that it was expedient to retain it, as the Indian population capable of using the franchise was very small.

Ten thousand signatures were obtained in the course of a fortnight. To secure this number of signatures from the whole of the province was no light task, especially when we consider that the men were perfect strangers to the work. Specially competent volunteers had to be selected for the work, as it had been decided not to take a single signature without the signatory fully understanding the petition. The villages were scattered at long distances. The work could be done promptly only if a number of workers put their whole heart into it. And this they did. All carried out their allotted task with enthusiasm. Sheth Dawud Muhammad, Rustomji, Adamji, Miyakhan, and Amad Jiva brought in the largest number of signatures. Dawud Sheth kept going about in his carriage the whole day. And it was all a labour of love, not one of them asking for even his out-of-pocket expenses. Dada Abdulla's house became at once a caravanserai and a public office. A number of educated friends who helped me and many others had their food there. Thus every helper was put to considerable expense.

The petition was at last submitted. A thousand copies had been printed for circulation and distribution. **It acquainted the Indian public for the first time with conditions in Natal.** I sent copies to all the newspapers and publicists I knew.

The Times of India, in a leading article on the petition, strongly supported the Indian demands. Copies were sent to journals and, publicists in England representing different parties. The London *Times* supported our claims, and we began to entertain hopes of the Bill being vetoed.

Continuing the Stay

It was now impossible for me to leave Natal. The Indian friends surrounded me on all sides and importuned me to remain there permanently. I expressed my difficulties. I had made up my mind not to stay at public expense. I felt it necessary to set up an independent household. I thought that the house should be good and situated in a good locality. I also had the idea that I could not add to the credit of the community, unless I lived in a style usual for barristers. And it seemed to me to be impossible to run such a household with anything less than £ 300 a year. I therefore decided that I could stay only if the members of the community guaranteed legal work to the extent of that minimum, and I communicated my decision to them.

'But,' said they, 'we should like you to draw that amount for public work, and we can easily collect it. Of course this is apart from the fees you must charge for private legal work.'

'No, I could not thus charge you for public work,' said I. 'The work would not involve the exercise on my part of much skill as barrister. **My work would be mainly to make you all work. And how could I charge you for that?** And then I should have to appeal to you frequently for funds for the work, and if I were to draw my maintenance from you, I should find myself at a disadvantage in making an appeal for large amounts, and we should ultimately find ourselves at a standstill. Besides I want the community to find more than £ 300 annually for public work.'

The upshot of this discussion was that about twenty merchants gave me retainer for one year for their legal work. Besides this, Dada Abdulla purchased me the necessary furniture in lieu of a purse he had intended to give me on my departure. Thus I settled in Natal.

Enrolled as an Advocate

I applied for admission as an advocate of the Supreme Court. I held a certificate of admission from the Bombay High Court, the English certificate I had to deposit with the Bombay High Court when I was enrolled there. It was necessary to attach two certificates of character to the application for admission, and thinking that these would carry more weight if given by Europeans, I secured them from two well-known European merchants whom I knew through Sheth Abdulla.

The Law Society sprang a surprise on me by serving me with a notice opposing my application for admission. One of their objections was that the original English certificate was not attached to my application. But the main objection was that, when the regulations regarding admission of advocates were made, the possibility of a coloured man applying could not have been contemplated. Natal owed its growth to European enterprise, and therefore it was necessary that the European element should predominate in the bar. If coloured people were admitted, they might gradually outnumber the Europeans, and the bulwark of their protection would break down.

The Law Society had engaged a distinguished lawyer to support their opposition. As he too was connected with Dada Abdulla and Co., he sent me word through Sheth Abdulla to go and see him. He talked with me quite frankly, and inquired about my antecedents, which I gave. Then he said:

Sheth Abdulla's affidavit was prepared and duly submitted to the counsel for the Law Society. He said he was satisfied. But not so the Law Society. It opposed my application before the Supreme Court, which ruled out the opposition without even calling upon Mr. Escombe to reply. The Chief Justice said in effect:

'Court has no authority to prevent Mr. Gandhi from being enrolled as an advocate. We admit his application. Mr. Gandhi, you can now take the oath.'

I stood up and took the oath before the Registrar. As soon as I was sworn in, the Chief Justice, addressing me, said:

'You must now take off your turban, Mr. Gandhi. You must submit to the rules of the Court with regard to the dress to be worn by practising barristers.'

I saw my limitations. The turban that I had insisted on wearing in the District Magistrate's Court I took off in obedience to the order of the Supreme Court. Not that, if I had resisted the order, the resistance could not have been justified. But I wanted to reserve my strength for fighting bigger battles.

All my life through, **the very insistence on truth has taught me to appreciate the beauty of compromise. I saw in later life that this spirit was an essential part of Satyagraha.** It has often meant endangering my life and incurring the displeasure of friends. But truth is hard and adamant and tender as a blossom.

The opposition of the Law Society gave me another advertisement in South Africa. Most of the newspapers condemned the opposition and accused the Law Society of jealousy. The advertisement, to some extent, simplified my work.

Forming of the Natal Indian Congress

The despatch of the petition regarding the disfranchising bill was not sufficient in itself. Sustained agitation was essential for making an impression on the Secretary of State for the Colonies. For this purpose it was thought necessary to bring into being a permanent organization.

To find out a name to be given to the new organization perplexed me sorely. It was not to identify itself with any particular party. The name 'Congress', I new, was in bad odour with the Conservatives in England, and yet the Congress was the very life of India. I wanted to popularize it in Natal. Therefore, I recommended that the organization should be called the Natal Indian Congress, and on the 22nd May the Natal Indian Congress came into being.

Dada Abdulla's spacious room was packed to the full on that day. The Congress received the enthusiastic approval of all present. Its constitution was simple, the subscription was heavy. Only he who paid five shillings monthly could be a member. The well-to-do classes were persuaded to subscribe as much as they could. Abdulla Sheth headed the list with £ 2 per month. Two other friends also put down the same. I thought I should not stint my subscription, and put down a pound per month. We got a considerable number of members who subscribed £ 1 per month. The number of those who put down 10s. was even larger. Besides this, there were donations.

Experience showed that no one paid his subscription for the mere asking. It was impossible to call frequently on members outside Durban. The enthusiasm of one moment seemed to wear away the next. Even the members in Durban had to be considerably dunned before they would pay in their subscriptions.

The task of collecting subscriptions lay with me, I being the secretary. And we came to a stage when I had to keep my clerk engaged all day long in the work of collection. The man got tired of the job, and I felt that, if the situation was to be improved, the subscriptions should be made payable annually and not monthly, and that too strictly in advance. So I called a meeting of the Congress. Everyone welcomed the proposal for making the subscription annual instead of monthly and for fixing the minimum at £ 3. Thus the work of collection was considerably facilitated.

I had learnt at the outset not to carry on public work with borrowed money. **One could rely on people's promises in most matters except in respect of money.**

Meetings used to be held once a month or even once a week if required. Minutes of the proceedings would be read, and all sorts of questions would be discussed. People had no experience of taking part in public discussions or of speaking briefly and to the point. Everyone hesitated to stand up to speak. I explained to them the rules of procedure at meetings, and they respected them. They realized that it was an education for them, and many who had never been accustomed to speaking before an audience soon acquired the habit of thinking and speaking publicly about matters of public interest.

Knowing that in public work minor expenses at times absorbed large amounts, I had decided not to have even the receipt books printed in the beginning. I had a cyclostyle machine in my office, on which I took copies of receipts and reports. Such things I began to get printed only when the Congress coffers were full, and when the number of members and work had increased. Such economy is essential for every organization, and yet I know that it is not always exercised. That is why I have thought it proper to enter into these little details of the beginnings of a small but growing organization.

People never cared to have receipts for the amounts they paid, but we always insisted on the receipts being given. Every pie was thus clearly accounted for, and I dare say the account books for the year 1894 can be found intact even today in the records of Natal Indian Congress. Carefully kept accounts are a *sine qua non* for any organization. Without them it falls into disrepute. Without properly kept accounts it is impossible to maintain truth in its pristine purity.

Another feature of the Congress was service of Colonial-born educated Indians. **The Colonial-born Indian Educational Association was founded under the auspices of the Congress.** The members consisted mostly of these educated youths. They had to pay a nominal subscription. The Association served to ventilate their needs and grievances, to stimulate thought amongst them, to bring them into touch with Indian merchants and also to afford them scope for service of the community. It was a sort of debating society. The members met regularly and spoke or read papers on different subjects. A small library was also opened in connection with the Association.

The third feature of the Congress was propaganda. This consisted in acquainting the English in South Africa and England and people in India with the real state of things in Natal. With that end in view I wrote two pamphlets. The first was *An Appeal to Every Briton in South Africa*. It contained a statement, supported by evidence, of the general condition of Natal Indians. The other was entitled *The Indian Franchise—*

An Appeal. They were widely circulated.

All this activity resulted in winning the Indians numerous friends in South Africa and in obtaining the active sympathy of all parties in India. It also opened out and placed before the South African Indians a definite line of action.

A Successful Case

The heart's earnest and pure desire is always fulfilled. In my own experience I have often seen this rule verified. Service of the poor has been my heart's desire, and it has always thrown me amongst the poor and enabled me to identify myself with them.

Although the members of the Natal Indian Congress included the Colonial-born Indians and the clerical class, the unskilled wage-earners, the indentured labourers were still outside its pale. The Congress was not yet theirs. They could not afford to belong to it by paying the subscription and becoming its members. The Congress could win their attachment only by serving them. An opportunity offered itself when neither the Congress nor I was really ready for it. I had put in scarcely three or four months' practice, and the Congress also was still in its infancy, when a Tamil man in tattered clothes, head-gear in hand, two front teeth broken and his mouth bleeding, stood before me trembling and weeping. He had been heavily belaboured by his master.

I sent him to a doctor. In those days only white doctors were available. I wanted a certificate from the doctor about the nature of the injury Balasundaram had sustained. I secured the certificate, and straightway took the injured man to the magistrate, to whom I submitted his affidavit. The magistrate was indignant when he read it, and issued a summons against the employer.

It was far from my desire to get the employer punished. I simply wanted Balasundaram to be released from him.

There were only two ways of releasing Balasundaram: either by getting the Protector of Indentured Labourers to cancel his indenture or transfer him to someone else, or by getting Balasundaram's employer to release him. I called on the latter and said to him: 'I do not want to proceed against you and get you punished. I shall be satisfied if you will transfer the indenture to someone else.' To this he readily agreed. I next saw the Protector. He also agreed, on condition that I found a new employer.

So I went off in search of an employer. He had to be a European, as no Indians could employ indentured labour. At that time I knew very few Europeans. I met one of them. He very kindly agreed to take on Balasundaram. I gratefully acknowledged his kindness. The magistrate convicted Balasundaram's employer, and recorded that he had undertaken to transfer the indenture to someone else.

Balasundaram's case reached the ears of every indentured labourer, and I came to be regarded as their friend. I hailed this connection with delight. A regular stream of indentured labourers began to pour into my office, and I got the best opportunity of learning their joys and sorrows. The echoes of Balasundaram's case were heard in far off Madras.

There was nothing extraordinary in the case itself, but the fact that there was someone in Natal to espouse their cause and publicly work for them gave the indentured labourers a joyful surprise and inspired them with hope.

I have said that Balasundaram entered my office, head-gear in hand. There was a peculiar pathos about the circumstances which also showed our humiliation. A practice had been forced upon every indentured labourer and every Indian stranger to take off his head-gear when visiting a European, whether the head-gear were a cap, a turban or a scarf wrapped round the head. A salute even with both hands was not sufficient. Balasundaram thought that he should follow the practice even with me. This was the first case in my experience. I felt humiliated and asked him to tie up his scarf. He did so, not without a certain hesitation, but I could perceive the pleasure of his face.

The £ 3 Tax on Indentured Labour

In the same year, 1894, the Natal Government sought to

impose an annual tax of £ 25 on the indentured Indians. The proposal astonished me. I put the matter before the Congress for discussion, and it was immediately resolved to organize the necessary opposition.

About the year 1860 the Europeans in Natal, finding that there was considerable scope for sugarcane cultivation, felt themselves in need of labour. Without outside labour the cultivation of cane and the manufacture of sugar were impossible, as the Natal Zulus were not suited to this form of work. The Natal Government therefore corresponded with the Indian Government, and secured their permission to recruit Indian labour. These recruits were to sign an indenture to work in Natal for five years, and at the end of the term they were to be at liberty to settle there and to have full rights of ownership of land.

The Indians gave more than had been expected of them. They grew large quantities of vegetables. They introduced a number of Indian varieties and made it possible to grow the local varieties cheaper. They also introduced the mango. Nor did their enterprise stop at agriculture. They entered trade. They purchased land for building, and many raised themselves from the status of labourers to that of owners of land and houses. Merchants from India followed them and settled there for trade. The late Sheth Abubakar Amod was first among them. He soon built up an extensive business. The white traders were alarmed. When they first welcomed the Indian labourers, they had not reckoned with their business skill. They might be tolerated as independent agriculturists, but their competition in trade could not be brooked.

This sowed the seed of the antagonism to Indians. Many other factors contributed to its growth. Our different ways of living, our simplicity, our contentment with small gains, our indifference to the laws of hygiene and sanitation, our slowness in keeping our surroundings clean and tidy, and our stinginess in keeping our houses in good repair—all these, combined with the difference in religion, contributed to fan the flame of antagonism. Through legislation this antagonism found its expression in the disfranchising bill and the bill to impose a tax on the indentured Indians. Independent of legislation a number of pinpricks had already been started.

The first suggestion was that the Indian labourers should be forcibly repatriated, so that the term of their indentures might expire in India. The Government of India was not likely to accept the suggestion. Another proposal was therefore made to the effect that

1. the indentured labourer should return to India on the expiry of his indenture; or that

2. he should sign a fresh indenture every two years, an increment being given at each renewal; and that

3. in the case of his refusal to return to India or renew the indenture he should pay an annual tax of £ 25.

A deputation composed of Sir Henry Binns and Mr. Mason was sent to India to get the proposal approved by the Government there. The Viceroy at that time was Lord Elgin. He disapproved of the £ 25 tax, but agreed to a poll tax of £ 3. I thought then, that this was a serious blunder on the part of the Viceroy. In giving his approval he had in no way thought of the interest of India. It was no part of his duty thus to accommodate the Natal Europeans. In the course of three or four years an indentured labourer with his wife and each male child over 16 and female child over 13 came under the impost. To levy a yearly tax of £ 12 from a family of four—husband, wife and two children—when the average income of the husband was never more than 14 s. a month, was atrocious and unknown anywhere else in the world.

We organized a fierce campaign against this tax. If the Natal Indian Congress had remained silent on the subject, the Viceroy might have approved of even the £ 25 tax.

The Congress could not regard it as any great achievement to have succeeded in getting the tax reduced from £ 25 to £ 3; The regret was still there that it had not completely safeguarded the interests of the indentured Indians. It ever remained its determination to get the tax remitted, but it was twenty years before the determination was realized. And when it was realized, it came as a result of the labours of not only the Natal Indians but of all the Indians in South Africa. The breach of faith with Mr. Gokhale became the occasion of the final campaign, in which the indentured Indians took their full share, some of them losing their lives as a result of the firing that was resorted to, and over ten thousand suffering imprisonment.

Study of Religions

If I found myself entirely absorbed in the service of the community, the reason behind it was my desire for self-realization. **I had made the religion of service my own, as I felt that God could be realized only through service.** And service for me was the service of India, because it came to me without my seeking, because I had an aptitude for it. I had gone to South Africa for travel, for finding an escape from Kathiawad intrigues and for gaining my own livelihood. But as I have said, I found myself in search of God and striving for self-realization.

Christian friends had whetted my appetite for knowledge, which had become almost insatiable, and they would not leave me in peace, even if I desired to be indifferent. In Durban Mr. Spencer Walton, the head of the South Africa General Mission, found me out. I became almost a member of his family.

This friendship kept alive my interest in religion. My religious correspondence continued. Raychandbhai was guiding me. Some friend sent me Narmadashanker's book *Dharma Vichar.* I came to like the book, and read it from cover to cover with attention. I read with interest Max Muller's book, *India—What Can It Teach Us?* and the translation of the *Upanishads* published by the Theosophical Society. All this enhanced my regard for Hinduism, and its beauties began to grow upon me. It did not, however, prejudice me against other religions. I read Washington Irving's *Life of Mahomet and His Successors* and Carlyle's panegyric on the prophet. These books raised Muhammad in my estimation. I also read a book called

The Sayings of Zarathustra.

I began some of the Yogic practices, as well as I could understand them from a reading of the Hindu books. But I could not get on very far, and decided to follow them with the help of some expert when I returned to India. The desire has never been fulfilled.

I made an intensive study of Tolstoy's books. *The Gospels in Brief, What to Do?* and other books made a deep impression on me. I began to realize more and more the infinite possibilities of universal love.

About the same time I came in contact with another Christian family. At their suggestion I attended the Wesleyan church every Sunday. For these days I also had their standing invitation to dinner. The church did not make a favourable impression on me. The sermons seemed to be uninspiring. They were not an assembly of devout souls; they appeared rather to be worldly-minded people going to church for recreation and in conformity to custom.

Meat or Fruit

My connection with the family I used to visit every Sunday was abruptly broken. It happened thus. My hostess was a good and simple woman, but somewhat narrow-minded. We always discussed religious subjects. I was then rereading Arnold's *Light of Asia.* Once we began to compare the life of Jesus with that of Buddha. 'Look at Gautama's compassion!' said I. 'It was not confined to mankind, it was extended to all living beings. Does not one's heart overflow with love to think of the lamb joyously perched on his shoulders? One fails to notice this love for all living beings in the life of Jesus.' The comparison pained the good lady. I cut the matter short, and we went to the dining-room. Her son, a cherub aged scarcely five was also with us. I spoke derisively of the piece of meat on his plate and in high praise of the apple on mine. The innocent boy was carried away and joined in my praise of the fruit. But the mother? She was dismayed. I checked myself and changed the subject.

The following week I visited the family as usual, I did not see that I should stop going there, I did not think it proper either. But the good lady made my way easy.

'Mr. Gandhi,' she said, 'please don't take it ill if I feel obliged to tell you that my boy is none the better for your company. Everyday he hesitates to eat meat and asks for fruit, reminding me of your argument. This is too much. If he gives up meat, he is bound to get weak, if not ill.'

'Mrs.—,' I replied, 'I am sorry. I can understand your feelings as a parent, for I too have children. We can very easily end this unpleasant state of things. What I eat and omit to eat is bound to have a greater effect on the child that what I say. The best way therefore, is for me to stop these visits.' 'I thank you,' she said with evident relief.

A Prostitute in the House

To set up a household was no new experience for me. But the establishment in Natal was different from the ones that I had had in Bombay and London. This time part of the expense was solely for the sake of prestige. I thought it necessary to have a household in keeping with my position as an Indian barrister in Natal and as a representative. So I had a nice little house in a prominent locality. It was also suitably furnished. Food was simple, but as I used to invite English friends and Indian co-workers, the housekeeping bills were always fairly high.

A good servant is essential in every household. But I have never known how to keep anyone as a servant. I had a friend as companion and help, and a cook who had become a member of the family. I also had office clerks boarding and lodging with me.

The companion was very clever and, I thought, faithful to me. But in this I was deceived. He became jealous of an office clerk who was staying with me, and wove such a tangled web that I suspected the clerk. This clerical friend had a temper of his own. Immediately he saw that he had been the object of my suspicion, he left both the house and the office.

In the meanwhile, the cook needed a few days' leave, or for some other cause was away. It was necessary to procure another during his absence. Of this new man I learnt later that he was a perfect scamp. But for me he proved a godsend. Within two or three days of his arrival, he discovered certain irregularities that were going on under my roof without my knowledge, and he made up his mind to warn me. At about twelve o'clock one day the cook came panting to the office and said, 'Please come home at once. There is a surprise for you;

'Now, what is this?' I asked. 'How can I leave the office at this hour to go and see it?'

'You will regret it, if you don't come. That is all I can say.'

I felt an appeal in his persistence. I went home accompanied by a clerk and the cook who walked ahead of us. He took me straight to the upper floor, pointed at my companion's room, and said, 'Open this door and see for yourself.'

I knocked at the door. No reply! I knocked heavily so as to make the very walls shake. The door was opened. I saw a prostitute inside. I asked her to leave the house, never to return.

To the companion I said, 'From this moment I cease to have anything to do with you. I have been thoroughly deceived and have made a fool of myself. That is how you have requited my trust in you?'

Instead of coming to his senses, he threatened to expose me.

I said to the clerk standing downstairs, 'Please go and inform the Police Superintendent, with my compliments, that a person living with me has misbehaved himself. I do not want to keep him but he refuses to leave. I shall be much obliged if police help can be sent me.'

This showed him that I was in earnest. His guilt unnerved him. He apologized to me. entreated me not to inform the police, and agreed to leave the house immediately, which he did.

The incident came as a timely warning in my life. I had known that the companion was a bad character, and yet I believed in his faithfulness to me. In the attempt to reform him I was ruining myself. I had disregarded the warnings of kind friends.

But God came to the rescue as before. The cook had been almost a messenger sent from Heaven. This was not the first time, as I subsequently learnt, that the woman had been brought into my house. She had come often before, but no one had the courage of this cook. For everyone knew how blindly I trusted the companion. The cook had, as it were, been sent to me just to do this service, for he begged leave of me that very moment.

'I cannot stay in your house,' he said. 'You are so easily misled. This is no place for me.'

By now I had been three years in South Africa. In 1896 I asked permission to go home for six months, for I saw that I was in for a long stay there. I had established a fairly good practice, and could see that people felt the need of my presence. So I made up my mind to go home, fetch my wife and children, and then return and settle out there. I also saw that, if I went home, I might be able to do there some public work by educating public opinion and creating more interest in the Indians of South Africa.

But who was to take charge of the Congress work and Education Society in my absence? I could think of two men—Adamji Miyakhan and Parsi Rustomji. Experience showed that the choice was a very happy one. Adamji Miyakhan satisfied all with his perseverance, liberality, amiability and courtesy, and proved to every one that the secretary's work did not require a man with a barrister's degree or high English education.

About the middle of 1896 I sailed for home in the *S.S. Pongola* which was bound for Calcutta.

•••

5

Promoting the S. Africa Cause in India

On my way to Bombay the train stopped at Allahabad for forty-five minutes. I decided to utilize the interval for a drive through the town. I also had to purchase some medicine at a chemist's shop. The chemist was half asleep, and took an unconscionable time in dispensing the medicine, with the result that when I reached the station, the train had just started. The Station Master had kindly detained the train one minute for my sake, but not seeing me coming, had carefully ordered my luggage to be taken out of the train.

In Allahabad

I took a room at Kellner's, and decided to start work there and then. I had heard a good deal about *The Pioneer* published from Allahabad, and I had understood it to be an opponent of Indian aspirations. I have an impression that Mr. Cheseny Jr. was the editor at that time. I wanted to secure the help of every party, so I wrote a note to Mr. Chesney, telling him how I bad missed the train, and asking for an appointment so as to enable me to leave the next day. He immediately gave me one, at which I was very happy, especially when I found that he gave me a patient hearing. He promised to notice in his paper anything that I might write, but added that he could not promise to endorse all the Indian demands inasmuch as he was bound to understand and give due weight to the viewpoint of the Colonials as well.

'It is enough,' I said, 'that you should study the question and discuss it in your paper. I ask and desire nothing but the barest justice that is due to us.'

The rest of the day was spent in having a look round admiring the magnificent confluence of the three rivers, the Triveni, and planning the work before me.

This unexpected interview with the editor of *The Pioneer* laid the foundation of the series of incidents which ultimately led to my being lynched in Natal.

Work in Rajkot

I went straight to Rajkot without halting at Bombay and began to make preparations for writing a pamphlet on the situation in South Africa. The writing and publication of the pamphlet took about a month. It had a green cover and came to be known afterwards as the Green Pamphlet. In it I drew a purposely subdued picture of the condition of Indians in South Africa. The language I used was more moderate than that of the two pamphlets which I have referred to before, as I knew that things heard of from a distance appear bigger than they are.

Ten thousand copies were printed and sent to all the papers and leaders of every party in India. *The Pioneer* was the first to notice it editorially. A summary of the article was cabled by Reuter to England, and a summary of that summary was cabled to Natal by Reuter's London Office. This cable was not longer than three lines in print. It was a miniature, but exaggerated, edition of the picture I had drawn of the treatment accorded to the Indians in Natal, and it was not in my words. We shall see later on the effect this had in Natal. In the meanwhile every paper of note commented at length on the question.

To get these pamphlets ready for posting was no small matter. It would have been expensive too, if I had employed paid help for preparing wrapper, etc. But I hit upon a much simpler plan. I gathered together all the children in my locality and asked them to volunteer two or three hours' labour of a morning, when they had no school. This they willingly agreed to do. I promised to bless them and give them, as a reward, used postage stamps which I had collected. They got through the work in no time. **That was my first experiment of having little children as volunteers.** Two of those little friends are my co-workers today.

Hardly ever have I known anybody to cherish such loyalty as I did to the British Constitution. I can see now that my love of truth was at the root of this loyalty. It has never been possible for me to simulate loyalty or, for that matter, any other virtue. The National Anthem used to be sung at every meeting that I attended in Natal. I then felt that I must also join in the singing. Not that I was unaware of the defects in British rule, but I thought that it was on the whole acceptable. **In those days I believed that British rule was on the whole beneficial to the ruled.**

The colour prejudice that I saw in South Africa was, I thought, quite contrary to British traditions, and I believed that it was only temporary and local. I therefore vied with Englishmen in loyalty to the throne. With careful perseverance I learnt the tune of the National Anthem and joined in the singing whenever it was sung. Whenever there was an occasion for the expression of loyalty without fuss or ostentation, I readily took part in it.

Preparations were going on for the celebration of Queen Victoria's Diamond Jubilee when I reached India. I was invited to join the committee appointed for the purpose in Rajkot. I accepted the offer, but had a suspicion that the celebrations would be largely a matter of show. I discovered much humbug about them and was considerably pained. I began to ask myself whether I should remain on the committee or not, but ultimately decided to rest content with doing my part of the business.

I taught the National Anthem to the children of my family. I recollect having taught it to students of the local Training College, but I forget whether it was on the occasion of the Jubilee or of King Edward VII's coronation as Emperor of India. Later on the text began to jar on me. As my conception of ahimsa went on maturing, I became more vigilant about my thought and speech.

Like loyalty an aptitude for nursing was also deeply rooted in my nature. I was fond of nursing people, whether friends or strangers.

Visit to Bombay

Whilst busy in Rajkot with the pamphlet on South Africa, I had an occasion to pay a flying visit to Bombay. It was my intention to educate public opinion in cities on this question by organizing meetings, and Bombay was the first city I chose. First of all I met Justice Ranade, who listened to me with attention, and advised me to meet Sir Pherozeshah Mehta. Justice Badruddin Tyabji, whom I met next, also gave the same advice. 'Justice Ranade and I can guide you but little,' he said. 'You know our position. We cannot take an active part in public affairs, but our sympathies are with you. The man who can effectively guide you is Sir Pherozeshah Mehta.'

I certainly wanted to see Sir Pherozeshah Mehta, but the fact that these senior men advised me to act according to his advice gave me a better idea of the immense influence that Sir Pherozeshah had on the public. In due course I met him. I was prepared to be awed by his presence. I had heard of the popular titles that he had earned, and knew that I was to see the 'Lion of Bombay', the 'Uncrowned King of the Presidency'. But the king did not overpower me. He met me as a loving father would meet his grown up son. Our meeting took place at his chamber. He was surrounded by a circle of friends and followers. Amongst them were Mr. D. E. Wacha and Mr. Qama, to whom I was introduced. I had already heard of Mr. Wacha. He was regarded as the right-hand man of Sir Pherozeshah, and Sjt. Virchand Gandhi had described him to me as a great statistician. Mr. Wacha said, 'Gandhi, we must meet again.'

These introductions could scarcely have taken two minutes. Sir Pherozeshah carefully listened to me. I told him that I had seen Justices Ranade and Tyabji. 'Gandhi,' said he, 'I see that I must help you. I must call a public meeting here.' With this he turned to Mr. Munshi, the secretary, and told him to fix up the date of the meeting. The date was settled, and he bade me good-bye, asking me to see him again on the day previous to the meeting. The interview removed my fears, and I went home delighted.

First Meeting

In accordance with Sir Pherozeshah's instructions I reported myself at his office at 5 p.m. on the eve of the meeting.

'Is your speech ready, Gandhi?' he asked.

'No, sir,' said I, trembling with fear, 'I think of speaking *extempore.*'

'That will not do in Bombay. Reporting here is bad, and if we would benefit by this meeting, you should write out your speech, and it should be printed before daybreak tomorrow. I hope you can manage this?'

I felt rather nervous, but I said I would try.

'Then, tell me, what time Mr. Munshi should come to you for the manuscript?'

'Eleven o'clock tonight,' said I.

On going to the meeting the next day, I saw the wisdom of Sir Pherozeshah's advice. The meeting was held in the hall of Sir Cowasji Jehangir Institute. I had heard that when Sir Pherozeshah Mehta addressed meetings the hall was always packed, chiefly by the students intent on hearing him, leaving not an inch of room. This was the first meeting of the kind in my experience. I saw that my voice could reach only a few. **I was trembling as I began to read my speech. Sir Pherozeshah cheered me up continually by asking me to speak louder and still louder.**

My old friend Sjt. Keshavrao Deshpande came to my rescue. I handed my speech to him. His was just the proper voice. But the audience refused to listen. The hall rang with the cries of 'Wacha', 'Wacha'. So Mr. Wacha stood up and read the speech, with wounderful results. The audience became perfectly quiet, and listened to the speech to the end, punctuating it with applause and cries of "shame" where necessary. This gladdened my heart.

Sir Pherozeshah liked the speech. I was supremely happy.

The meeting won me the active sympathy of Sjt. Deshpande and a Parsi friend. Both expressed their resolve to accompany me to South Africa. Mr. C. M. Cursetji, who was then Small Causes Court Judge, however, moved the Parsi friend from his resolve, as he had plotted his marriage. He had to choose between marriage and going to South Africa, and he chose the former. But Parsi Rustomji made amends for the broken resolve, and a number of Parsi sisters are now making amends for the lady who helped in the breach by dedicating themselves to Khadi work. I have therefore gladly forgiven that couple. Sjt. Deshpande had no temptations of marriage, but he too could not come. Today he is himself doing enough reparation for the broken pledge. On my way back to South Africa I met one of the Tyabjis at Zanzibar. He also promised to come and help me, but never came. Mr. Abbas Tyabji is atoning for that offence. **Thus none of my three attempts to induce barristers to go to South Africa bore any fruit.**

In Poona

Sir Pherozeshah had made my way easy. So from Bombay I went to Poona. Here there were two parties. I wanted the help of people of every shade of opinion. First I met Lokamanya Tilak. He said:

'You are quite right in seeking the help of all parties. There can be no difference of opinion on the South African question. But you must have a non-party man for your President. Meet Professor Bhandarkar. He has been taking no part of late in any public movement. But this question might possibly draw him out. See him and let me know what he says. I want to help you to the fullest extent. Of course you will meet me whenever you like. I am at your disposal.'

This was my first meeting with the Lokamanya. It revealed to me the secret of his unique popularity.

Next I met Gokhale. I found him on the Fergusson College grounds. He gave me an affectionate welcome, and his manner immediately won my heart. With him too this was my first meeting, and yet it seemed as though we were renewing an old friendship. **Sir Pherozeshah had seemed to me like the Himalaya, the Lokamanya like the ocean. But Gokhale was as the Ganges. One could have a refreshing bath in the holy river.** The Himalaya was unscalable, and one could not easily launch forth on the sea, but the Ganges invited one to its bosom. It was a joy to be on it with a boat and an oar. Gokhale closely examined me, as a schoolmaster would examine a candidate seeking admission to a school. He told me whom to approach and how to approach them. He asked to have a look at my speech. He showed me over the college, assured me that he was always at my disposal, asked me to let him know the result of the interview with Dr. Bhandarkar, and sent me away exultantly happy. In the sphere of politics the place that Gokhale occupied in my heart during his lifetime and occupies even now was and is absolutely unique.

Dr. Bhandarkar received me with the warmth of a father. It was noon when I called on him. The very fact that I was busy seeing people at that hour appealed greatly to this indefatigable savant, and my insistence of a non-party man for the president of the meeting had his ready approval, which was expressed in the spontaneous exclamation, 'That's it,' 'That's it.'

After he had heard me out he said: 'Anyone will tell you that I do not take part in politics. But I cannot refuse you. Your case is so strong and your industry is so admirable that I cannot decline to take part in your meeting. You did well in consulting Tilak and Gokhale. Please tell them that I shall be glad to preside over the meeting to be held under the joint auspices of the two Sabhas. You need not have the time of the meeting from me. Any time that suits them will suit me.' With this he bade me good-bye with congratulations and blessings.

Without any ado this erudite and selfless band of workers in Poona held a meeting in an unostentatious little place, and sent me away rejoicing and more confident of my mission.

In Madras

I next proceeded to Madras. It was wild with enthusiasm. The Balasundaram incident made a profound impression on the meeting. My speech was printed and was, for me, fairly long. But the audience listened to every word with attention. At the close of the meeting there was a regular run on the 'Green Pamphlet'. I brought out a second and revised edition of 10,000 copies. They sold like hot cakes, but I saw that it was not necessary to print such a large number. In my enthusiasm I had over- calculated the demand. It was the English-speaking public to which my speech had been addressed, and in Madras that class alone could not take the whole ten thousand.

The greatest help here came to me from the late Sjt. G. Parameshvaran Pillay, the editor of *The Madras Standard.* He had made a careful study of the question, and he often invited me to his office and gave me guidance. Sjt. G. Subrahmaniam of *The Hindu* and Dr. Subrahmaniam also were very sympathetic. But Sjt. G. Parame- shvaran Pillay placed the columns of *The Madras Standard* entirely at my disposal, and I freely availed myself of the offer. The meeting in Pachaiappa Hall, so far as I can recollect, was with Dr. Subrahmaniam in the chair.

The affection showered on me by most of the friends I met and their enthusiasm for the cause were so great that, in spite of my having to communicate with them in English, I felt myself entirely at home. What barrier is there that love cannot break?

In Calcutta

From Madras I proceeded to Calcutta where I found myself hemmed in by difficulties. I knew no one there. So I took a room in the Great Eastern Hotel. Here I became acquainted with Mr. Ellerthorpe, a representative of *The Daily Telegraph.* He invited me to the Bengal Club, where he was staying. He did not then realize that an Indian could not be taken to the drawing-room of the club. Having discovered the restriction, he took me to his room. He expressed his sorrow regarding this prejudice of the local Englishmen and apologized to me for not having been able to take me to the drawing-room.

I had of course to see Surendranath Banerji, the 'Idol of Bengal'. When I met him, he was surrounded by a number of friends. He said:

'I am afraid people will not take interest in your work. As you know, our difficulties here are by no means few. But you must try as best you can. You will have to enlist the sympathy of Maharajas. Mind you meet the representatives of the British Indian Association. You should meet Raja Sir Pyarimohan Mukarji and Maharaja Tagore. Both are liberal-minded and take a fair share in public work.'

I met these gentlemen, but without success. Both gave me a cold reception and said it was no easy thing to call a public meeting in Calcutta, and if anything could be done, it would practically all depend on Surendranath Banerji.

I saw that my task was becoming more and more difficult. I called at the office of *The Amrita Bazar Patrika.* **The gentleman whom I met there took me to be a wandering Jew. *The Bangabasi* went even one better. The editor kept me waiting for an hour.** He had evidently many interviewers, but he would not so much as look at me, even when he had disposed of the rest. On my venturing to broach my subject after the long wait, he said: 'Don't you see our hands are full? There is no end to the number of visitors like you. You had better go. I am not disposed to listen to you.' For a moment I felt offended, but I quickly understood the editor's position. I had heard of the fame of *The Bangabasi.* 'I could see that there was a regular stream of visitors there. And they were all people acquainted with him. His papers had no lack of topics to discuss, and South Africa was hardly known at that time.

But I was not discouraged. I kept on seeing editors of other papers. As usual I met the Anglo-Indian editors also. *The Statesman* and *The Englishman* realized the importance of the question. I gave them long interviews, and they published them in full.

Mr. Saunders, editor of *The Englishman,* claimed me as

his own. He placed his office and paper at my disposal. He even allowed me the liberty of making whatever changes I liked in the leading article he had written on the situation, the proof of which he sent me in advance. It is no exaggeration to say that a friendship grew up between us. He promised to render me all the help he could, carried out the promise to the letter, and kept on his correspondence with me until the time when he was seriously ill.

Throughout my life I have had the privilege of many such friendships, which have sprung up quite unexpectedly. What Mr. Saunders liked in me was my freedom from exaggeration and my devotion to truth. He subjected me to a searching cross-examination before he began to sympathize with my cause, and he saw that I had spared neither will nor pains to place before him an impartial statement of the case even of the white man in South Africa and also to appreciate it.

My experience has shown me that we win justice quickest by rendering justice to the other party.

The unexpected help of Mr. Saunders had begun to encourage me to think that I might succeed after all in holding a public meeting in Calcutta, when I received the following cable from Durban: 'Parliament opens January. Return soon.'

So I addressed a letter to the press, in which I explained why I had to leave Calcutta so abruptly, and set off for Bombay. Before starting I wired to the Bombay agent of Dada Abdulla and Co., to arrange for my passage by the first possible boat to South Africa. Dada Abdulla had just then purchased the steamship *Courland,* and insisted on my travelling on that boat, offering to take me and my family free of charge. I gratefully accepted the offer, and in the beginning of December set sail a second time for South Africa, now with my wife and two sons and the only son of my widowed sister. Another steamship *Naderi* also sailed for Durban at the same time. The agents of the Company were Dada Abdulla and Co. The total number of passengers these boats carried must have been about eight hundred, half of whom were bound for the Transvaal.

•••

6

WITH FAMILY IN S. AFRICA

This was my first voyage with my wife and children. An account of child marriages amongst middle class Hindus, the husband will be literate whilst the wife remains practically unlettered. A wide gulf thus separates them, and the husband has to become his wife's teacher. So I had to think out the details of the dress to be adopted by my wife and children, the food they were to eat, and the manners which would be suited to their new surroundings.

A Hindu wife regards implicit obedience to her husband as the highest religion. A Hindu husband regards himself as lord and master of his wife who must ever dance attendance upon him. I believed, at the time of which I am writing, that in order to look civilized, our dress and manners had as far as possible to approximate to the European standard. Because, I thought, only thus could we have some influence, and without influence it would not be possible to serve the community.

I therefore determined the style of dress for my wife and children. How could I like them to be known as Kathiawad Banias? **The Parsis used then to be regarded as the most civilized people amongst Indians, and so, when the complete European style seemed to be unsuited, we adopted the Parsi style.** Accordingly my wife wore the Parsi *sari,* and the boys the Parsi coat and trousers. Of course no one could be without shoes and stockings. It was long before my wife and children could get used to them. The shoes cramped their feet and the stockings stank with perspiration. The toes often got sore. I always had my answers ready to all these objections. But I have an impression that it was not so much the answers as the force of authority that carried conviction. They agreed to the changes in dress as there was no alternative. In the same spirit and with even more reluctance they adapted the use of knives and forks. When my infatuation for these signs of civilization wore away, they gave up the knives and forks. After having become long accustomed to the new style, it was perhaps no less irksome for them to return to the original mode. But I can see today that we feel all the freer and lighter for having cast off the tinsel of 'civilization'.

On board the same steamer with us were some relatives and acquaintances. These and other deck passengers I frequently met, because, the boat belonging to my client friends, I was free to move about anywhere and everywhere I liked.

Since the steamer was making straight for Natal, without calling at intermediate ports, our voyage was of only eighteen days. But as though to warn us of the coming real storm on land, a terrible gale overtook us, whilst we were only four days from Natal. The gale in which we were caught was so violent and prolonged that the passengers became alarmed. It was a solemn scene. All became one in face of the common danger. They forgot their differences and began to think of the one and only God—Musalmans, Hindus, Christians and all. Some took various vows. The captain also joined the passengers in their prayers. 'His will be done' was the only cry on every lip. So far as I can recollect, we must have been in this plight for about twenty-four hours. At last the sky cleared, the sun made his appearance, and the captain said that the storm had blown over. People's faces beamed with gladness, and with the disappearance of danger disappeared also the name of God from their lips. Eating and drinking, singing and merry-making again became the order of the day.

The ship cast anchor in the port of Durban on the 18th or 19th of December. The *Naderi* also reached the same day.

But the real storm was still to come.

Ships Stopped

We have seen that the two ships cast anchor in the port

of Durban on or about the 18th of December. No passengers are allowed to land at any of the South African ports before being subjected to a thorough medical examination. If the ship has any passenger suffering from a contagious disease, she has to undergo a period of quarantine. As there had been plague in Bombay when we set sail, we feared that we might have to go through a brief quarantine. Before the examination every ship has to fly a yellow flag, which is lowered only when the doctor has certified her to be healthy. Relatives and friends of passengers are allowed to come on board only after the yellow flag has been lowered.

Accordingly our ship was flying the yellow flag, when the doctor came and examined us. He ordered a five days' quarantine because, in his opinion, plague germs took twenty-three days at the most to develop. Our ship was therefore ordered to be put in quarantine until the twenty-third day of our sailing from Bombay.

But this quarantine order had more than health reasons behind it. The white residents of Durban had been agitating for our repatriation, and the agitation was one of the reasons for the order. Dada Abdulla and Co. kept us regularly informed about the daily happenings in the town. The whites were holding monster meetings every day. They were addressing all kinds of threats and at times offering even inducements to Dada Abdulla and Co. They were ready to indemnify the Company if both the ships should be sent back. But Dada Abdulla and Co. were not the people to be afraid of threats. Sheth Abdul Karim Haji Adam was then the managing partner of the firm. He was determined to moor the ships at the wharf and disembark the passengers at any cost. He was daily sending me detailed letters. Fortunately the late Sjt. Mansukhlal Naazar was then in Durban, having gone there to meet me. He was capable and fearless and guided the Indian community. Their advocate Mr. Laughton was an equally fearless man. He condemned the conduct of the white residents and advised the community, not merely as their paid advocate, but also as their true friend.

Thus Durban had become the scene of an unequal duel. On one side there was a handful of poor Indians and a few of their English friends, and on the other were ranged the white men, strong in arms, in numbers, in education and in wealth. They had also the backing of the State, for the Natal Government openly helped them. Mr. Harry Escombe, who was the most influential of the members of the Cabinet, openly took part in their meetings.

Now threats began to be addressed to us: 'If you do not go back, you will surely be pushed into the sea. But if you consent to return, you may even get your passage money back.' I constantly moved amongst my fellow-passengers cheering them up. I also sent messages of comfort to the passengers of the *Naderi.* All of them kept calm and courageous.

We arranged all sorts of games on the ship for the entertainment of the passengers. On Christmas Day the captain invited the saloon passengers to dinner. The principal among these were my family and I. In the speeches after dinner I spoke on Western civilization. I knew that this was not an occasion for a serious speech. But mine could not be otherwise. I took part in the merriment, but my heart was in the combat that was going on in Durban. For I was the real target. **There were two charges against me:**

1. that whilst in India I had indulged in unmerited condemnation of the Natal whites;

2. that with a view to swamping Natal with Indians I had specially brought the two shiploads of passengers to settle there.

I was conscious of my responsibility. I knew that Dada Abdulla and Co. had incurred 'grave risks on my account, the lives of the passengers were in danger, and by bringing my family with me I had put them likewise in jeopardy.

But I was absolutely innocent. I had induced no one to go to Natal. I did not know the passengers when they embarked. And with the exception of a couple of relatives, I did not know the name and address of even one of the hundreds of passengers on board. Neither had I said, whilst in India, a word about the whites in Natal that I had not already said in Natal itself. And I had ample evidence in support of all that I had said.

I therefore deplored the civilization of which the Natal whites were the fruit, and which they represented and championed. This civilization had all along been on my mind, and I therefore offered my views concerning it in my speech before that little meeting. The captain and other friends gave me a patient hearing, and received my speech in the spirit in which it was made. I do not know that it in any way affected the course of their lives, but afterwards I had long talks with the captain and other officers regarding the civilization of the West. **I had in my speech described Western civilization as being, unlike the Eastern, predominantly based on force.** The questioners pinned me to my faith, and one of them—the captain so far as I recollect—said to me:

'Supposing the whites carry out their threats, **how will you stand by our principle of non-violence?' To which I replied: 'I hope God will give me the courage and the sense to forgive them and to refrain from bringing them to law. I have no anger against them. I know that they are sorry for their ignorance and their narrowness.** I know that they sincerely believe that what they are doing today is right and proper. I have no reason therefore to be angry with them.'

The questioner smiled, possibly distrustfully.

Thus the days dragged on their weary length. When the quarantine would terminate was still uncertain. The Quarantine Officer said that the matter had passed out of his hands and that, as soon as he had orders from the Government, he would permit us to land.

At last ultimatums were served on the passengers and me. We were asked to submit, if we would escape with our lives. In our reply the passengers and I both maintained our right to land at Port Natal, and intimated our determination to enter Natal at any risk.

At the end of twenty-three days the ships were permitted to enter the harbour, and orders permitting the passengers to land were passed.

Attacks on Gandhi

So the ships were brought into the dock and the passengers began to go ashore. But Mr. Escombe had sent word to the captain that, as the whites were highly enraged against me and my life was in danger, my family and I should be advised to land at dusk, when the Port Superintendent Mr. Tatum would escort us home. The captain communicated the message to me, and I agreed to act accordingly. But scarcely half an hour after this Mr. Laughton came to the captain. He said: 'I would like to take Mr. Gandhi with me, should he have no objection. As the legal adviser of the Agent Company I tell you that you are not bound to carry out the message you have received from Mr. Escombe.' After this he came to me and said somewhat to this effect: **'If you are not afraid, I suggest that Mrs. Gandhi and the children should drive to Mr. Rustomji's house, whilst you and I follow them on foot. I do not like the idea of your entering the city like a thief in the night.** I do not think there is any fear of anyone hurting you. Everything is quiet now. The whites have all dispersed. But in any case I am convinced that you ought not to enter the city stealthily.' I readily agreed. My wife and children drove safely to Mr. Rustomji's place. With the captain's permission I went ashore with Mr. Laughton. Mr. Rustomji's house was about two miles from the dock.

As soon as we landed, some youngsters recognized me and shouted 'Gandhi, Gandhi'. About half a dozen men rushed to the spot and joined in the shouting. Mr. Laughton feared that the crowd might swell and hailed a rickshaw. I had never liked the idea of being in a rickshaw. This was to be my first experience. But the youngsters would not let me get into it. They frightened the rickshaw-boy out of his life, and he took to his heels. As we went ahead, the crowd continued to swell, until it became impossible to proceed further. They first caught hold of Mr. Laughton and separated us. **Then they pelted me**

with stones, brick-bats and rotten eggs. Someone snatched away my turban, whilst others began to batter and kick me. I fainted and caught hold of the front railings of a house and stood there to get my breath. But it was impossible. They came upon me boxing and battering. The wife of the Police Superintendent, who knew me, happened to be passing by. The brave lady came up, opened her parasol though there was no sun then, and stood between the crowd and me. This checked the fury of the mob, as it was difficult for them to deliver blows on me without harming Mrs. Alexander.

Meanwhile, an Indian youth who witnessed the incident had run to the police station. The Police Superintendent Mr. Alexander sent a posse of men to ring me round and escort me safely to my destination. They arrived in time. The police station lay on our way. As we reached there, the Superintendent asked me to take refuge in the station, but I gratefully declined the offer. 'They are sure to quiet down when they realize their mistake,' I said. 'I have trust in their sense of fairness.' Escorted by the police, I arrived without further harm at Mr. Rustomji's place. I had bruises all over, but no abrasions except in one place. Dr. Dadibarjor, the ship's doctor, who was on the spot, rendered the best possible help.

There was quiet inside, but outside the whites surrounded the house. Night was coming on, and the yelling crowd was shouting, 'We must have Gandhi.' The quick-sighted Police Superintendent was already there trying to keep the crowds under control, not by threats, but by humouring them. But he was not entirely free from anxiety. He sent me a message to this effect: 'If you would save your friend's house and property and also your family, you should escape from the house in disguise, as I suggest.'

Thus on one and the same day I was faced with two contradictory positions. When danger to life had been no more than imaginary, Mr. Laughton advised me to launch forth openly. I accepted the advice. When the danger was quite real, another friend gave me the contrary advice, and I accepted that too. **Who can say whether I did so because I saw that**

my life was in jeopardy, or because I did not want to put my friend's life and property or the lives of my wife and children in danger? Who can say for certain that I was right both when I faced the crowd in the first instance bravely, as it was said, and when I escaped from it in disguise?

It is idle to adjudicate upon the right and wrong of incidents that have already happened. It is useful to understand them and, if possible, to learn a lesson from them for the future. It is difficult to say for certain how a particular man would act in a particular set of circumstances. We can also see that judging a man from his outward act is no more than a doubtful inference, inasmuch as it is not based on sufficient data.

Escape in Disguise

Be that as it may, the preparations for escape made me forget my injuries. As suggested by the Superintendent, I put on an Indian constable's uniform and wore on my head a Madrasi scarf, wrapped round a plate to serve as a helmet. Two detectives accompanied me, one of them disguised as an Indian merchant and with his face painted to resemble that of an Indian. I forget the disguise of the other. We reached a neighbouring shop by a bylane and, making our way through the gunny bags piled in the godown, escaped by the gate of the shop and threaded our way through the crowd to a carriage that had been kept for me at the end of the street. In this we drove off to the same police station where Mr. Alexander had offered me refuge a short time before, and I thanked him and the detective officers.

Whilst I had been thus effecting my escape, Mr. Alexander had kept the crowd amused by singing the tune:

Hang old Gandhi
On the sour apple tree.

When he was informed of my safe arrival at the police station, he thus broke the news to the crowd: 'Well, your victim has made good his escape through a neighbouring shop. You had better go home now.' Some of them were angry, others laughed, some refused to believe the story.

'Well then,' said the Superintendent, 'if you do not believe me, you may appoint one or two representatives, whom I am ready to take inside the house. If they succeed in finding out Gandhi, I will gladly deliver him to you. But if they fail, you must disperse. I am sure that you have no intention of destroying Mr. Rustomji's house or of harming Mr. Gandhi's wife and children.'

The crowd sent their representatives to search the house. They soon returned with disappointing news, and the crowd broke up at last, most of them admiring the Superintendent's tactful handling of the situation, and a few fretting and fuming.

'I'll not Prosecute Anyone'

The late Mr. Chamberlain, who was then Secretary of State for the Colonies, cabled asking the Natal Government to prosecute my assailants. Mr. Escombe sent for me, expressed his regret for the injuries I had sustained, and said: 'Believe me, I cannot feel happy over the least little injury done to your person. You had a right to accept Mr. Laughton's advice and to face the worst, but I am sure that, if you had considered my suggestion favourably, these sad occurrences would not have happened. If you can identify the assailants, I am prepared to arrest and prosecute them. Mr. Chamberlain also desires me to do so.'

To which I gave the following reply:

'I do not want to prosecute anyone. It is possible that I may be able to identify one or two of them, but what is the use of getting them punished? Besides, I do not hold the assailants to blame. They were given to understand that I had made exaggerated statements in India about the whites in Natal and caluminated them. If they believed these reports, it is no wonder that they were enraged. **The leaders, and, if you will permit me to say so, you are to blame. You could have guided the people properly, but you also believed Reuter and assumed that must have indulged in exaggeration.** I do no want to bring anyone to book. I am sure that, when the truth becomes known, they will be sorry for their conduct.'

'Would you mind giving me this in writing?' said Mr. Escombe. 'Because I shall have to cable to Mr. Chamberlain to that effect. I do not want you to make any statement in haste. You may, if you like, consult Mr. Laughton and your other friends, before you come to a final decision. I may confess, however, that, if you waive the right of bringing your assailants to book, you will considerably help me in restoring quiet, besides enhancing your own reputation.'

'Thank you,' said I. 'I need not consult anyone. I had made my decision in the matter before I came to you. It is my conviction that I should not prosecute the assailants, and I am prepared this moment to reduce my decision to writing.'

With this I gave him the necessary statement.

Calm After the Storm

I had not yet left the police station, when, after two days, I was taken to see Mr. Escombe. Two constables were sent to protect me, though no such precaution was then needed.

On the day of landing, as soon as the yellow flag was lowered, a representative of *The Natal Advertiser* had come to interview me. He had asked me a number of questions, and in reply I had been able to refute everyone of the charges that had been levelled against me. Thanks to Sir Pherozeshah Mehta, I had delivered only written speeches in India, and I had copies of them all, as well as of my other writings. I had given the interviewer all this literature and showed him that in India I had said nothing which I had not already said in South Africa in stronger language. I had also shown him that I had had no hand in bringing the passengers of the *Courland* and *Naderi* to South Africa. Many of them were old residents, and most of them, far from wanting to stay in Natal, meant to go to the Transvaal. In those days the Transvaal offered better prospects than Natal to those coming in search of wealth, and most Indians, therefore, preferred to go there.

This interview and my refusal to prosecute the assailants produced such a profound impression that the Europeans of Durban were ashamed of their conduct. The press declared me to be innocent and condemned the mob. **Thus the lynching ultimately proved to be a blessing for me that is, for the cause. It enhanced the prestige of the Indian community in South Africa and made my work easier.**

In three or four days I went to my house, and it was not long before I settled down again. The incident added also to my professional practice. But if it enhanced the prestige of the community, it also fanned the flame of prejudice against it. As soon as it was proved that the Indian could put up a manly fight, he came to be regarded as a danger. Two bills were introduced in the Natal Legislative Assembly, one of them calculated to affect the Indian trader adversely, and the other to impose a stringent restriction on Indian immigration. Fortunately, the fight for the franchise had resulted in a decision to the effect that no enactment might be passed against the Indians as such, that is to say, that the law should make no distinctions of colour or race. The language of the bills above mentioned made them applicable to all, but their object undoubtedly was to impose further restrictions on the Indian residents of Natal.

The bills considerably increased my public work and made the community more alive than ever to their sense of duty. They were translated into Indian languages and fully explained, so as to bring home to the community their subtle implications. We appealed to the Colonial Secretary, but he refused to interfere and the bills became law.

Public work now began to absorb most of my time. Sjt. Mansukhlal Naazar came to stay with me, and as he gave his time to public work, he lightened my burden to some extent.

Sheth Adamji Miyakhan had, in my absence, discharged his duty with great credit. He had increased the membership and added about £ 1,000 to the coffers of the Natal Indian Congress. The awakening caused by the bills and the demonstration against the passengers I turned to good account by making an appeal for membership and funds, which now amounted to £ 5,000. My desire was to secure for the Congress a permanent fund, so that it might procure property of its own and then carry on its work out of the rent of the property.

This was my first experience of managing a public institution. I placed my proposal before my co-workers, and they welcomed it. The property that was purchased was leased out, and the rent was enough to meet the current expenses of the Congress. The property was vested in a strong body of trustees and is still there today, but it has become the source of much internecine quarrelling with the result that the rent of the property now accumulates in the court.

This sad situation developed after my departure from South Africa, but my idea of having permanent funds for public institutions underwent a change long before this difference arose. And now after considerable experience with the many public institutions which I have managed, it has become my firm conviction that it is not good to run public institutions on permanent funds. A permanent fund carries in itself the seed of the moral fall of the institution. A public institution means an institution conducted with the approval, and from the funds, of the public. When such an institution ceases to have public support, it forfeits its right to exist. Institutions maintained on permanent funds are often found to ignore public opinion, and are frequently responsible for acts contrary to it.

These views were confirmed during the days of the Satyagraha in South Africa. That magnificent campaign extending over six years was carried on without permanent funds, though lakhs of rupees were necessary for it. I can recollect times when I did not know what would happen the next day if no subscriptions came in.

Education of Children

When I landed at Durban in January 1897, I had three children with me, my sister's son ten years old, and my own sons nine and five years of age. Where was I to educate them?

I could have sent them to the schools for European children, but only as a matter of favour and exception. No other Indian children were allowed to attend them. For these there were schools established by Christian missions, but I was not prepared to send my children there, as I did not like the education imparted in those schools. For one thing, the medium of instruction would be only English, or perhaps incorrect Tamil or Hindi; this too could only have been arranged with difficulty. I could not possibly put up with this and other disadvantages. In the meantime I was making my own attempt to teach them. But that was at best irregular, and I could not get hold of a suitable Gujarati teacher.

I was at my wits' end. I advertised for an English teacher who should teach the children under my direction. Some regular instruction was to be given them by this teacher, and for the rest they should be satisfied with what little I could give them irregularly. So I engaged an English governess on £7 a month. This went on for some time, but not to my satisfaction. The boys acquired some knowledge of Gujarati through my conversation and intercourse with them, which was strictly in the mother-tongue. I was loathe to send them back to India, for I believed even then that young children should not be separated from their parents. I did send my nephew and elder son to be educated at residential schools in India for a few months, but I soon had to recall them. Later, the eldest son, long after he had come of age, broke away from me, and went to India to join a High School in Ahmedabad. The other three of my sons have never been at a public school, though they did get some regular schooling in an improvised school which I started for the children of Satyagrahi parents in South Africa.

These experiments were all inadequate. I could not devote to the children all the time I had wanted to give them. My inability to give them enough attention and other unavoidable causes prevented me from providing them with the literary education I had desired, and all my sons have had complaints to make against me in this matter. Whenever they come across an M.A. or a B.A., or even a matriculate, they seem to feel the handicap of a want of school education.

Therefore, though I have not been able to give them a literary education either to their or to my satisfaction, I am not quite sure, as I look back on my past years, that I have not done my duty by them to the best of my capacity. Nor do I regret not having sent them to public schools. I have always felt that the undesirable traits I see today in my eldest son are an echo of my own undisciplined and unformulated early life.

But the ultimate result of my experiments is in the womb of the future. The purpose of this chapter is to show the lengths to which a votary of truth is driven by his experiments with truth, as also to show the votary of liberty how many are the sacrifices demanded by that stern goddess.

The youths whom I called out in 1920 from those citadels of slavery— their schools and colleges—and whom I advised that it was far better to remain unlettered and break stones for the sake of liberty than to go in for a literary education in the chains of slaves will probably be able to trace my advice to its source.

Spirit of Service

My profession progressed satisfactorily, but that was far from satisfying me. The question of further simplifying my life and of doing some concrete act of service to my fellowmen had been constantly agitating me, when a leper came to my door. I had not the heart to dismiss him with a meal. So I offered him shelter, dressed his wounds, and began to look after him. But I could not go on like that indefinitely. I could not afford, I lacked the will to keep him always with me. So I sent him to the Government Hospital for indentured labourers.

But I was still ill at ease. I longed for some humanitarian work of a permanent nature. Dr. Booth was the head of the St. Aidan's Mission. He was a kind-hearted man and treated his patients free. Thanks to Parsi Rustomji's charities, it was possible to open a small charitable hospital under Dr. Booth's charge. I felt strongly inclined to serve as a nurse in this hospital. The work of dispensing medicines took from one to two hours daily, and I made up my mind to find that time from my office-work, so as to be able to fill the place of a compounder in the dispensary attached to the hospital.

This work brought me some peace. It consisted in ascertaining the patient's complaints, laying the facts before the doctor and dispensing the prescriptions. It brought me in close touch with suffering Indians, most of them indentured Tamil, Telugu or North India men.

The experience stood me in good stead, when during the Boer War I offered my services for nursing the sick and wounded soldiers.

The question of the rearing of children had been ever before me. I had two sons born in South Africa, and my service in the hospital was useful in solving the question of their upbringing. I studied the things necessary for safe labour. I read Dr. Tribhuvandas' book, *Ma-ne Shikhaman*—Advice to a Mother—and I nursed both my children according to the instructions given in the book, tempered here and there by such experience as I had gained elsewhere. The services of a nurse were utilized—not for more than two months each time—chiefly for helping my wife, and not for taking care of the babies, which I did myself.

The birth of the last child put me to the severest test. The travail came on suddenly. The doctor was not immediately available, and some time was lost in fetching the midwife. Even if she had been on the spot, she could not have helped delivery. I had to see through the safe delivery of the baby. My careful study of the subject in Dr. Tribhuvandas' work was of inestimable help. I was not nervous.

The couple who realize these things will never have sexual union for the fulfilment of their lust, but only when they desire issue. I think it is the height of ignorance to believe that the sexual act is an independent function necessary like sleeping or eating. The world depends for its existence on the act of generation, and as the world is the playground of God and a reflection of His glory, the act of generation should be controlled for the ordered growth of the world.

Brahmacharya

We now reach the stage in this story when I began seriously to think of taking the *brahmacharya* vow. It was in South Africa that I came to realize the importance of observing *brahmacharya* even with respect to my wife.

What should be my relation with my wife? Did my faithfulness consist in making my wife the instrument of my lust? So long as I was the slave of lust, my faithfulness was worth nothing. To be fair to my wife, I must say that she was never the temptress. It was therefore the easiest thing for me to take the vow of *brahmacharya,* if only I willed it. It was my weak will or lustful attachment that was the obstacle.

Even after my conscience had been roused in the matter, I failed twice. I failed because the motive that actuated the effort was none the highest. My main object was to escape having more children. Whilst in England I had read something about contraceptives. I have referred to Dr. Allinson's birth control propaganda. If it had some temporary effect on me, Mr. Hill's opposition to those methods and his advocacy of internal efforts as opposed to outward means, in a word, of self-control, had a far greater effect, which in due time came to be abiding. Seeing, therefore, that I did not desire more children I began to strive after self control. There was endless difficulty in the task. We began to sleep in separate beds. I decided to retire to bed only after the day's work had left me completely exhausted. All these efforts did not seem to bear much fruit.

The final resolution could only be made as late as 1906. Satyagraha had not then been started. I was practising in Johannesburg at the time of the Zulu 'Rebellion' in Natal, which came soon after the Boer War. I felt that I must offer my services to the Natal Government on that occassion. The offer was accepted. But the work set me furiously thinking in the direction of self-control, and according to my wont I discussed my thoughts with my co-workers. It became my conviction that procreation and the consequent care of children were inconsistent with public service. I had to break up my household at Johannesburg to be able to serve during the

'Rebellion'. I took my wife and children to Phoenix and led the Indian ambulance corps attached to the Natal forces. During the difficult marches that had then to be performed, the idea flashed upon me that, if I wanted to devote myself to the service of the community in this manner, I must relinquish the desire for children and wealth and live the life of a *vanaprastha*—of one retired from household cares.

After full discussion and mature deliberation I took the vow in 1906. I had not shared my thoughts with my wife until then, but only consulted her at the time of taking the vow. She had no objection. But I had great difficulty in making the final resolve. I had not the necessary strength. How was I to control my passions? The elimination of carnal relationship with one's wife seemed then a strange thing. But I launched forth with faith in the sustaining power of God.

As I look back upon the twenty years of the vow, I am filled with pleasure and wonderment. The more or less successful practice of self-control had been going on since 1901. But the freedom and joy that came to me after taking the vow had never been experienced before 1906. Before the vow I had been open to being overcome by temptation at any moment. Now the vow was a sure shield against temptation.

The knowledge that a perfect observance of *brahmacharya* means realization of *brahman,* I did not owe to a study of the Shastras. It slowly grew upon me with experience. The shastraic texts on the subject I read only later in life. Every day of the vow has taken me nearer the knowledge that in *brahmacharya* lies the protection of the body, the mind and the soul. For *brahmacharya* was now no process of hard penance, it was a matter of consolation and joy. Every day revealed a fresh beauty in it.

But if it was a matter of ever-increasing joy, let no one believe that it was an easy thing for me. Even when I am past fifty-six years, I realize how hard a thing it is. Every day I realize more and more that it is like walking on the sword's edge, and I see every moment the necessity for eternal vigilance.

Control of the palate is the first essential in the observance of the vow. I found that complete control of the palate made the observance very easy, and so I now pursued my dietetic experiments not merely from the vegetarian's but also from the *brahmachari's* point of view. As the result of these experiments I saw that the *brahmachari's* food should be limited, simple, spiceless, and, if possible, uncooked. Six years of experiment have showed me that the *brahmachari's* ideal food is fresh fruit and nuts. *Brahmacharya* needed no effort on my part in South Africa when I lived on fruits and nuts alone.

As an external aid to *brahmacharya,* fasting is as necessary as selection and restriction in diet. So overpowering are the senses that they can be kept under control only when they are completely hedged in on all sides, from above and from beneath. It is common knowledge that they are powerless without food, and so fasting undertaken with a view to control of the senses is, I have no doubt, very helpful.

Brahmacharya means control of the senses in thought, word and deed. So long as thought is not under complete control of the will, *brahmacharya* in its fulness is absent. Involuntary thought is an affection of the mind, and curbing of thought, therefore, means curbing of the mind which is even more difficult to curb than the wind. Nevertheless the existence of God within makes even control of the mind possible.

I had started on a life of ease and comfort, but the experiment was shortlived. Although I had furnished the house with care, yet it failed to have any hold on me. So no sooner had I launched forth on that life, than I began to cut down expenses. The washerman's bill was heavy, and as he was besides by no means noted for his punctuality, even two or three dozen shirts and collars proved insufficient for me. Collars had to be changed daily and shirts, if not daily, at least every alternate day. This meant a double expense, which appeared to me unnecessary. So I equipped myself with a washing outfit to save it. I bought a book on washing, studied the art and taught it also to my wife. This no doubt added to my work, but its novelty made it a pleasure.

In course of time I became an expert washerman so far as my own work went, and my washing was by no means inferior to laundry washing. My collars were no less stiff or shiny than others.

When Gokhale came to South Africa, he had with him a scarf which was a gift from Mahadeo Govind Ranade. He treasured the memento with the utmost care and used it only on special occasions. One such occasion was the banquet given in his honour by the Johannesburg Indians. The scarf was creased and needed ironing. It was not possible to send it to the laundry and get it back in time. I offered to try my art.

'I can trust to your capacity as a lawyer but not as a washerman,' said Gokhale. 'What if you should soil it? Do you know what it means to me?'

With this he narrated, with much joy, the story of the gift. I still insisted, guaranteed good work, got his permission to iron it, and won his certificate. After that I did not mind if the rest of the world refused me its certificate.

In the same way, I threw off dependence on the barber. All people who go to England learn there at least the art of shaving, but none, to my knowledge, learn to cut their own hair. I had to learn that too. I once went to an English haircutter in Pretoria. He contemptuously refused to cut my hair. I certainly felt hurt, but immediately purchased a pair of clippers and cut my hair before the mirror. I succeeded more or less in cutting the front hair, but I spoiled the back. The friends in the court shook with laughter.

'What's wrong with your hair, Gandhi? Rats have been at it?'

'No. The white barber would not condescend to touch my black hair,' said I, 'so I preferred to cut it myself, no matter how badly.'

Serving in the Boer War : A New Idea

I must skip many other experiences of the period between 1897 and 1899 and come straight to the Boer War.

When the war was declared, my personal sympathies were all with the Boers, but I believed then that I had yet no right, in such cases to enforce my individual convictions. My loyalty to the British rule drove me to participation with the British in that war. **I felt that, if I demanded rights as a British citizen, it was also my duty as such, to participate in the defence of the British Empire. I held then that India could achieve her complete emancipation only within and through the British Empire.** So I collected together as many comrades as possible, and with very great difficulty got their services accepted as an ambulance corps.

The average Englishman believed that the Indian was a coward, incapable of taking risks or looking beyond his immediate self-interest. Many English friends, therefore, threw cold water on my plan. But Dr. Booth supported it wholeheartedly. He trained us in ambulance work. We secured medical certificates of fitness for service. Mr. Laughton and the late Mr. Escombe enthusiastically supported the plan, and we applied at last for service at the front. The Government thankfully acknowledged our application, but said that our services were not then needed.

I would not rest satisfied, however, with this refusal. Through the introduction of Dr. Booth, I called on the Bishop of Natal. There were many Christian Indians in our corps. The Bishop was delighted with my proposal and promised to help us in getting our services accepted. Time too was working with us. The Boer had shown more pluck, determination and bravery than had been expected; and our services were ultimately needed.

Our corps was 1,100 strong, with nearly 40 leaders. About three hundred were free Indians, and the rest indentured. Dr. Booth was also with us. The corps acquitted itself well. Though our work was to be outside the firing line, and though we had the protection of the Red Cross, we were asked at a critical moment to serve within the firing line. The reservation had not been of our seeking. The authorities did not want us to be within the range of fire. The situation, however, was changed after the repulse at Spion Kop, and General Buller sent the message that, though we were not bound to take the risk, Government would be thankful if we would do so and fetch the wounded from the field. We had no hesitation, and so the action at Spion Kop found us working within the firing line. During these days we had to march from twenty to twenty-five miles a day, bearing the wounded on stretchers. Amongst the wounded we had the honour of carrying soldiers like General Woodgate.

The corps was disbanded after six weeks' service. After the reverses at Spion Kop and Vaalkranz, the British Commander-in-Chief abandoned the attempt to relieve Ladysmith and other places by summary procedure, and decided to proceed slowly, awaiting reinforcements from England and India.

Our humble work was at the moment much applauded, and the Indians' prestige was enhanced. The newspapers published laudatory rhymes with the refrain, 'We are sons of Empire after all.' General Buller mentioned with appreciation the work of the corps in his despatch, and the leaders were awarded the War Medal.

The Indian community became better organized. I got into closer touch with the indentured Indians. There came a greater awakening amongst them, and the feeling that Hindus, Musalmans, Christians, Tamilians, Gujaratis and Sindhis were all Indians and children of the same motherland took deep root amongst them. Everyone believed that the Indians' grievances were now sure to be redressed. At the moment the white man's attitude seemed to be distinctly changed. The relations formed with the whites during the war were of the sweetest. We had come in contact with thousands of tommies. They were friendly with us and thankful for being there to serve them.

Sanitary Reform

It has always been impossible for me to reconcile myself to any one member of the body politic remaining out of use. I have always been loathe to hide or connive at the weak points of the community or to press for its rights without having purged it of its blemishes. Therefore, ever since my settlement in Natal, I had been endeavouring to clear the community of a charge that had been levelled against it, not without a certain amount of truth. The charge had often been made that the Indian was slovenly in his habits and did not keep his house and surroundings clean. House-to-house inspection was undertaken when plague was reported to be imminent in Durban. This was done after consulting, and gaining the approval of the city fathers, who had desired our co-operation.

But I had some bitter experiences. I saw that I could not so easily count on the help of the community in getting it to do its own duty, as I could in claiming for it rights. At some places I met with insults, at others with polite indifference. It was too much for people to bestir themselves to keep their surroundings clean. To expect them to find money for the work was out of the question. These experiences taught me, better than ever before, that **without infinite patience it was impossible to get the people to do any work. It is the reformer who is anxious for the reform, and not society,** from which he should expect nothing better than opposition, abhorrence and even mortal persecution. Why may not society regard as retrogression what the reformer holds dear as life itself?

Nevertheless the result of this agitation was that the Indian community learnt to recognize more or less the necessity for keeping their houses and environments clean. I gained the esteem of the authorities. They saw that, though I had made it my business to ventilate grievances and press for rights, I was no less keen and insistent upon self-purification.

There was one thing, however, which still remained to be done, namely, the awakening in the Indian settler of a sense of duty to the motherland. India was poor, the Indian settler went to South Africa in search of wealth, and he was bound to contribute part of his earnings for the benefit of his countrymen in the hour of their adversity. This the settler did during the terrible famines of 1897 and 1899. They contributed handsomely for famine relief, and more so in 1899 than 1897.

We had appealed to Englishmen also for funds, and they had responded well. Even the indentured Indians gave their share to the contribution, and the system inaugurated at the time of these famines had been continued ever since.

On my relief from war-duty I felt that my work was no longer in South Africa but in India. Not that there was nothing to be done in South Africa, but I was afraid that my main business might become merely money-making. Friends at home were also pressing me to return and I felt that I should be of more service in India. And for the work in South Africa, there were, of course, Messrs Khan and Mansukhlal Naazar. So I requested my co-workers to relieve me. After very great difficulty my request was conditionally accepted, the condition being that I should be ready to go back to South Africa if, within a year, the community should need me.

Costly Gifts

At this time I was intimately connected only with Natal. The Natal Indians bathed me with the nectar of love. Farewell meetings were arranged at every place, and costly gifts were presented to me. The gifts of course included things in gold and silver, but there were articles of costly diamond as well.

What right had I to accept all these gifts? Accepting them, how could I persuade myself that I was serving the community without remuneration? The evening I was presented with the bulk of these things I had a sleepless night. I walked up and down my room deeply agitated, but could find no solution. It was difficult for me to forego gifts worth hundreds, it was more difficult to keep them.

And even if I could keep them, what about my children? What about my wife? They were being trained to a life of service and to an understanding that service was its own reward.

I decided that I could not keep these things. I drafted a letter, creating a trust of them in favour of the community and appointing Parsi Rustomji and others trustees. In the morning I held a consultation with my wife and children and finally got rid of the heavy incubus.

I knew that I should have some difficulty in persuading my wife, and I was sure that I should have none so far as the children were concerned. So I decided to constitute them my attorneys.

The children readily agreed to my proposal.

I was delighted. 'Then you will plead with mother, won't you?' I asked them.

'Certainly,' said they. 'That is our business. She does not need to wear the ornaments. She would want to keep them for us, and if we don't want them, why should she not agree to part with them?'

But it was easier said than done.

'You may not need them,' said my wife. 'Your children may not need them. Cajoled, they will dance to your tune. I can understand your not permitting me to wear them. But what about my daughters-in-law? They will be sure to need them. And who knows what will happen tomorrow? I would be the last person to part with gifts so lovingly given.'

And thus the torrent of argument went on, reinforced, in the end, by tears. But the children were adamant. And I was unmoved.

I mildly put in: 'The children have yet to get married. We do not want to see them married young. When they are grown up, they can take care of themselves. And surely we shall not have, for our sons, brides who are fond of ornaments. And if, after all, we need to provide them with ornaments, I am there. You will ask me then.'

'Ask you? I know you by this time. You deprived me of my ornaments, you would not leave me in peace with them. Fancy you offering to get ornaments for the daughters-in-law! You who are trying to make *sadhus* of my boys from today! No, the ornaments will not be returned. And pray what right have you to my necklace?'

'But,' I rejoined, 'is the necklace given you for your service or for my service?'

'I agree. But service rendered by you is as good as rendered by me. I have toiled and moiled for you day and night. Is that no service? You forced all and sundry on me, making me weep bitter tears, and I slaved for them!'

These were pointed thrusts, and some of them went home. But I was determined to return the ornaments. I somehow succeeded in extorting a consent from her. The gifts were all returned.

Often, when I was in need of funds for public purposes, and felt that I must draw upon the trust, I have been able to raise the requisite amount, leaving the trust money intact. The fund is still there, being operated upon in times of need, and it has regularly accumulated.

I have never since regretted the step, and as the years have gone by, my wife has also seen its wisdom. It has saved us from many temptations.

I am definitely of opinion that a public worker should accept no costly gifts.

•••

7

At the Congress Session in India

I sailed for home. Mauritius was one of the ports of call, and as the boat made a long halt there, I went ashore and acquainted myself fairly well with the local conditions. For one night I was the guest of Sir Charles Bruce, the Governor of the Colony.

After reaching India I spent some time in going about the country. It was the year 1901 when the Congress met at Calcutta under the presidentship of Mr. (later Sir) Dinshaw Wacha. And I of course attended it. It was my first experience of the Congress.

From Bombay I travelled in the same train as Sir Pherozeshah Mehta, as I had to speak to him about conditions in South Africa. I knew the kingly style in which he lived. He had engaged a special saloon for himself, and I had orders to take my opportunity of speaking to him by travelling in his saloon for one stage. I, therefore, went to the saloon and reported myself at the appointed station. With him were Mr. Wacha, and Mr. (now Sir) Chimanlal Setalvad. They were discussing politics.

As soon as Sir Pherozeshah saw me, he said, 'Gandhi, it seems nothing can be done for you. Of course we will pass the resolution you want. But what rights have we in our own country? I believe that, so long as we have no power in our own land, you cannot fare better in the Colonies.'

I was taken aback. Mr. Setalvad seemed to concur in the view; Mr. Wacha cast a pathetic look at me.

I tried to plead with Sir Pherozeshah, but it was out of the question for one like me to prevail upon the uncrowned king of Bombay. I contented myself with the fact that I should be allowed to move my resolution.

'You will of course show me the resolution,' said Mr. Wacha, to cheer me up. I thanked him and left them at the next stop.

So we reached Calcutta. The President was taken to his camp with great *eclat* by the Reception Committee. I asked a volunteer where I was to go. He took me to the Ripon College, where a number of delegates were being put up. Fortune favoured me. Lokamanya was put up in the same block as I. I have a recollection that he came a day later.

And as was natural, Lokamanya would never be without his darbar. Were I a painter, I could paint him as I saw him seated on his bed—so vivid is the whole scene in my memory. Of the numberless people that called on him, I can recollect today only one, namely, the late Babu Motilal Ghose, editor of the *Amrita Bazar Patrika.* Their loud laughter and their talks about the wrong doings of the ruling race cannot be forgotten.

But I propose to examine in some detail the appointments in this camp. The volunteers were clashing against one another. You asked one of them to do something. He delegated it to another, and he in his turn to a third, and so on; and as for the delegates, they were neither here nor there.

I made friends with a few volunteers. I told them some things about South Africa, and they felt somewhat ashamed. I tried to bring home to them the secret of service. They seemed to understand, but service is no mushroom growth. It presupposes the will first and then experience. There was no lack of will on the part of those good simple-hearted young men, but their experience was nil. The Congress would meet three days every year and then go to sleep. What training could one have out of a three days' show once a year? And the delegates were of a piece with the volunteers. They had no better or longer training. They would do nothing themselves. 'Volunteer, do this,' 'Volunteer, do that,' were their constant orders.

Even here **I was face to face with untouchability in a fair measure. The Tamilian kitchen was far away from the rest. To the Tamil delegates even the sight of others, whilst they were dining, meant pollution.** So a special kitchen had to be made for them in the College compound, walled in by wickerwork. It was full of smoke which choked you. It was a kitchen, dining room, washroom, all in one—a close safe with no outlet. To me this looked like a travesty of *Varnadharma.* **If, I said to myself, there was such untouchability between the delegates of the Congress, one could well imagine the extent to which it existed amongst their constituents. I heaved a sigh at the thought.**

There was no limit to insanitation. Pools of water were everywhere. There were only a few latrines, and the recollection of their stink still oppresses me. I pointed it out to the volunteers. They said pointblank: 'That is not our work, it is the scavenger's work.' **I asked for a broom. The man stared at me in wonder. I procured one and cleaned the latrine.** But that was for myself. The rush was so great, and the latrines were so few, that they needed frequent cleaning; but that was more than I could do. So I had to content myself with simply ministering to myself. And the others did not seem to mind the stench and the dirt.

But that was not all. **Some of the delegates did not scruple to use the verandahs outside their rooms for calls of nature at night. In morning I pointed out the spots to the volunteers. No one was ready to undertake the cleaning, and I found no one to share the honour with me of doing It.** Conditions have since considerably improved, but even today thoughtless delegates are not wanting who disfigure the Congress camp by committing nuisance wherever they choose, and all the volunteers are not always ready to clean up after them.

I saw that, **if the Congress session were to be prolonged, conditions would be quite favourable for the outbreak of an epidemic.**

Worked as a Clerk

There were yet two days for the Congress session to begin. I had made up my mind to offer my services to the Congress office in order to gain some experience. So as soon as I had finished the daily ablutions on arrival at Calcutta, I proceeded to the Congress office.

Babu Bhupendranath Basu and Sjt. Ghosal were the secretaries. I went to Bhupenbabu and offered my services. He looked at me, and said: 'I have no work, but possibly Ghosalbabu might have something to give you. Please go to him.'

So I went to him. He scanned me and said with a smile: 'I can give you only clerical work. Will you do it?'

'Certainly,' said I. 'I am here to do anything that is not beyond my capacity.'

'That is the right spirit, young man,' he said. Addressing the volunteers who surrounded him, he added, 'Do you hear what this young man says?'

Then turning to me he proceeded: 'Well then, here is a heap of letters for disposal. Take that chair and begin. As you see, hundreds of people come to see me. What am I to do? Am I to meet them, or am I to answer these busybodies inundating me with letters? I have no clerks to whom I can entrust this work. Most of these letters have nothing in them, but you will please look them through. Acknowledge those that are worth it, and refer to me those that need a considered reply.'

I was delighted at the confidence reposed in me.

Sjt. Ghosal did not know me when he gave me the work. Only later did he enquire about my credentials.

I found my work very easy—the disposal of that heap of correspondence. I had done with it in no time, and Sjt. Ghosal was very glad. He was talkative. He would talk away for hours together. **When he learnt something from me about my history, he felt rather sorry to have given me clerical work.** But I reassured him: 'Please don't worry. What am I before you? You have grown gray in the service of the Congress, and are as an elder to me. I am but an inexperienced youth. You have put me under a debt of obligation by entrusting me with this work. For I want to do Congress work, and you have given me the rare opportunity of understanding the details.'

'To tell you the truth,' said Sjt. Ghosal, 'that is the proper spirit. But young men of today do not realize it. Of course I have known the Congress since its birth. In fact I may claim a certain share with Mr. Hume in bringing the Congress into being.'

And thus we became good friends. He insisted on my having lunch with him.

Sjt. Ghosal used to get his shirt buttoned by his bearer. I volunteered to do the bearer's duty, and I loved to do it, as my regard for elders was always great. When he came to know this, he did not mind my doing little acts of personal service for him. In fact he was delighted. **Asking me to button his shirt, he would say, 'You see now, the Congress secretary has no time even to button his shirt.** He has always some work to do.' Sjt. Ghosal's naivete amused me, but did not create any dislike in me for service of that nature. The benefit I received from this service is incalculable.

In a few days I came to know the working of the Congress. I met most of the leaders. I observed the movements of stalwarts like Gokhale and Surendranath. I also noticed the huge waste of time there. I observed too, with sorrow even then, the prominent place that the English language occupied in our affairs. There was little regard for economy of energy. More than one did the work of one, and many an important thing was no one's business at all.

Critical as my mind was in observing these things, there was enough charity in me, and so I always thought that it might, after all, be impossible to do better in the circumstances, and that saved me from undervaluing any work.

The Resolution on S. Africa

In the Congress at last. The immense pavilion and the volunteers in stately array, as also the elders seated on the dais, overwhelmed me. I wondered where I should be in that vast assemblage.

The presidential address was a book by itself. To read it from cover to cover was out of the question. Only a few passages were therefore read. After this came the election of the Subjects Committee. Gokhale took me to the Committee meetings.

Sir Pherozeshah had of course agreed to admit my resolution, but I was wondering who would put it before the Subjects Committee, and when. For there were lengthy speeches to every resolution, all in English to boot, and every resolution had some well-known leader to back it. Mine was but a feeble pipe amongst those veteran drums, and as the night was closing in, my heart beat fast. The resolutions coming at the fagend were, so far as I can recollect, rushed through at lightning speed. Everyone was hurrying to go. It was 11 o'clock. I had not the courage to speak. **I had already met Gokhale, who had looked at my resolution. So I drew near his chair and whispered to him: 'Please do something for me.'** He said: 'Your resolution is not out of my mind. You see the way they are rushing through the resolutions. But I will not allow yours to be passed over.'

'So we have done?' said Sir Pherozeshah Mehta.

'No, no, there is still the resolution on South Africa. Mr. Gandhi has been waiting long,' cried out Gokhale.

'Have you seen the resolution?' asked Sir Pherozeshah.

'Of course.'

'Do you like it?'

'It is quite good.'

'Well then, let us have it, Gandhi.'

I read it trembling. Gokhale supported it.

'Unanimously passed,' cried out everyone.

'You will have five minutes to speak, Gandhi,' said Mr. Wacha.

The procedure was far from pleasing to me. **No one had troubled to understand the resolution, everyone was in a**

hurry to go and, because Gokhale had seen the resolution, it was not thought necessary for the rest to see it or understand it!

The morning found me worrying about my speech. What was I to say in five minutes? I had prepared myself fairly well, but the words would not come to me. I had decided not to read my speech but to speak *extempore.* **But the facility for speaking that I had acquired in South Africa seemed to have left me for the moment.**

As soon as it was time for my resolution, Mr. Wacha called out my name. I stood up. **My head was reeling. I read the resolution somehow.** Someone had printed and distributed amongst the delegates copies of a poem he had written in praise of foreign emigration. I read the poem and referred to the grievances of the settlers in South Africa.

Just at this moment Mr. Wacha rang the bell. I was sure I had not yet spoken for five minutes. I did not know that the bell was rung in order to warn me to finish in two minutes more. I had heard others speak for half an hour or three quarters of an hour, and yet no bell was rung for them. I felt hurt and sat down as soon as the bell was rung. There was no question about the passing of the resolution. In those days there was hardly any difference between visitors and delegates. Everyone raised his hand and all resolutions passed unanimously. My resolution also fared in this wise and so lost all its importance for me. And yet the very fact that it was passed by the Congress was enough to delight my heart.

British Darbars

The Congress was over, but as I had to meet the Chamber of Commerce and various people in connection with work in South Africa, I stayed in Calcutta for a month. Rather than stay this time in a hotel, I arranged to get the required introduction for a room in the India Club. Among its members were some prominent Indians, and I looked forward to getting into touch with them and interesting them in the work in South Africa. Gokhale frequently went to this Club to play billiards, and when he knew that I was to stay in Calcutta for some time, he invited me to stay with him. I thankfully accepted the invitation, but did not think it proper to go there by myself. He waited for a day or two and then took me personally. He discovered my reserve and said. 'Gandhi, you have to stay in the country and this sort of reserve will not do. You must get into touch with as many people as possible. I want you to do Congress work.'

I shall record here an incident in the India Club, before I proceed to talk of my stay with Gokhale.

Lord Curzon held his darbar about this time. Some Rajas and Maharajas who had been invited to the darbar were members of the Club. In the Club I always found them wearing fine Bengali *dhotis* and shirts and scarves. On the darbar day they put on trousers befitting *khansamas* and shining boots. I was pained and inquired of one of them the reason for the change.

'We alone know our unfortunate condition. We alone know the insults we have to put up with, in order that we may possess our wealth and titles,' he replied.

'But what about these *khansama* turbans and these shining boots?' I asked.

'Do you see any difference between *khansamas* and us?' he replied, and added, 'they are our *khansamas,* **we are Lord Curzon's khansamas**. If I were to absent myself from the *levee,* I should have to suffer the consequences. **If I were to attend it in my usual dress, it would be an offence.** And do you think I am going to get any opportunity there of talking to Lord Curzon? Not a bit of it!'

I was moved to pity for this plainspoken friend.

This reminds me of another darbar.

At the time when Lord Hardinge laid the foundation stone of Hindu University, there was a darbar. There were Rajas and Maharajas of course, but Pandit Malaviyaji specially invited me also to attend it, and I did so.

I was distressed to see the Maharajas bedecked like women—silk *pyjamas* and silk *achkans,* pearl necklaces round their necks, bracelets on their wrists, pearl and diamond tassels on their turbans and, besides all this, swords with golden hilts hanging from their waistbands.

I discovered that these were insignia not of their royalty, but of their slavery. I had thought that they must be wearing these badges of impotence of their own free will, but **I was told that it was obligatory for these Rajas to wear all their costly jewels at such functions.** I also gathered that some of them had a positive dislike for wearing these jewels, and that they never wore them except on occasions like the darbar.

I do not know how far my information was correct. But whether they wear them on other occasions or not, it is distressing enough to have to attend viceregal darbars in jewels that only some women wear.

How heavy is the toll of sins and wrongs that wealth, power and prestige exact from man!

A Month with Gokhale

From the very first day of my stay with him Gokhale made me feel completely at home. He treated me as though I were his younger brother, he acquainted himself with all my requirements and arranged to see that I got all I needed. Fortunately my wants were few, and as I had cultivated the habit of self-help, I needed very little personal attendance. He was deeply impressed with my habit of fending for myself, my personal cleanliness, perseverance and regularity, and would often overwhelm me with praise.

He seemed to keep nothing private from me. He would introduce me to all the important people that called on him. Of these the one who stands foremost in memory is Dr. (now Sir) P. C. Ray. He lived practically next door and was a very frequent visitor.

This is how he introduced Dr. Ray: 'This is Prof. Ray who, having a monthly salary of Rs. 800, keeps just Rs. 40 for himself and devotes the balance to public purposes. He is not, and does not want to get married.'

To see Gokhale at work was as much a joy as an education.

He never wasted a minute. His private relations and friendships were all for public good. All his talks had reference only to the good of the country and were absolutely free from any trace of untruth or insincerity. India's poverty and subjection were matters of constant and intense concern to him. Various people sought to interest him in different things. But he gave everyone of them the same reply: 'You do the thing yourself. Let me do my own work. What I want is freedom for my country. After that is won, we can think of other things. Today that one thing is enough to engage all my time and energy.'

During these days I walked up and down the streets of Calcutta. I went to most places on foot. I met Justice Mitter and Sir Gurudas Banerji, whose help I wanted in my work in South Africa. And about this time I met Raja Pyarimohan Mukarji.

Visit to Kali Temple

Kalicharan Banerji had spoken to me about the Kali temple, which I was eager to see, especially as I had read about it in books. So I went there one day. Justice Mitter's house was in the same locality, and I therefore went to the temple on the same day that I visited him. On the way I saw a stream of sheep going to be sacrificed to Kali. Rows of beggars lined the lane leading to the temple. There were religious mendicants too, and **even in those days I was sternly opposed to giving alms to sturdy beggars.** A crowd of them pursued me. One of such men was found seated on a verandah. He stopped me, and accosted me: 'Whither are you going, my boy?'

I replied to him. He asked my companion and me to sit down, which we did.

I asked him: 'Do you regard this sacrifice as religion?'

'Who would regard killing of animals as religion?'

'Then, why don't you preach against it?'

'That's not my business. Our business is to worship God.'

'But could you not find any other place in which to worship God?'

'All places are equally good for us. The people are like a flock of sheep, following where leaders lead them. It is no business of us *sadhus.*'

We did not prolong the discussion but passed on to the temple. We were greeted by rivers of blood. I could not bear to stand there. I was exasperated and restless. **I have never forgotten that sight.**

That very evening I had an invitation to dinner at a party of Bengali friends. There I spoke to a friend about this cruel form of worship. He said: 'The sheep don't feel anything. The noise and the drumbeating there deaden all sensation of pain.'

I could not swallow this. I told him that, if the sheep had speech, they would tell a different tale. **I felt that the cruel custom ought to be stopped. I thought of the story of Buddha but I also saw that the task was beyond my capacity.**

I hold today the same opinion as I held then. To my mind the life of a lamb is no less precious than that of a human being. I should be unwilling to take the life of a lamb for the sake of the human body. **I hold that, the more helpless a creature, the more entitled it is to protection by man from the cruelty of man.** But he who has not qualified himself for such service is unable to afford to it any protection. I must go through more self-purification and sacrifice, before I can hope to save these lambs from this unholy sacrifice. Today I think I must die pining for this self-purification and sacrifice. **It is my constant prayer that there may be born on earth some great spirit, man or woman, fired with divine pity, who will deliver us from this heinous sin, save the lives of the innocent creatures, and purify the temple.**

How is that Bengal with all its knowledge, intelligence, sacrifice, and emotion tolerates this slaughter?

The terrible sacrifice offered to Kali in the name of religion enhanced my desire to know Bengali life. I had read and heard a good deal about the Brahmo Samaj. I knew something about the life of Pratap Chandra Mazumdar. I had attended some of the meetings addressed by him. I secured his life of Keshav

Chandra Sen, read it with great interest, and understood the distinction between Sadharan Brahmo Samaj and Adi Brahmo Samaj. I met Pandit Shivanath Shastri and in company with Prof. Kathavate went to see Maharshi Devendranath Tagore, but as no interviews with him were allowed then, we could not see him. We were, however, invited to a celebration of the Brahmo Samaj held at his place, and there we had the privilege of listening to fine Bengali music. Ever since I have been a lover of Bengali music.

Having seen enough of the Brahmo Samaj, it was impossible to be satisfied without seeing Swami Vivekanand. So with great enthusiasm **I went to Belur Math, mostly, or maybe all the way, on foot. I loved the sequestered site of the Math. I was disappointed and sorry to be told that the Swami was at his Calcutta house, lying ill, and could not be seen.**

I then ascertained the place of residence of Sister Nivedita, and met her in a Chowringhee mansion. I was taken aback by the splendour that surrounded her, and even in our conversation there was not much meeting ground. I spoke to Gokhale about this, and he said he did not wonder that there could be no point of contact between me and a volatile person like her.

I met her again at Mr. Pestonji Padshah's place. I happened to come in just as she was talking to his old mother, and so I became an interpreter between the two. In spite of my failure to find any agreement with her, I could not but notice and admire her overflowing love for Hinduism. I came to know of her books later.

I must needs skip over many a reminiscence of this memorable month. Let me simply mention my flying visit to Burma, and the *foongis* (monks) there. **I was pained by their lethargy. I saw the golden pagoda. I did not like the innumerable little candles burning in the temple, and the rats running about the sanctum** brought to my mind thoughts of Swami Dayanand's experience at Morvi. The freedom and energy of the Burmese women charmed just as the indolence of the men pained me. I also saw, during my brief sojourn, that just as Bombay was not India, Rangoon was not Burma, and that just as we in India have become commission agents of English merchants, even so in Burma have we combined with the English merchants, in making the Burmese people our commission agents.

On my return from Burma I took leave of Gokhale. The separation was a wrench, but my work in Bengal, or rather Calcutta, was finished, and I had no occasion to stay any longer.

Tour through India

Before settling down I had thought of making a tour through India travelling third class, and of acquainting myself with the hardships of third class passengers. I spoke to Gokhale about this. To begin with, he ridiculed the idea, but when I explained to him what I hoped to see, he cheerfully approved. I planned to go first to Benares to pay my respects to Mrs. Besant, who was then ill.

It was necessary to equip myself anew for the third class tour. Gokhale himself gave me a metal tiffin-box and got it filled with sweet balls and *puris.* I purchased a canvas bag worth twelve annas and a long coat made of coarse Chhaya wool. The bag was to contain this coat, a *dhoti,* a towel and a shirt. I had a blanket as well to cover myself with and a water jug. Thus equipped I set forth on my travels. Gokhale and Dr. Ray came to the station to see me off. I had asked them both not to trouble to come, but they insisted. 'I should not have come if you had gone first class, but now I had to,' said Gokhale.

No one stopped Gokhale from going on to the platform. He was in his silk turban, jacket and *dhoti.* Dr. Ray was in his Bengali dress. He was stopped by the ticket collector; but on Gokhale telling him that he was his friend, he was admitted.

Thus with their good wishes I started on my journey.

The journey was from Calcutta to Rajkot, and I planned to halt at Benares, Agra, Jaipur and Palanpur *en route.* I had not the time to see any more places than these. In each city I stayed one day and put up in *dharmashalas* or with *pandas* like the ordinary pilgrims, excepting at Palanpur. So far as I can remember, I did not spend more than Rs. 31 (including the train fare) on this journey.

In travelling third class I mostly preferred the ordinary to the mail trains, as I knew that the latter were more crowded and the fares in them higher. The third class compartments are practically as dirty, and the closet arrangements as bad, today as they were then. There may be a little improvement now, but the difference between the facilities provided for the first and the third classes is out of all proportion to the difference between the fares for the two classes. In Europe I travelled third—and only once first, just to see what it was like—but there I noticed no such difference between the first and the third classes. In South Africa third class passengers are mostly Negroes, yet the third class comforts are better there than here.

Benares Temples

I arrived in Benares in the morning. I had decided to put up with a *panda.* Numerous Brahmins surrounded me, as soon as I got out of the train, and I selected one who struck me to be comparatively cleaner and better than the rest. It proved to be a good choice. There was a cow in the courtyard of his house and an upper storey where I was given a lodging. I did not want to have any food without ablution in the Ganges in the proper orthodox manner. The *panda* made preparations for it. I had told him beforehand that on no account could I give him more than a rupee and four annas as *dakshina,* and that he should therefore keep this in mind while making the preparations.

The *panda* readily assented. 'Be the pilgrim rich or poor,' said he, 'the service is the same in every case. But the amount of *dakshina* we receive depends upon the will and the ability of the pilgrim.' I did not find that the *panda* at all abridged the usual formalities in my case. The *puja* was over at twelve o'clock and I went to the Kashi Vishvanath temple for *darshan.* I was deeply pained by what I saw there. When practising as a barrister in Bombay in 1891, I had occasion to attend a lecture on 'Pilgrimage to Kashi' in the Prarthana Samaj hall. I was therefore prepared for some measure of disappointment. But the actual disappointment was greater than I had bargained for.

The approach was through a narrow and slippery lane. Quiet there was none. The swarming flies and the noise made by the shopkeepers and pilgrims were perfectly insufferable.

Where one expected an atmosphere of meditation and communion, it was conspicuous by its absence. One had to seek that atmosphere in oneself. I did observe devout sisters, who were absorbed in meditation, entirely unconscious of the environment. But for this the authorities of the temple could scarcely claim any credit. The authorities should be responsible for creating and maintaining about the temple a pure, sweet and serene atmosphere, physical as well as moral. Instead of this I found a *bazar* where cunning shopkeepers were selling sweets and toys of the latest fashion.

When I reached the temple, I was greeted at the entrance by a stinking mass of rotten flowers. The floor was paved with fine marble, which was however broken by some devotee innocent of aesthetic taste, who had set it with rupees serving as an excellent receptacle for dirt.

I went near the *Jnana-vapi* (Well of Knowledge). **I searched here for God but failed to find Him.** I was not therefore in a particularly good mood. The surroundings of the *Jnana-vapi* too I found to be dirty. I had no mind to give any *dakshina.* So I offered a pie. The *panda* in charge got angry and threw away the pie. **He swore at me and said, 'This insult will take you straight to hell.'**

This did not perturb me. 'Maharaj', said I, 'whatever fate has in store for me, it does not behove one of your class to indulge in such language. You may take this pie if you like, or you will lose that too.'

'Go away,' he replied, 'I don't care for your pie.' And then followed a further volley of abuse.

I took up the pie and went my way, flattering myself that the Brahmin had lost a pie and I had saved one. But the Maharaj was hardly the man to let the pie go. He called me back and said, 'All right, leave the pie here, I would rather not be as you are. If I refuse your pie, it will be bad for you.'

I silently gave him the pie and, with a sigh, went away.

Since then I have twice been to Kashi Vishvanath but that has been after I had already been afflicted with the title of *Mahatma* and experiences such as I have detailed above had become impossible. People eager to have my *darshan* would not permit me to have *darshan* of the temple. Otherwise the dirt and the noise were the same as before.

After this visit to the temple, I waited upon Mrs. Besant. I knew that she had just recovered from an illness. I sent in my name. She came at once. As I wished only to pay my respects to her, I said, 'I am aware that you are in delicate health. I only wanted to pay my respects. I am thankful that you have been good enough to receive me in spite of your indifferent health. I will not detain you any longer.'

So saying, I took leave of her.

In Bombay

Gokhale was very anxious that I should settle down in Bombay, practise at the bar and help him in public work. Public work in those days meant Congress work, and the chief work of the institution which he had assisted to found was carrying on the Congress administration.

I liked Gokhale's advice, but I was not overconfident of success as a barrister. The unpleasant memories of past failure were yet with me, and I still hated as poison the use of flattery for getting briefs.

I therefore decided to start work first at Rajkot. Kevalram Mavji Dave, my old wellwisher, who had induced me to go to England, was there, and he started me straightaway with three briefs. Two of them were appeals before the Judicial Assistant to the Political Agent in Kathiawad and one was an original case in Jamnagar. This last was rather important. On my saying that I could not trust myself to do it justice, Kevalram Dave exclaimed: 'Winning or losing is no concern of yours. You will simply try your best, and I am of course there to assist you.

The counsel on the other side was Sjt. Samarth. I was fairly well prepared. Not that I knew much of Indian law, but Kevalram Dave had instructed me very thoroughly. I won the case and gained some confidence. I had no fear about the appeals, which were successful. All this inspired a hope in me that after all I might not fail even in Bombay. In Bombay, I took chambers in Payne, Gilbert and Sayani's offices, and it looked as though I had settled down.

No Allopathy

But though I had hired chambers in the Fort and a house in Girgaum, God would not let me settle down. Scarcely had I moved into my new house when my second son Manilal, who had already been through an acute attack of smallpox some years back, had a severe attack of typhoid, combined with pneumonia and signs of delirium at night.

The doctor was called in. He said medicine would have little effect, but eggs and chicken broth might be given with profit.

The doctor was a very good Parsi. I told him that we were all vegetarians and that I could not possibly give either of the two things to my son. Would he therefore recommend something else?

'Your son's life is in danger,' said the good doctor. 'We could give him milk diluted with water, but that will not give him enough nourishment. As you know, I am called in by many Hindu families, and they do not object to anything I prescribe. I think you will be well advised not to be so hard on your son.'

'What you say is quite right,' said I. 'As a doctor you could not do otherwise. But my responsibility is very great. To my mind it is only on such occasions, that a man's faith is truly tested. Religion, as I understand it, does not permit me to use meat or eggs even on occasions like this, and I must therefore take the risk that you say is likely. But I beg of you one thing. As I cannot avail myself of your treatment, I propose to try some hydropathic remedies which I happen to know. But I shall not know how to examine the boy's pulse, chest, lungs, etc. If you will kindly look in from time to time to examine him and keep me informed of his condition, I shall be grateful to you.'

The good doctor appreciated my difficulty and agreed to my request.

I knew Kuhne's treatment and had tried it, too. I knew as well that fasting also could be tried with profit. So I began to give Manilal hip baths according to Kuhne, never keeping him in the tub for more than three minutes, and kept him on orange juice mixed with water for three days. But the temperature persisted, going up to 104°. At night he would be delirious. I began to get anxious. What would people say of me? What would my elder brother think of me? Could we not call in another doctor? Why not have an Ayurvedic physician? What right had the parents to inflict their fads on their children?

I was haunted by thoughts like these. Then a contrary current would start. God would surely be pleased to see that I was giving the same treatment to my son as I would give myself. I had faith in hydropathy, and little faith in allopathy. The doctors could not guarantee recovery. The thread of life was in the hands of God. Why not trust it to Him and in His name go on with what I thought was the right treatment?

My mind was torn between these conflicting thoughts. It was night. I was in Manilal's bed lying by his side. I decided to give him a wet sheet pack. I got up, wetted a sheet, wrung the water out of it and wrapped it about Manilal, keeping only his head out, and then covered him with two blankets. To the head I applied a wet towel. The whole body was burning like hot iron, and quite parched. There was absolutely no perspiration.

I was sorely tired. I left Manilal in the charge of his mother, and went out for a walk on Chaupati to refresh myself. It was about ten o'clock. Very few pedestrians were out. Plunged in deep thought, I scarcely looked at them. 'My honour is in

Thy keeping, oh Lord, in this hour of trial,' I repeated to myself. *Ramanama* was on my lips. After a short time I returned, my heart beating within my breast.

No sooner had I entered the room than Manilal said, 'You have returned, Bapu?'

'Yes, darling.'

'Do please pull me out. I am burning.'

'Are you perspiring, my boy?'

'I am simply soaked. Do please take me out.'

I felt his forehead. It was covered with beads of perspiration. The temperature was going down. I thanked God.

The perspiration streamed down his forehead. I undid the pack and dried his body. Father and son fell asleep.

And each slept like a log. Next morning Manilal had much less fever. He went on thus for forty days on diluted milk and fruit juices. I had no fear now. It was an obstinate type of fever, but it had been got under control. Today Manilal is the healthiest of my boys.

To South Africa Again

Manilal was restored to health, but I saw that the Girgaum house was not habitable. It was damp and ill-lighted. So in consultation with Shri Revashankar Jagjivan I decided to hire some well-ventilated bungalow in a suburb of Bombay. I wandered about in Bandra and Santa Cruz. The slaughter house in Bandra prevented our choice falling there. Ghatkopar and places near it were too far from the sea. At last we hit upon a fine bungalow in Santa Cruz, which we hired as being the best from the point of view of sanitation.

I took a first class season ticket from Santa Cruz to Churchgate, and remember having frequently felt a certain pride in being the only first class passenger in my compartment. Often I walked to Bandra in order to take the fast train from there direct to Churchgate.

I prospered in my profession better than I had expected. My South African clients often entrusted me with some work, and it was enough to enable me to pay my way.

Thus whilst on the one hand I began to feel somewhat at ease about my profession, on the other handæ Gokhale, whose eyes were always on me, had been busy making his own plans on my behalf. He peeped in at my chambers twice or thrice every week, often in company with friends whom he wanted me to know, and he kept me acquainted with his mode of work. But it may be said that God has never allowed any of my own plans to stand. He has disposed them in His own way.

Just when I seemed to be settling down as I had intended, I received an unexpected cable from South Africa: 'Chamberlain expected here. Please return immediately.' I remembered my promise and cabled to say that I should be ready to start the moment they put me in funds. They promptly responded, I gave up the chambers and started for South Africa.

I had an idea that the work there would keep me engaged for at least a year, so I kept the bungalow and left my wife and children there. I believed then that enterprising youths who could not find an opening in the country should emigrate to other lands. I therefore took with me four or five such youths, one of whom was Maganlal Gandhi.

The separation from wife and children, the breaking up of a settled establishment, and the going from the certain to the uncertain—all this was for a moment painful, but I had inured myself to an uncertain life. **I think it is wrong to expect certainties in this world, where all else but God that is Truth is an uncertainty.**

I reached Durban not a day too soon. There was work waiting for me. The date for the deputation to wait on Mr. Chamberlain had been fixed. I had to draft the memorial to be submitted to him and accompany the deputation.

•••

8

In South Africa

Mr. Chamberlain had come to get a gift of 35 million pounds from South Africa, and to win the hearts of Englishmen and Boers. So he gave a cold shoulder to the Indian deputation.

'You know,' he said, 'that the Imperial Government has little control over self-governing Colonies. Your grievances seem to be genuine. I shall do what I can, but you must try your best to placate the Europeans, if you wish to live in their midst.'

The reply cast a chill over the members of the deputation. I was also disappointed. It was an eye-opener for us all, and I saw that we should start with our work *de novo*. I explained the situation to my colleagues.

As a matter of fact there was nothing wrong about Mr. Chamberlain's reply. It was well that he did not mince matters. He had brought home to us in a rather gentle way the rule of might being right or the law of the sword.

But sword we had none. We scarcely had the nerve and the muscle even to receive sword-cuts.

From Natal he hastened to the Transvaal. I had to prepare the case for the Indians there as well and submit it to him. But how was I to get to Pretoria? Our people there were not in a position to procure the necessary legal facilities for my getting to them in time. The War had reduced the Transvaal to a howling wilderness. There were neither provisions nor clothing available. Empty or closed shops were there, waiting to be replenished or opened, but that was a matter of time. Even refugees could not be allowed to return until the shops were ready with provisions. Every Transvaaller had therefore to obtain a permit. The European had no difficulty in getting one, but the Indian found it very hard.

During the War many officers and soldiers had come to South Africa from India and Ceylon, and it was considered to be the duty of the British authorities to provide for such of them as decided to settle there. They had in any event to appoint new officers, and these experienced men came in quite handy. The quick ingenuity of some of them created a new department. It showed their resourcefulness. There was a special department for the Negroes. Why then should there not be one for the Asiatics? The argument seemed to be quite plausible. When I reached the Transvaal, this new department had already been opened and was gradually spreading its tentacles. The officers who issued permits to the returning refugees might issue them to all, but how could they do so in respect of the Asiatics without the intervention of the new department? And if the permits were to be issued on the recommendation of the new department, some of the responsibility and burden of the permit officers could thus be lessened. This was how they had argued. The fact, however, was that the new department wanted some apology for work, and the men wanted money. If there had been no work, the department would have been found unnecessary and would have been discontinued. So they found this work for themselves.

The Indians had to apply to this department. A reply would be vouchsafed many days after. And as there were large numbers wishing to return to the Transvaal, there grew up an army of intermediaries or touts, who, with the officers, looted the poor Indians to the tune of thousands. I was told that no permit could be had without influence, and that in some cases one had to pay up to hundred pounds in spite of the influence which one might bring to bear. Thus there seemed to be no way open to me. I went to my old friend, the Police Superintendent of Durban, and said to him: 'Please introduce me to the Permit Officer and help me to obtain a permit. You know that I have been a resident of the Transvaal.' He immediately put on his hat, came out and secured me a permit. There was hardly an hour left before my train was to start. I had kept my luggage ready. I thanked Superintendent Alexander and started for Pretoria.

I now had a fair idea of the difficulties ahead. On reaching Pretoria I drafted the memorial. In Durban I do not recollect the Indians having been asked to submit in advance the names of their representatives, but here there was the new department and it asked to do so. The Pretoria Indians had already come to know that the officers wanted to exclude me.

The officers at the head of the new department were at a loss to know how I had entered the Transvaal. They inquired of the Indians who used to go to them, but these could say nothing definite. The officers only ventured a guess that I might have succeeded in entering without a permit on the strength of my old connections. If that was the case, I was liable to be arrested!

It is a general practice, on the termination of a big war, to invest the Government of the day with special powers. This was the case in South Africa. The Government had passed a Peace Preservation Ordinance, which provided that anyone entering the Transvaal without a permit should be liable to arrest and imprisonment. The question of arresting me under this provision was mooted, but no one could summon up courage enough to ask me to produce my permit.

The officers had of course sent telegrams to Durban, and when they found that I had entered with a permit, they were disappointed. But they were not the men to be defeated by such disappointment. They could still successfully prevent me from waiting on Mr. Chamberlain.

So the community was asked to submit the names of the representatives who were to form the Deputation. In South Africa the public departments were maintained for the good of the people and were responsible to public opinion. Hence officials in charge had a certain courtesy of manner and humility about them, and coloured people also got the benefit of it more or less. With the coming of the officers from Asia, came also its autocracy, and the habits that the autocrats had imbibed there. In South Africa there was a kind of responsible government or democracy, whereas the commodity imported from Asia was autocracy pure and simple.

I was first summoned to see the chief of the department, an officer from Ceylon. No written order was sent to me. Indian leaders often had to visit the Asiatic officers. Among these was the late Sheth Tyeb Haji Khanmahomed. The chief of the office asked him who I was and why I had come there.

'He is our adviser,' said Tyeb Sheth, 'and he has come here at our request.'

'Then what are we here for? Have we not been appointed to protect you? What can Gandhi know of the conditions here?' asked the autocrat.

Tyeb Sheth answered the charge as best he could. The Sahib ordered Tyeb Sheth to fetch me before him. No seats were offered, we were all kept standing.

'What brings you here?' said the Sahib addressing me.

'I have come here at the request of my fellow countrymen to help them with my advice,' I replied.

'But don't you know that you have no right to come here? The permit you hold was given you by mistake. You cannot be regarded as a domiciled Indian. You must go back. You shall not wait on Mr. Chamberlain. Well, you may go.' With this he bade me good-bye, giving me no opportunity for a reply.

But he detained my companions. He gave them a sound scolding and advised them to send me away.

They returned chagrined. We were now confronted with an unexpected situation.

We had a letter from the Chief of the Asiatic Department to the effect that, as I had seen Mr. Chamberlain in Durban, it had been found necessary to omit my name from the deputation which was to wait on him.

The letter was more than my co-workers could bear. They proposed to drop the idea of the deputation altogether. I pointed out to them the awkward situation of the community.

'If you do not represent your case before Mr. Chamberlain,' said I, 'it will be presumed that you have no case at all. After all, the representation has to be made in writing, and we have got it ready. It does not matter in the least, whether I read it or someone else reads it. Mr. Chamberlain is not going to argue the matter with us.'

I had scarcely finished speaking when Tyeb Sheth cried out, 'Does not an insult to you amount to an insult to the community? How can we forget that you are our representative?'

'Too true,' said I. 'But even the community will have to pocket insults like these. Have we any alternative?'

'Come what may, why should we swallow a fresh insult? Nothing worse can possibly happen to us. Have we many rights to lose?' asked Tyeb Sheth.

It was a spirited reply, but of what avail was it? I was fully conscious of the limitations of the community. I pacified my friends and advised them to have, in my place, Mr. George Godfrey, an Indian barrister.

So Mr. Godfrey led the deputation. Mr. Chamberlain referred in his reply to my exclusion. 'Rather than hear the same representative over and over again, is it not better to have someone new?' he said, and tried to heal the wound.

But all this, far from ending the matter, only added to the work of the community and also to mine. We had to start afresh.

So I set the ball rolling, discussed things with Indians in Pretoria and Johannesburg, and ultimately decided to set up office in Johannesburg.

It was indeed doubtful whether I would be enrolled in the Transvaal Supreme Court. But the Law Society did not oppose my application and the Court allowed it. It was difficult for an Indian to secure rooms for office in a suitable locality. But I had come in fairly close contact with Mr. Ritch, who was then one of the merchants there. Through the good offices of a house agent known to him, I succeeded in securing suitable rooms for my office in the legal quarters of the city, and I started on my professional work.

Studying the Gita

When, in 1893, I came in close contact with Christian friends, I was a mere novice. They tried hard to bring home to me, and make me accept, the message of Jesus, and I was a humble and respectful listener with an open mind. At that time I naturally studied Hinduism to the best of my ability and endeavoured to understand other religions.

In 1903 the position was somewhat changed. Theosophist friends certainly intended to draw me into their society, but that was with a view to getting something from me as a Hindu. Theosophical literature is replete with Hindu influence, and so these friends expected that I should be helpful to them. I explained that my Samskrit study was not much to speak of, that I had not read the Hindu scriptures in the original, and that even my acquaintance with the translations was of the slightest. But being believers in *sanskara* (tendencies caused by previous births) and *punarjanma* (rebirth), they assumed that I should be able to render at least some help. And so I felt like a Triton among the minnows. I started reading Swami Vivekananda's *Rajayoga* with some of these friends and M. N. Dwivedi's *Rajayoga* with others. I had to read Patanjali's *Yoga Sutras* with one friend and the *Bhagavadgita* with quite a number.

We formed a sort of Seekers' Club where we had regular readings. 'I already had faith in the Gita, which had a fascination for me. Now I realized the necessity of diving deeper into it. I decided also to get by heart one or two verses every day. For this purpose I employed the time of my morning ablutions. I used to do these standing in western fashion. So on the wall opposite I stuck slips of paper on which were written the Gita verses and referred to them now and then to help my memory. This time was found sufficient for memorizing the daily portion and recalling the verses already learnt. **I remember having committed to memory thirteen chapters.**

What effect this reading of the Gita had on my friends only they can say, but to me the Gita became an infallible guide of conduct. It became my dictionary of daily reference. Just as I turned to the English dictionary for the meanings of English words that I did not understand, I turned to this dictionary of conduct for a ready solution of all my troubles and trials. Words like *aparigraha* (non-possession) and *samabhava* (equability) gripped me. How to cultivate and preserve that equability was the question. How was one to treat alike insulting, insolent and corrupt officials, co-workers of yesterday raising meaningless opposition, and men who had always been good to one? How was one to divest oneself of all possessions? Was not the body itself possession enough? Were not wife and children possessions? Was I to destroy all the cupboards of books I had? Was I to give up all I had and follow Him? Straight came the answer: I could not follow Him unless I gave up all I had. I understood more clearly in the light of the Gita teaching the implication of the word 'trustee'. My regard for jurisprudence increased, I discovered in it religion. I understood the Gita teaching of non possession to mean that those who desired salvation should act like the trustee who, though having control over great possessions, regards not an iota of them as his own. It became clear to me as daylight that non possession and equability presupposed a change of heart, a change of attitude.

A Sacrifice of Vegetarianism

As the ideals of sacrifice and simplicity were becoming more and more realized, and the religious consciousness was becoming more and more quickened in my daily life, the passion for vegetarianism as a mission went on increasing. I have known only one way of carrying on missionary work, by personal example and discussions with searchers for knowledge.

There was in Johannesburg a vegetarian restaurant conducted by a German who believed in Kuhne's hydropathic treatment. I visited the restaurant myself and helped it by taking English friends there. But I saw that it could not last as it was always in financial difficulties. I assisted it as much as I thought it deserved, and spent some money on it, but it had ultimately to be closed down.

Most theosophists are vegetarians more or less, and an enterprising lady belonging to that society now came upon the scene with a vegetarian restaurant on a grand scale. She was fond of art, extravagant and ignorant of accounts. Her circle of friends was fairly large. She had started in a small way, but later decided to extend the venture by taking large rooms, and asked me for help. I knew nothing of her finances when she thus approached me, but I took it that her estimate must be fairly accurate. And I was in a position to accommodate her. My clients used to keep large sums as deposits with me. Having received the consent of one of these clients, I lent about a thousand pounds from the amount to his credit. This client was most large-hearted and trusting. He had originally come to South Africa as an indentured labourer. He said: 'Give away the money, if you like. I know nothing in these matters. I only know you.' His name was Badri. He afterwards took a prominent part in Satyagraha, and suffered imprisonment as well. So I advanced the loan assuming that this consent was enough.

In two or three months' time I came to know that the amount would not be recovered. I could ill afford to sustain such a loss. There were many other purposes to which I could have applied this amount. The loan was never repaid. But how could trusting Badri be allowed to suffer? He had known me only. I made good the loss.

Tussle with Power

Johannesburg was the stronghold of the Asiatic officers. I had been observing that, far from protecting the Indians, Chinese and others, these officers were grinding them down. Every day I had complaints like this: 'The rightful ones are not admitted, whilst those who have no right are smuggled in on payment of £ 100. If you will not remedy this state of things, who will?'

So I began to collect evidence, and as soon as I had

gathered a fair amount, I approached the Police Commissioner. He appeared to be a just man. Far from giving me the cold shoulder, he listened to me patiently and asked me to show him all the evidence in my possession. He examined the witnesses himself and was satisfied, but he knew as well as I that it was difficult in South Africa to get a white jury to convict a white offender against coloured men. 'But,' said he, 'let us try at any rate. It is not proper either, to let such criminals go scotfree for fear of the jury acquitting them. I must get them arrested. I assure you I shall leave no stone unturned.'

I suspected quite a number of officers, but as I had no unchallenge-able evidence against them all, warrants of arrest were issued against the two about whose guilt I had not the slightest doubt.

My movements could never be kept secret. Many knew that I was going to the Police Commissioner practically daily. The two officers against whom warrants had been issued had spies more or less efficient. They used to patrol my office and report my movements to the officers. I must admit, however, that these officers were so bad that they could not have had many spies. Had the Indians and the Chinese not helped me, they would never have been arrested.

One of these absconded. The Police Commissioner obtained an extradition warrant against him and got him arrested and brought to the Transvaal. They were tried, and although there was strong evidence against them, and in spite of the fact that the jury had evidence of one of them having absconded, both were declared to be not guilty and acquitted.

However, the guilt of both these officers was so patent that in spite of their acquittal the Government could not harbour them. Both were cashiered, and the Asiatic Department became comparatively clean and the Indian community was somewhat reassured.

The event enhanced my prestige and brought me more business. The bulk, though not all, of the hundreds of pounds that the community was monthly squandering in speculation, was saved.

I must say that, though these officers were so bad, I had nothing against them personally. They were aware of this themselves, and when in their straits they approached me, I helped them too. They had a chance of getting employed by the Johannesburg Municipality in case I did not oppose the proposal. A friend of theirs saw me in this connection and I agreed not to thwart them, and they succeeded.

This attitude of mine put the officials with whom I came in contact perfectly at ease, and though I had often to fight with their department and use strong language, they remained quite friendly with me. **I was not then quite conscious that such behaviour was part of my nature. I learnt later that it was an essential part of Satyagraha, and an attribute of ahimsa.**

Man and his deed are two distinct things. Whereas a good deed should call forth approbation and a wicked deed disapprobation, the doer of the deed, whether good or wicked, always deserves respect or pity as the case may be. 'Hate the sin and not the sinner' is a precept which, though easy enough to understand, is rarely practised, and that is why the poison of hatred spreads in the world.

This ahimsa is the basis of the search for truth. I am realizing every day that the search is vain unless it is founded on ahimsa as the basis. It is quite proper to resist and attack a system, but to resist and attack its author is tantamount to resisting and attacking oneself.

Clash with Kasturba

A variety of incidents in my life have conspired to bring me in close contact with people of many creeds and many communities, and my experience with all of them warrants the statement that I have known no distinction between relatives and strangers, countrymen and foreigners, white and coloured, Hindus and Indians of other faiths, whether Musalmans, Parsis, Christians or Jews. I may say that my heart has been incapable of making any such distinctions.

When I was practising in Durban, my office clerks often

stayed with me, and there were among them Hindus and Christians, or to describe them by their provinces, Gujaratis and Tamilians. I treated them as members of my family, and had unpleasantness with my wife if ever she stood in the way of my treating them as such.

One of the clerks was a Christian, born of Panchama parents. The house was built after the Western model and the rooms rightly had no outlets for dirty water. Each room had therefore chamber-pots. Rather than have these cleaned by a servant or a sweeper, my wife or I attended to them. The clerks who made themselves completely at home would naturally clean their own pots, but the Christian clerk was a newcomer, and it was our duty to attend to his bedroom. My wife managed the pots of the others, but to clean those used by one who had been a Panchama seemed to her to be the limit, and we fell out. She could not bear the pots being cleaned by me, neither did she like doing it herself. Even today I can recall the picture of her chiding me, her eyes red with anger, and pearl drops streaming down her cheeks, as she descended the ladder, pot in hand. But I was a cruelly kind husband. I regarded myself as her teacher, and so harassed her out of my blind love for her.

I was far from being satisfied by her merely carrying the pot. I would have her do it cheerfully. So I said, raising my voice: 'I will not stand this nonsense in my house.'

The words pierced her like an arrow. She shouted back: 'Keep your house to yourself and let me go.'

I forgot myself, and the spring of compassion dried up in me. I caught her by the hand, dragged the helpless woman to the gate, which was just opposite the ladder, and proceeded to open it with the intention of pushing her out. The tears were running down her cheeks in torrents, and she cried: 'Have you no sense of shame? Must you so far forget yourself? Where am I to go? I have no parents or relatives here to harbour me. Being your wife, you think I must put up with your cuffs and kicks? For Heaven's sake behave yourself, and shut the gate. Let us not be found making scenes like this!'

I put on a brave face, but was really ashamed and shut the gate. If my wife could not leave me, neither could I leave her. We have had numerous bickerings, but the end has always been peace between us. The wife, with her matchless powers of endurance, has always been the victor.

Today I am in a position to narrate the incident with some detachment, as it belongs to a period out of which I have fortunately emerged. I am no longer a blind, infatuated husband, I am no more my wife's teacher. Kasturba can, if she will, be as unpleasant to me today, as I used to be to her before. We are tried friends, the one no longer regarding the other as the object of lust. She has been a faithful nurse throughout my illnesses, serving without any thought of reward.

The European Workers

In Johannesburg I had at one time as many as four Indian clerks. But even these were not enough for my work. It was impossible to do without typewriting, which, among us, if at all, only I knew. I taught it to two of the clerks, but they never came up to the mark because of their poor English.

I was at my wits' end. Arrears were fast mounting up, so much so that it seemed impossible for me, however much I might try, to cope with, professional and public work. I was quite willing to engage a European clerk, but I was not sure to get a white man or woman to serve a coloured man like myself. However I decided to try. I approached a typewriter's agent whom I knew, and asked him to get me a stenographer. There were girls available, and he promised to try to secure the services of one. He came across a Scotch girl called Miss Dick, who had just come fresh from Scotland. She had no objection to earning an honest livelihood, wherever available, and she was in need. So the agent sent her on to me. She immediately prepossessed me.

'Don't you mind serving under an Indian?' I asked her.

'Not at all,' was her firm reply.

When can you join?'

'This moment, if you wish.'

I was very pleased and straightaway started dictating letters to her.

Before very long she became more a daughter or a sister to me than a mere stenotypist. I had scarcely any reason to find fault with her work. She was often entrusted with the management of funds amounting to thousands of pounds, and she was in charge of account books. She won my complete confidence, but what was perhaps more, she confided to me her innermost thoughts and feelings. She sought my advice in the final choice of her husband, and **I had the privilege to give her away in marriage.** As soon as Miss Dick became Mrs. Macdonald, she had to leave me, but even after her marriage she did not fail to respond, whenever under pressure I made a call upon her.

But a permanent stenotypist was now needed in her place, and I was fortunate in getting another girl. She was Miss Schlesin, introduced to me by Mr. Kallenbach. She was about seventeen when she came to me. Some of her idiosyncrasies were at times too much for Mr. Kallenbach and me. She had come less to work as a stenotypist than to gain experience. Colour prejudice was foreign to her temperament. She seemed to mind neither age nor experience. She would not hesitate even to the point of insulting a man and telling him to his face what she thought of him. Her impetuosity often landed me in difficulties, but her open and guileless temperament removed them as soon as they were created. I have often signed without revision letters typed by her, as I considered her English to be better than mine, and had the fullest confidence in her loyalty.

Her sacrifice was great. For a considerable period she did not draw more than £6, and refused ever to receive more than £ 10 a month. When I urged her to take more, she would give me a scolding and say, 'I am not here to draw a salary from you. I am here because I like to work with you and I like your ideals.'

She had once an occasion to take £ 40 from me, but she insisted having it as a loan, and repaid the full amount. Her courage was equal to her sacrifice. She is one of the few women

I have been privileged to come across with a character as clear as crystal and courage that would shame a warrior.

She knew neither night nor day in toiling for the cause. She ventured out on errands in the darkness of the night all by herself, and angrily scouted any suggestion of an escort. Thousands of stalwart Indians looked up to her for guidance. When during the Satyagraha days almost every one of the leaders was in jail, she led the movement single-handed. She had the management of thousands, a tremendous amount of correspondence, and *Indian Opinion* in her hands, but she never wearied.

Gokhale knew every one of my co-workers. He was pleased with many of them, and would often give his opinion of them. He gave the first place to Miss Schlesin amongst all the Indian and European co-workers. 'I have rarely met with the sacrifice, the purity and the fearlessness I have seen in Miss Schlesin,' said he. 'Amongst your co-workers, she takes the first place in my estimation.'

The appointment of Miss Dick was not enough for my purpose. I needed more assistance. I have referred to Mr. Ritch. I knew him well. He was manager in a commercial firm. He approved my suggestion of leaving the firm and getting articled under me, and he considerably lightened my burden.

Launching *Indian Opinion*

About this time Sjt. Madanjit approached me with a proposal to start *Indian Opinion* and sought my advice. He had already been conducting a press, and I approved of his proposal. The journal was launched in 1904, and Sjt. Mansukhlal Naazar became the first editor. But I had to bear the brunt of the work, having for most of the time to be practically in charge of the journal. The journal has been until this day a weekly. In the beginning it used to be issued in Gujarati, Hindi, Tamil and English. I saw, however, that the Tamil and Hindi sections were a make-believe. They did not serve the purpose for which they were intended, so I discontinued them.

I had no notion that I should have to invest any money in this journal, but I soon discovered that it could not go on without my financial help. I kept on pouring out my money, until ultimately I was practically sinking all my savings in it. I remember a time when I had to remit £ 75 each month.

But after all these years I feel that the journal has served the community well. It was never intended to be a commercial concern. So long as it was under my control, the changes in the journal were indicative of changes in my life. *Indian Opinion* in those days, like *Young India* and *Navajivan* today, was a mirror of part of my life. Week after week I poured out my soul in its columns, and expounded the principles and practice of Satyagraha as I understood it. During ten years, that is, until 1914, excepting the intervals of my enforced rest in prison, there was hardly an issue of *Indian Opinion* without an article from me. Satyagraha would probably have been impossible without *Indian Opinion.* The readers looked forward to it for a trustworthy account of the Satyagraha campaign as also of the real condition of Indians in South Africa. I was inundated with letters containing the outpourings of my correspondents' hearts. They were friendly, critical or bitter, according to the temper of the writer. It was a fine education for me to study, digest and answer all this correspondence. It was as though the community thought audibly through this correspondence with me. It made me thoroughly understand the responsibility of a journalist, and the hold I secured in this way over the community made the future campaign workable, dignified and irresistible.

In the very first month of *Indian Opinion,* I realized that the sole aim of journalism should be service. The newspaper press is a great power, but just as an unchained torrent of water submerges whole countrysides and devastates crops, even so an uncontrolled pen serve but to destroy. If the control is from without, it proves more poisonous than want of control. It can be profitable only when exercised from within.

Coolie Ghettoes

Some of the classes which render us the greatest social

service, but which we Hindus have chosen to regard as 'untouchables', are relegated to remote quarters of a town or a village, called in Gujarati *dhedvado,* and the name has acquired a bad odour. Even so in Christian Europe the Jews were once 'untouchables', and the quarters that were assigned to them had the offensive name of 'ghettoes'. In a similar way today we have become the untouchables of South Africa.

The ancient Jews regarded themselves as the chosen people of God, to the exclusion of all others, with the result that their descendants were visited with a strange and even unjust retribution. Almost in a similar way the Hindus have considered themselves Aryas or civilized, and a section of their own kith and kin as Anaryas or untouchables, with the result that a strange, if unjust, nemesis is being visited not only upon the Hindus in South Africa, but the Musalmans and Parsis as well, inasmuch as they belong to the same country and have the same colour as their Hindu brethren.

In South Africa we have acquired the odious name of 'coolies'. The word 'coolie' in India means only a porter or hired workman, but in South Africa it has a contemptuous connotation. It means what a pariah or an untouchable means to us, and the quarters assigned to the 'coolies' are known as 'coolie locations'. Johannesburg had one such location, but unlike other places with locations where the Indians had tenancy rights, in the Johannesburg location the Indians had acquired their plots on a lease of 99 years. People were densely packed in the location, the area of which never increased with the increase in population. Beyond arranging to clean the latrines in the location in a haphazard way, the Municipality did nothing to provide any sanitary facilities, much less good roads or lights. It was hardly likely that it would safeguard its sanitation, when it was indifferent to the welfare of the residents. Usually people migrate abroad in search of wealth and trade, but the bulk of the Indians who went to South Africa were ignorant, pauper agriculturists. The traders and educated Indians who followed them were very few.

The criminal negligence of the Municipality and the

ignorance of the Indian settlers thus conspired to render the location thoroughly_insanitary. The Municipality used the insanitation as a pretext for destroying the location, and for that purpose obtained from the local legislature authority to dispossess the settlers. This was the condition of things when I settled in Johannesburg.

The settlers, having proprietary rights in their land, were naturally entitled to compensation. A special tribunal was appointed to try the land acquisition cases. If the tenant was not prepared to accept the offer of the Municipality, he had a right to appeal to the tribunal, and if the latter's award exceeded the Municipality's offer, the Municipality had to bear the costs.

Most of the tenants engaged me as their legal adviser. I had no desire to make money out of these cases, so I told the tenants that I should be satisfied with whatever costs the tribunal awarded, in case they won, and a fee of £ 10 on every lease, irrespective of the result of the case. I also told them that I proposed to set apart half of the money paid by them for the building of a hospital or similar institution for the poor. This naturally pleased them all.

Out of about 70 cases only one was lost. So the fees amounted to a fairly big figure. But *Indian Opinion* was there with its persistent claim and devoured, so far as I can recollect, a sum of £ 1,600. For the redress of their tenants' grievances they had formed an association of their own, separate from that of the free Indian merchants and traders. Some of them were open-hearted, liberal men and had high character.

It may be of some interest to know how the Indians used to name me. Abdulla Sheth refused to address me as Gandhi. None, fortunately, ever insulted me by calling or regarding me as 'saheb'. Abdulla Sheth hit upon a fine appellation—'bhai', i.e., brother. Others followed him and continued to address me as 'bhai' until the moment I left South Africa.

The Black Plague

While the Indians were fretting over this state of things, there was a sudden outbreak of the black plague, also called pneumonic plague, more terrible and fatal than the bubonic.

Fortunately, it was not the location but one of the gold mines in the vicinity of Johannesburg that was responsible for the outbreak. The workers in this mine were for the most part negroes, for whose cleanliness their white employers were solely responsible. There were a few Indians also working in connection with the mine, twenty-three of whom suddenly caught the infection, and returned one evening to their quarters in the location with an acute attack of the plague. Sjt. Madanjit, who was then canvassing subscribers for *Indian Opinion* and realizing subscriptions, happened to be in the location at this moment. He was a remarkably fearless man. His heart wept to see these victims of the scourge, and he sent a pencil-note to me to the following effect: 'There has been a sudden outbreak of the black plague. You must come immediately and take prompt measures, otherwise we must be prepared for dire consequences. Please come immediately.'

Sjt. Madanjit bravely broke open the lock of a vacant house, and put all the patients there. I cycled to the location, and wrote to the Town Clerk to inform him of the circumstances in which we had taken possession of the house. Dr. William Godfrey, who was practising in Johannesburg, ran to the rescue as soon as he got the news, and became both nurse and doctor to the patients. But twenty-three patients were more than three of us could cope with.

It is my faith, based on experience, that if one's heart is pure, calamity brings in its train men and measures to fight it. I had at that time four Indians in my office—Sjts. Kalyandas, Maneklal, Gunvantrai Desai and another whose name I cannot recollect. I decided to sacrifice all four—call them clerks, co-workers or sons.

So far as I can recollect, we pulled all the patients through that night! The next day they placed a vacant godown at my disposal, and suggested that the patients be removed there. We cleaned it up ourselves, raised a few beds and other necessaries through the offices of charitable Indians, and improvised a temporary hospital. The Municipality lent the services of a nurse, who came with brandy and other hospital equipment.

The nurse was a kindly lady and would fain have attended to the patients, but we rarely allowed her to touch them, lest she should catch the contagion. We had instructions to give the patients frequent doses of brandy. The nurse even asked us to take it for precaution, just as she was doing herself. But none of us would touch it. I put three patients, who were prepared to do without brandy, under the earth treatment, applying wet earth bandages to their heads and chests. Two of these were saved. The other twenty died in the godown.

In the course of a few days we learnt that the good nurse had had an attack and immediately succumbed. It is impossible to say how the two patients were saved and how we remained immune, but the experience enhanced my faith in earth treatment, as also my scepticism of the efficacy of brandy, even as a medicine. I know that neither this faith nor this scepticism is based upon any solid grounds, but I still retain the impression which I then received, and have therefore thought it necessary to mention it here.

On the outbreak of the plague, I had addressed a strong letter to the press, holding the Municipality guilty of negligence after the location came into its possession and responsible for the outbreak of the plague itself. This letter secured me Mr. Henry Polak, and was partly responsible for the friendship of the late Rev. Joseph Doke.

I used to have my meals at a vegetarian restaurant. Here I met Mr. Albert West. We used to meet every evening and go out walking after dinner. Mr. West was a partner in a small printing concern. He read my letter in the press about the outbreak of the plague and, not finding me in the restaurant for a day or two, knocked at my door early one morning just as I was getting ready to go out for a walk. As I opened the door Mr. West said: 'I did not find you in the restaurant and was really afraid lest something should have happened to you; so I decided to come and see you. I am ready to help in nursing the patients. You know that I have no one depending on me.'

I expressed my gratitude, and without taking even a second to think, replied: 'I will not have you as a nurse. If there are no more cases, we shall be free in a day or two. There is one thing however.'

'Yes, what is it?'

'Could you take charge of the *Indian Opinion* press at Durban? Mr. Madanjit is likely to be engaged here, and someone is needed at Durban. If you could go, I should feel quite relieved on that score.'

'You know that I have a press. Most probably I shall be able to go, but may I give my final reply in the evening?'

I was delighted. We had the talk. He agreed to go. Salary was no consideration to him, as money was not his motive. But a salary of £ 10 per month and a part of the profits, if any, was fixed up. The very next day Mr. West left for Durban by the evening mail, entrusting me with the recovery of his dues. From that day until the time I left the shores of South Africa, he remained a partner of my joys and sorrows.

The location, after the plague, was put under a strong guard, passage in and out being made impossible without permission. The decision was to make the whole location population vacate, and live under canvas for three weeks in an open plain about thirteen miles from Johannesburg, and then to set fire to the location.

The people were in a terrible fright, but my constant presence was a consolation to them. Many of the poor people used to hoard their scanty savings underground. This had to be unearthed. They had no bank, they knew none. I became their banker. Streams of money poured into my office. I could not possibly charge any fees for my labours in such a crisis. I coped with the work somehow. I knew my bank manager very well. I told him that I should have to deposit these moneys with him. The banks were by no means anxious to accept large amounts of copper and silver. There was also the fear of bank clerks refusing to touch money coming from a plague-affected area. But the manager accommodated me in every way. It was decided to disinfect all the money before sending it to the bank. So far as I can remember, nearly sixty thousand pounds were thus deposited. I advised such of the people as had enough money to place it as fixed deposit, and they accepted the advice. The result was some of them became accustomed to invest their money in banks.

The location residents were removed by special train to Klipspruit Farm near Johannesburg, where they were supplied with provisions by the Municipality at public expense. This city under canvas looked like a military camp.

The Municipality had to incur heavy expenditure, but it successfuly arrested the further progress of the plague and the city once more breathed freely.

The Magic Book: *Unto this Last*

The black plague enhanced my influence with the poor Indians, and increased my business and my responsibility. Some of the new contacts with Europeans became so close that they added considerably to my moral obligations.

I made the acquaintance of Mr. Polak in the vegetarian restaurant, just as I had made that of Mr. West. One evening a young man dining at a table a little way off sent me his card expressing a desire to see me. I invited him to come to my table, which he did.

'I am sub-editor of *The Critic'*, he said. 'When I read your letter to the press about the plague, I felt a strong desire to see you. I am glad to have this opportunity.'

Mr. Polak's candour drew me to him. We seemed to hold closely similar views on the essential things of life. He liked simple life. He had a wonderful faculty of translating into practice anything that appealed to his intellect. Some of the changes that he had made in his life were as prompt as they were radical.

Indian Opinion was getting more and more expensive every day. The very first report from Mr. West was alarming. He wrote: 'I do not expect the concern to yield the profit that you had thought probable. I am afraid there may be even a loss. The books are not in order. There are heavy arrears to be recovered, but one cannot make head or tail of them. Considerable overhauling will have to be done. But all this need not alarm you. I shall try to put things right as best I can. I remain on, whether there is profit or not.'

On receipt of Mr. West's letter I left for Natal. I had taken Mr. Polak into my fullest confidence. He came to see me off at the station, and left with me a book to read during the journey, which he said I was sure to like. It was Ruskin's *Unto This Last.*

The book was impossible to lay aside, once I had begun it. It gripped me. Johannesburg to Durban was a twenty-four hours' journey. The train reached there in the evening. I could not get any sleep that night. I determined to change my life in accordance with the ideals of the book.

This was the first book of Ruskin I had ever read. It was the one that brought about an instantaneous and practical transformation in my life. I translated it later into Gujarati, entitling it *Sarvodaya* (the welfare of all).

I discovered some of my deepest convictions reflected in this great book of Ruskin, and that is why it so captured me and made me transform my life.

The teachings of *Unto This Last* I understood to be:

1. That the good of the individual is contained in the good of all.

2. That a lawyer's work has the same value as the barber's, inasmuch as all have the same right of earning their livelihood from their work.

3. That a life of labour, i.e., the life of the tiller of the soil and the handicraftsman, is the life worth living.

The first or these I knew. The second I had dimly realized. The third had never occurred to me. *Unto This Last* made it as clear as daylight for me that the second and the third were contained in the first. I arose with the dawn, ready to reduce these principles to practice.

The Phoenix Settlement

I talked over the whole thing with Mr. West, described to him the effect *Unto This Last* had produced on my mind, and proposed that *Indian Opinion* should be removed to a farm, on which everyone should labour, drawing the same living wage, and attending to the press work in spare time. Mr. West approved of the proposal, and £ 3 was laid down as the monthly allowance per head, irrespective of colour or nationality.

But it was a question whether all the ten or more workers in the press would agree to go and settle on an out-of-the-way farm, and be satisfied with bare maintenance. We therefore proposed that those who could not fit in with the scheme should continue to draw their salaries and gradually try to reach the ideal of becoming members of the settlement.

I talked to the workers in the terms of this proposal. It did not appeal to Sjt. Madanjit, who considered my proposal to be foolish and held that it would ruin a venture on which he had staked his all; that the workers would bolt, *Indian Opinion* would come to a stop, and the press would have to be closed down.

Among the men working in the press was Chhaganlal Gandhi, one of my cousins. I had put the proposal to him at the same time as to West. He had a wife and children, but he had from childhood chosen to be trained and to work under me. He had full faith in me. So without any argument he agreed to the scheme and has been with me ever since. The machinist Govindaswami also fell in with the proposal. The rest did not join the scheme, but agreed to go wherever I removed the press.

I do not think I took more than two days to fix up these matters with the men. Thereafter I at once advertised for a piece of land situated near a railway station in the vicinity of Durban. An offer came in respect of Phoenix. Mr. West and I went to inspect the estate. Within a week we purchased twenty acres of land. It had a nice little spring and a few orange and mango trees. Adjoining it was a piece of 80 acres which had many more fruit trees and a dilapidated cottage. We purchased this too, the total cost being a thousand pounds.

Mr. Rustomji always supported me in such enterprises.

He liked the project. He placed at my disposal second-hand corrugated iron sheets of a big godown and other building material, with which we started work. Some Indian carpenters and masons, who had worked with me in the Boer War, helped me in erecting a shed for the press. This structure, which was 75 feet long and 50 feet broad, was ready in less than a month. Mr. West and others, at great personal risk, stayed with the carpenters and masons. The place, uninhabited and thickly overgrown with grass, was infested with snakes and obviously dangerous to live in. At first all lived under canvas. We carted most of our things to Phoenix in about a week. It was fourteen miles from Durban, and two and a half miles from Phoenix station.

Only one issue of *Indian Opinion* had to be printed outside, in the Mercury press.

I now endeavoured to draw to Phoenix those relations and friends who had come with me from India to try their fortune, and who were engaged in business of various kinds. They had come in search of wealth, and it was therefore difficult to persuade them, but some agreed. Of these I can single out here only Maganlal Gandhi's name. The others went back to business. Maganlal Gandhi left his business for good to cast in his lot with me, and by ability, sacrifice and devotion stands foremost among my original co-workers in my ethical experiments.

The First Night

It was no easy thing to issue the first number of *Indian Opinion* from Phoenix. Had I not taken two precautions, the first issue would hae had to be dropped or delayed. The idea of having an engine to work the press had not appealed to me. I had thought that hand-power would be more in keeping with an atmosphere where agricultural work was also to be done by hand. But as the idea had not appeared feasible, we had installed an oil-engine. I had, however, suggested to West to have something handy to fall back upon in case the engine failed. He had, therefore, arranged a wheel which could be worked by hand. The size of the paper, that of a daily, was considered unsuitable for an out-of-the-way place like Phoenix. It was reduced to foolscap size, so that, in case of emergency, copies might be struck off with the help of a treadle.

In the initial stages, we all had to keep late hours before the day of publication. Everyone, young and old, had to help in folding the sheets. We usually finished our work between ten o'clock and midnight. But the first night was unforgettable. The pages were locked, but the engine refused to work. We had got out an engineer from Durban to put up the engine and set it going. He and West tried their hardest, but in vain.

'Where have we the men to work?' he replied. 'We are not enough to cope with the job. It requires relays of four men each, and our own men are all tired.'

Building work had not yet been finished, so the carpenters were still with us. They were sleeping on the press floor. I said pointing to them, 'But can't we make use of these carpenters?'

'I dare not wake up the carpenters,' said West.

'Well, that's for me to negotiate,' said I.

I woke up the carpenters and requested their co-operation. They needed no pressure. They said, 'If we cannot be called upon in an emergency, what use are we? We will work the wheel. For us it is easy work.'

West was greatly delighted and started singing a hymn as we set to work. I partnered the carpenters, all the rest joined turn by turn, and thus we went on until 7 a.m. There was still a good deal to do. I therefore suggested to West that the engineer might now be asked to get up and try again to start the engine.

West woke him up, and he immediately went into the engine room. And lo and behold! the engine worked almost as soon as he touched it. The whole press rang with peals of joy.

The copies were despatched in time, and everyone was happy.

In order to enable everyone of us to make a living by manual labour, we parcelled out the land round the press in pieces of three acres each. One of these fell to my lot. On all these plots we, much against our wish, built houses with corrugated iron. Our desire had been to have mud huts thatched with straw or small brick houses such as would become ordinary peasants, but it could not be. They would have been more expressive and would have meant more time, and everyone was eager to settle down as soon as possible.

The editor was still Mansukhlal Naazar. He had not accepted the new scheme and was directing the paper from Durban where there was a branch office for *Indian Opinion.* Though we had paid compositors, the idea was for every member of the Settlement to learn typesetting, the easiest, if the most tedious, of the processes in a printing press. Those, therefore, who did not already know the work learnt it. I remained a dunce to the last. Maganlal Gandhi surpassed us all.

We had hardly settled down, the buildings were hardly ready, when I had to leave the newly constructed nest and go to Johannesburg. I informed Polak of the important changes I had made. His joy knew no bounds when he learnt that the loan of his book had been so fruitful. 'Is it not possible,' he asked, 'for me to take part in the new venture?' 'Certainly,' said I. 'You may if you like to join the Settlement.' 'I am quite ready,' he replied, 'if you will admit me.'

His determination captured me. He gave a month's notice to his chief to be relieved from *The Critic,* and reached Phoenix in due course. By his sociability he won the hearts of all and soon became a member of the family. Simplicity was so much a part of his nature that, far from feeling the life at Phoenix in any way strange or hard, he took to it like a duck takes to water. But I could not keep him there long. Mr. Ritch had decided to finish his legal studies in England, and it was impossible for me to bear the burden of the office singlehanded, so I suggested to Polak that he should join the office and qualify as an attorney. He wrote to me from Phoenix that though he loved tthe life there, was perfectly happy, and had hopes of developing the Settlement, still he was ready to leave and join the office to qualify as an attorney, if I thought that thereby we should more quickly realize our ideals.' Polak left Phoenix, came to Johannesburg and signed his articles with me.

About the same time a Scotch theosophist, whom I had been coaching for a local legal examination, also joined as an articled clerk, on my inviting him to follow Polak's example. His name was Mr. MacIntyre.

Thus, with the laudable object of quickly realizing the ideals at Phoemx, I seemed to be going deeper and deeper into a contrary current, and had God not willed otherwise, I should have found myself entrapped in this net spread in the name of simple life.

Whom God Protects

I had now given up all hope of returning to India in the near future. I had promised my wife that I would return home within a year. The year was gone without any prospect of my return, so I decided to send for her and the children.

On the boat bringing them to South Africa, Ramdas, my third son, broke his arm while playing with the ship's captain. The captain looked after him well and had him attended to by the ship's doctor. Ramdas landed with his hand in a sling. The doctor had advised that, as soon as we reached home, the wound should be dressed by a qualified doctor. But this was the time when I was full of faith in my experiments in earth treatment.

In fear and trembling I undid the bandage, washed the wound, applied a clean earth poultice and tied the arm up again. This sort of dressing went on daily for about a month until the wound was completely healed. There was no hitch, and the wound took no more time to heal than the ship's doctor had said it would under the usual treatment.

I invited Polak to come and stay with me, and we began to live like blood brothers. The lady who was soon to be Mrs. Polak and he had been engaged for some years, but the marriage had been postponed for a propitious time. I have an impression that Polak wanted to put some money by before he settled down to a married life. But I pleaded with him:

'When there is a heart union, as in your case, it is hardly right to postpone marriage merely for financial considerations. If poverty is a bar, poor men can never marry. And then you are now staying with me. There is no question of household expenses. I think you should get married as soon as possible.' He appreciated the force of my argument, and immediately opened correspondence on the subject with Mrs. Polak, who was then in England. She gladly accepted the proposal and in a few months reached Johannesburg. Any expense over the wedding was out of the question, not even a special dress was thought necessary. They needed no religious rites to seal the bond. Mrs. Polak was a Christian by birth and Polak a Jew. Their common religion was the religion of ethics.

The Registrar of European marriages in the Transvaal could not register marriages between black or coloured people. In the wedding in question, I acted as the best man. We three went to the Registrar of marriages. How could he be sure that the parties to a marriage in which I acted as the best man would be whites? He proposed to postpone registration pending inquiries. The next day was a Sunday. The day following was New Year's Day. To postpone the date on such a flimsy pretext was more than one could put up with. I knew the Chief Magistrate, who was head of the Registration Department. So I appeared before him with the couple. He laughed and gave me a note to the Registrar and the marriage was duly registered.

I had better celebrate West's wedding also in this chapter. At this stage of my life, my ideas about *brahmacharya* had not fully matured, so I was interesting myself in getting all my bachelor friends married. When, in due course, West made a pilgrimage to South to see his parents, I advised him to return married if possible. Phoenix was the common home, and as we were all supposed to have become farmers, we were not afraid of marriage and its usual consequences. West returned with Mrs. West, a beautiful young lady from Leicester. She came of a family of shoemakers working in a Leicester factory. Mrs. West had herself some experience of work in this factory. I have called her beautiful, because it was her moral beauty that at once attracted me. True beauty after all consists in purity of heart. With Mr. West had come his mother-in-law too. She put us all to shame by her industry and her buoyant, cheerful nature.

In the same way as I persuaded these European friends to marry, I encouraged the Indian friends to send for their families from home. Phoenix thus developed into a little village, half a dozen families having come and settled and begun to increase there.

It has already been seen that, though household expenses were heavy, the tendency towards simplicity began in Durban. But the Johannesburg house came in for much severer overhauling in the light of Ruskin's teaching.

I introduced as much simplicity as was possible in a barrister's house. It was impossible to do without a certain amount of furniture. The change was more internal than external. The liking for doing personally all the physical labour increased to bring my children also under that discipline.

Instead of buying baker's bread, we began to prepare unleavened wholemeal bread at home according to Kuhne's recipe. Common mill flour was no good for this, and the use of handground flour, it was thought, would ensure more simplicity, health and economy. So I purchased a hand-mill for £7. The iron wheel was too heavy to be tackled by one man, but easy for two. Polak and I and the children usually worked it. My wife also occasionally lent a hand, though the grinding hour was her usual time for commencing kitchen work.

We had engaged a servant to look after the house. He lived with us as a member of the family, and the children used to help him in his work. The municipal sweeper removed the night-soil, but we personally attended to the cleaning of the closet instead of asking or expecting the servant to do it.

Serving in the Zulu 'Rebellion'

Just when I felt that I should be breathing in peace, an unexpected event happened. The papers brought the news of the outbreak of the Zulu 'rebellion' in Natal. I bore no grudge against the Zulus, they had harmed no Indian. I had doubts about the 'rebellion' itself. But I then believed that the British Empire existed for the welfare of the world. A genuine sense of loyalty prevented me from even wishing ill to the Empire. The rightness or otherwise of the 'rebellion' was therefore not likely to affect my decision. Natal had a Volunteer Defence Force, and was open to it to recruit more men. I read that this force had already been mobilized to quell the 'rebellion'.

I considered myself a citizen of Natal, being intimately connected with it. So I wrote to the Governor, expressing my readiness, if necessary, to form an Indian Ambulance Corps. He replied immediately accepting the offer.

I went to Durban and appealed for men. A big contingent was not necessary. We were a party of twenty-four, of whom, besides me, four were Gujaratis. The rest were ex-indentured men from South India, excepting one who was a free Pathan.

The Chief Medical Officer appointed me to the temporary rank of Sergeant Major and three men selected by me to the rank of sergeants and one to that of corporal. We also received our uniforms from the Government. Our Corps was on active service for nearly six weeks.

On reaching the scene of the 'rebellion', I saw that there was nothing there to justify the name of 'rebellion'. There was no resistance that one could see. The reason why the disturance had been magnified into a rebellion was that a Zulu chief had advised non-payment of a new tax imposed on his people, and had assisted a sergeant who had gone to collect the tax. At any rate my heart was with the Zulus, and I was delighted, on reaching headquarters, to hear that our main work was to be the nursing of the wounded Zulus.

The Medical Officer in charge welcomed us. He said the white people were not willing nurses for the wounded Zulus, that their wounds were festering, and that he was at his wits' end. He hailed our arrival as a godsend for those innocent people, and he equipped us with bandages, disinfectants etc., and took us to the improvised hospital. The Zulus were delighted to see us. The white soldiers used to peep through the railings that separated us from them and tried to dissuade us from attending to the wounds. And as we would not heed them, they became enraged and poured unspeakable abuse on the Zulus.

Gradually I came into closer touch with these soldiers, and they ceased to interfere. Among the commanding officers were Col. Sparks and Col. Wylie, who had bitterly opposed me in 1896. They were surprised at my attitude and specially called and thanked me. They introduced me to General Mackenzie.

The wounded in our charge were not wounded in battle. A section of them had been taken prisoners as suspects. The General had sentenced them to be flogged. The flogging had caused severe sores. These, being unattended to, were festering. The others were Zulu friendlies. Although these had badges given them to distinguish them from the 'enemy', they had been shot at by the soldiers by mistake.

Besides this work I had to compound and dispense prescriptions for the white soldiers. This was easy enough for me as I had received a year's training in Dr. Booth's little hospital. This work brought me in close contact with many Europeans.

We were attached to a swift-moving column. It had orders to march wherever danger was reported. It was for the most part mounted infantry. As soon as our camp was moved, we had to follow on foot with our stretchers on our shoulders. Twice or thrice we had to march forty miles a day. But wherever we went, I am thankful that we had God's good work to do, having to carry to the camp on our stretchers those Zulu friendlies who had been inadvertently wounded, and to attend upon them as nurses.

The Zulu 'rebellion' was full of new experiences and gave me much food for thought. The Boer War had not brought home to me the horrors of war with anything like the vividness that the 'rebellion' did. This was no war but a man-hunt, not only in my opinion, but also in that of many Englishmen with whom I had occasion to talk. To hear every morning reports of the soldiers' rifles exploding like crackers in innocent hamlets, and to live in the midst of them was a trial. I could see that but for us the Zulus would have been uncared for. This work, therefore, eased my conscience.

But there was much else to set one thinking. It was a sparsely populated part of the country. Few and far between in hills and dales were the scattered Kraals of the simple and so-called 'uncivilized' Zulus. Marching, with or without the wounded, through there solemn solitudes, I often fell into deep thought.

I pondered over *brahmacharya* and its implications, and my convictions took deep root. I discussed it with my co-workers. I clearly saw that one aspiring to serve humanity with his whole soul could not do without it. It was borne in upon me that I should have more and more occasions for service of the kind I was rendering, and that I should find myself unequal to my task if I were engaged in the pleasures of family life and in the propagation and rearing of children.

On the present occasion, for instance, I should not have been able to throw myself into the fray, had my wife been expecting a baby. Without the observance of *brahmacharya* service of the family would be inconsistent with service of the community. So thinking, I became somewhat impatient to take a final vow. The prospect of the vow brought a certain kind of exultation.

A report then came to the effect that the work of suppressing the 'rebellion' was nearly over, and that we should soon be discharged. A day or two after this our discharge came and we got back to our homes.

Taking a Vow of Brahmacharya

On my arrival at Phoenix I eagerly broached the subject of *brahmacharya* with Chhaganlal, Maganlal, West and others. They liked the idea and accepted the necessity of taking the vow, but they also presented the difficulties of the task. Some of them set themselves bravely to observe it, and some, I know, succeeded also.

I too took the plunge—the vow to observe brahmacharya for life. I must confess that I had not then fully realized the magnitude and immensity of the task I undertook. The difficulties are even today staring me in the face. What formerly appeared to me to be extravagant praise of *brahmacharya* in our religious books seems now, with increasing clearness every day, to be absolutely proper and founded on experience.

In the first flush of enthusiasm, I found the observance quite easy. The very first change I made in my mode of life was to stop sharing the same bed with my wife or seeking privacy with her.

Thus *brahmacharya,* which I had been observing willy-nilly since 1900, was sealed with a vow in the middle of 1906.

The Birth of Satyagraha

Events were so shaping themselves in Johannesburg as to make this self-purification on my part a preliminary as it were to Satyagraha. I can now see that all the principal events of my life, culminating in the vow of *brahmacharya,* were secretly preparing me for it. The principle called Satyagraha came into being before that name was invented.

Indeed when it was born, I myself could not say what it was. In Gujarati also we used the English phrase 'passive resistance' to describe it. When in a meeting of Europeans I found that the term 'passive resistance' was too narrowly construed, that it was supposed to be a weapon of the weak, that it could be characterized by hatred, and that it could finally manifest itself as violence, I had to demur to all these statements and explain the real nature of the Indian movement. It was clear that a new word must be coined by the Indians to designate their struggle.

But I could not for the life of me find out a new name, and therefore offered a nominal prize through *Indian Opinion* to the reader who made the best suggestion on the subject. As a result Maganlal Gandhi coined the word 'Sadagraha' (Sat =

truth, Agraha = firmness) and won the prize. But in order to make it clearer I changed the word to 'Satyagraha' which has since become current in Gujarati as a designation for the struggle.

The history of this struggle is for all practical purposes a history of the remainder of my life in South Africa and especially of my experiments with truth in that sub-continent. I wrote the major portion of this history in Yeravda jail and finished it after I was released. It was published in *Navajivan* and subsequently issued in book form.

Giving up Milk and Fasting

Kasturbai's illness during this period was instrumental in bringing about some changes in my diet. At a later stage more changes were introduced for the sake of supporting *brahmacharya.*

The first of these was the giving up of milk. It was from Raychandbhai that I first learnt that milk stimulated animal passion. Books on vegetarianism strengthened the idea, but so long as I had not taken the *brahmacharya* vow I could not make up my mind to forego milk. I had long realized that milk was not necessary for supporting the body, but it was not easy to give it up. While the necessity for avoiding milk in the interests of self-restraint was growing upon me, I happened to come across some literature from Calcutta, describing the tortures to which cows and buffaloes were subjected by their keepers. This had a wonderful effect on me. I discussed it with Mr. Kallenbach.

We met quite by accident. He was a friend of Mr. Khan's, and as the later had discovered deep down in him a vein of other-worldliness he introduced him to me. When I came to know him I was startled at his love of luxury and extravagance. But at our very first meeting, he asked searching questions concerning matters of religion. We incidentally talked of Gautama Buddha's renunciation. Our acquaintance soon ripened into very close friendship, so much so that we thought alike, and he was convinced that he must carry out in his life the changes I was making in mine.

At that time he was single, and was expending Rs. 1,200 monthly on himself, over and above house rent. Now he reduced himself to such simplicity that his expenses came to Rs. 120 per month. After the breaking up of my household we began to live together. It was a fairly bad life that we led.

It was during this time that we had the discussion about milk. Mr. Kallenbach said, "We constantly talk about the harmful effects of milk. Why then do not we give it up? It is certainly not necessary. I was agreeably surprised at the suggestion, which I warmly welcomed, and both of us pledged ourselves to abjure milk there and then. This was at Tolstoy Farm in the year 1912.

But this denial was not enough to satisfy me. Soon after this I decided to live on a pure fruit diet, and that too composed of the cheapest fruit possible. Our ambition was to live the life of the poorest people.

I then commenced fasting as a means of self-restraint. In this Mr. Kallenbach also joined me. I had been used to fasting now and again, but for purely health reasons. That fasting was necessary for self-restraint I learnt from a friend. Having been born in a Vaishnava family and of a mother who was given to keeping all sorts of hard vows, I had observed, while in India, the *Ekadashi* and other fasts, but in doing so I had merely copied my mother and sought to please my parents.

When I started on this experiment, the Hindu month of Shravan and the Islamic month of Ramzan happened to coincide. These were undertaken while we were at Tolstoy Farm, where Mr. Kallenbach and I were staying with a few Satyagrahi families, including young people and children. Among them were four or five Musalmans. I always helped and encouraged them in keeping all their religious observances. I took care to see that they offered their daily *namaz.* There were Christian and Parsi youngsters too, whom I considered it my duty to encourage to follow their respective religious observances.

During this month, there, I persuaded the Musalman youngsters to observe the Ramzan fast. I had of course decided to observe *pradosha* myself, but I now asked the Hindu, Parsi and Christian youngsters to join me. I explained to them that it was always a good thing to join with others in any matter of self-denial. Many of the Farm inmates welcomed my proposal. The Hindu and the Parsi youngsters did not copy the Musalman ones in every detail; it was not necessary. The Musalman youngsters had to wait for their breakfast until sunset whereas the others did not do so, and were thus able to prepare delicacies for the Musalman friends and serve them. Nor had the Hindu and other youngsters to keep the Musalman company when they had their last meal before sunrise next morning, and of course all except the Musalmans allowed themselves water. The result of these experiments was that all were convinced of the value of fasting, and a splendid *esprit de corps* grew up among them.

We were all vegetarians on Tolstoy Farm, thanks, I must gratefully confess, to the readiness of all to respect my feelings. The Musalman youngsters delighted in and relished the vegetarian diet, and the Hindu youngsters often prepared vegetarian delicacies for them.

Schoolmaster

As the Farm grew, it was found necessary to make some provision for the education of its boys and girls. It was not possible, and I did not think it necessary, to engage special teachers for them. I did not believe in the existing system of education, and I had a mind to find out by experience and experiment the true system.

I had always given the first place to the culture of the heart or the building of character, and as I felt confident that moral training could be given to all alike, no matter how different their ages and their upbringing, I decided to live amongst them all the twenty-four hours of the day as their father. But as I fully appreciated the necessity of a literary training in addition, I started some classes with the help of Mr. Kallenbach and Sjt. Pragji Desai. Nor did I underrate the building up of the body. This they got in the course of their daily routine. For there were no servants on the Farm, and all the work, from cooking down to scavenging, was done by the inmates. There were many fruit trees to be looked after, and enough gardening to be done as well. Mr. Kallenbach was fond of gardening and had gained some experience of this work in one of the Governmental model gardens. It was obligatory on all, young and old, who were not engaged in the kitchen, to give some time to gardening. The children had the lion's share of this work, which included digging pits, felling timber and lifting loads. This gave them ample exercise. They took delight in the work, and so they did not generally need any other exercise or games.

It was my intention to teach every one of the youngsters some useful manual vocation. For this purpose Mr. Kallenbach went to a Trappist monastery and returned having learnt shoemaking. I learnt it from him and taught the art to such as were ready to take it up. Mr. Kallenbach had some experience of carpentry, and there was another inmate who knew it; so we had a small class in carpentry. Cooking almost all the youngsters knew.

All this was new to them. They had never even dreamt that they would have to learn these things some day. For generally, the only training that Indian children received in South Africa was in the three R's.

On Tolstoy Farm we made it a rule that the youngsters should not be asked to do what the teachers did not do and therefore, when they were asked to do any work, there was always a teacher co-operating and actually working with them. Hence whatever the youngsters learnt, they learnt cheerfully.

The spiritual training of the boys was a much more difficult matter than their physical and mental training. I relied little on religious books for the training of the spirit. Of course I believed that every student should be acquainted with the elements of his own religion and have a general knowledge of his own scriptures, and therefore I provided for such knowledge as best as I could. But that, to my mind, was part of the intellectual training. Long before I undertook the education of the youngsters of the Tolstoy Farm I had realized that the training of the sport was a thing by itself. To develop the spirit is to build character and to enable one to work towards a knowledge of God and self-realization. And I held that this was an essential part of the training of the young, and that all training without culture of the spirit was of no use, and might be even harmful.

How then was this spiritual training to be given? I made the children memorize and recite hymns, and read to them from books on moral training. But that was far from satisfying me. As I came into closer contact with them I saw that it was not through books that one could impart training of the spirit. Just as physical training was to be imparted through physical exercise, and through intellectual exercise, even so the training of the spirit was possible only through the exercise of the spirit. And the exercise of the spirit entirely depended on the life and character of the teacher. The teacher had always to be mindful of his p's and q's whether he was in the midst of his boys or not.

It is possible for a teacher situated miles away to affect the spirit of the pupils by his way of living. It would be idle for me, if I were a liar, to teach boys to tell the truth. A cowardly teacher would never succeed in making his boys valiant, and a stranger to self-restraint could never teach his pupils the value of self-restraint. I saw, therefore, that I must be an eternal object-lesson to the boys and girls living with me. They thus became my teachers, and I learnt I must be good and live straight, if only for their sakes. I may say that the increasing discipline and restraint I imposed on myself at Tolstoy Farm was mostly due to those wards of mine.

Fasting for a Purpose

Day by day it became increasingly clear to me how very difficult it was to bring up and educate boys and girls in the right way. If I was to be their real teacher and guardian, I must touch their hearts. I must share their joys and sorrows, I must help them to solve the problems that faced them, and I must take along the right channel the surging aspirations of their youth.

In those days. I had to move between Johannesburg and Phoenix. Once when I was in Johannesburg I received tidings of the moral fall of two of the inmates of the Ashram. News of an apparent failure or reverse in the Satyagraha struggle would not have shocked me, but this news came upon me like a thunderbolt. The same day I took the train for Phoenix. Mr. Kallenbach insisted on accompanying me. He had noticed the state I was in. He would not brook the thought of my going alone, for he happened to be the bearer of the tidings which had so upset me.

During the journey my duty seemed clear to me. I felt that the guardian or teacher was responsible, to some extent at least, for the lapse of his ward or pupil. So my responsibility regarding the incident in question became clear to me as daylight. My wife had already warned me in the matter, but being of a trusting nature, I had ignored her caution. **I felt that the only way the parties could be made to realize my distress and the depth of their own fall would be for me to do some penance. So I imposed upon myself a fast for seven days and a vow to have only one meal a day for a period of four months and a half.** Mr. Kallenbach tried to dissuade me, but in vain. He finally conceded the propriety of the penance, and insisted on joining me. I could not resist his transparent affection.

I felt greatly relieved, for the decision meant a heavy load off my mind. The anger against the guilty parties subsided and gave place to the purest pity for them. Thus considerably eased, I reached Phoenix. I made further investigation and acquainted myself with some more details I needed to know.

My penance pained everybody, but it cleared the atmosphere. Everyone came to realize what a terrible thing it was to be sinful, and the bond that bound me to the boys and girls became stronger and truer.

A circumstance arising out of this incident compelled me a little while after, to go into a fast for fourteen days, the results of which exceeded even my expectations.

It is not my purpose to make out from these incidents

that it is the duty of a teacher to resort to fasting whenever there is a delinquency on the part of his pupils. I hold, however, that some occasions do call for this drastic remedy. But it presupposes clearness of vision and spiritual fitness.

The first penance did not prove difficult for any of us. I had to suspend or stop none of my normal activities. It may be recalled that during the whole of this period of penance I was a strict fruitarian. The latter part of the second fast went fairly hard with me. I had not then completely understood the wonderful efficacy of *Ramanama,* and my capacity for suffering was to that extent less. Besides, I did not know the technique of fasting, especially the necessity of drinking plenty of water, however nauseating or distasteful it might be.

Then the fact that the first fast had been an easy affair had made me rather careless as to the second. Thus during the first I took Kuhne baths every day, but during the second I gave them up after two or three days, and drank very little water, as it was distasteful and produced nausea. The throat became parched and weak and during the last days I could speak only in a very low voice: In spite of this, however, my work was carried on through dictation where writing was necessary. I regularly listened to readings from the *Ramayana* and other sacred books. I had also sufficient strength to discuss and advise in all urgent matters.

(Gandhi used this most unusual method in fighting against the British rulers in India—*Ed.*)

World War

In 1914, I received Gokhale's instructions to return home via London. So in July Kasturbai, Kallenbach and I sailed for England.

I had now begun travelling third class. I therefore took third class passages for this voyage. But there was a good deal of difference between third class accommodation on the boat on this route and that provided on Indian coastal boats or railway trains. There is hardly sufficient sitting, much less sleeping, accommodation in the Indian service, and little cleanliness. During the voyage to London, on the other hand, there was enough room and cleanliness and the steamship company had provided special facilities for us. The company had provided reserved closet accommodation for us, and as we were fruitarians, the steward had orders to supply us with fruits and nuts. As a rule third class passengers get little fruit or nuts. These facilities made our eighteen days on the boat quite comfortable.

In Madeira we heard that the great War might break out at any moment. As we entered the English Channel, we received the news of its actual outbreak. We were stopped for some time. It was a difficult business to tow the boat through the submarine mines which had been laid throughout the Channel, and it took about two days to reach Southampton. War was declared on the 4th of August. We reached London on the 6th.

On arrival in England I learned that Gokhale had been stranded in Paris where he had gone for reasons of health, and as communication between Paris and London had been cut off, there was no knowing when he would return.

What then was I to do in the meanwhile? What was my duty as regards the war? Sorabji Adajania, my comrade in jail and a Satyagrahi, was then reading for the bar in London. As one of the best Satyagrahis he had been sent to England to qualify himself as a barrister, so that he might take my place on return to South Africa. Dr. Pranjivandas Mehta was paying his expenses. With him, and through him, I had conferences with Dr. Jivraj Mehta and others who were prosecuting their studies in England. In consultation with them, a meeting of the Indian residents in Great Britain and Ireland was called. I placed my views before them.

I felt that Indians residing in England ought to do their bit in the war. English students had volunteered to serve in the army, and Indians might do no less. A number of objections were taken to this line of argument. There was, it was contended, a world of difference between the Indians and the English. We were slaves and they were masters. How could a slave co-operate with the master in the hour of the latter's need? Was it not the duty of the slave seeking to be free, to make the master in the hour of the latter's need? **Was it not the duty of the slave, seeking to be free to make the master's need hus apportunity? This argument failed to appeal to me then. I knew the difference of status between an Indian and an Englishman, but I did not believe that we had been quite reduced to slavery. I felt then that it was more the fault of individual British officials than of the British system, and that we could convert them by love.** If we would improve our status through the help and co-operation of the British, it was our duty to win their help by standing by them in their hour of need.

Offering Service

I therefore adhered to my advice and invited those who would to enlist as volunteers. There was a good response, practically all the provinces and all the religions being represented among the volunteers. I wrote a letter to Lord Crewe, acquainting him with these facts and expressing our readiness to be trained for ambulance work, if that should be considered a condition precedent to the acceptance of our offer. He accepted the offer after some hesitation, and thanked us for having tendered our services to the Empire at that critical hour.

The volunteers began their preliminary training in first aid to the wounded under the well-known Dr. Cantlie. It was a short course of six weeks, but it covered the whole course of first aid. We were a class of about 80. In six weeks we were examined, and all except one passed. For these the Government now provided military drill and other training. Colonel Baker was placed in charge of this work.

London in these days was a sight worth seeing. There was no panic, but all were busy helping to the best of their ability. Able-bodied adults began training as combatants, but what were the old, the infirm and the women to do? There was enough work for them, ıf they wanted. So they employed themselves in cutting and making clothes and dressings for the wounded.

The Lyceum, a ladies' club, undertook to make as many clothes for the soldiers as they could. Shrimati Sarojini Naidu was a member of this club, and threw herself whole-heartedly into the work. This was my first acquaintance with her. She placed before me a heap of clothes which had been cut to pattern, and asked me to get them all sewn up and return them to her. I welcomed her demand and with assistance of friends got as many clothes made as I could manage during my training for first aid.

An officer was appointed in charge of our training, as soon as our names were approved and enlisted. We were all under the impression that this Commanding Officer was to be our chief only so far as technical matters were concerned, and that in all other matters I was the head of our Corps, which was directly responsible to me in matters of internal discipline, that is to say, the Commanding Officer had to deal with the Corps through me. But from the first the Officer left us under no such delusion.

Mr. Sorabji Adajania was a shrewd man. He warned me. 'Beware of this man,' he said. 'He seems inclined to lord it over us. We will have none of his orders. We are prepared to look upon him as our instructor. But the youngsters he has appointed to instruct us also feel as though they had come as our masters.' These youngsters were Oxford students who had come to instruct us and whom the Commanding Officer had appointed to be our section leaders.

I also had not failed to notice the high-handedness of the Commanding Officer, but I asked Sorabji not to be anxious and tried to pacify him. But he was not the man to be easily convinced. 'You are too trusting. These people will deceive you with wretched words, and when at last you see through them, you will ask us to resort to Satyagraha, and so come to grief, and bring us all to grief along with you,' said he with a smile.

In a very few days our relations with him reached the breaking point. I had hardly regained my strength after the fourteen days' fast, when I began to take part in the drill, often walking to the appointed place about two miles from home. This gave me pleurisy and laid me low. In this condition I had to go weekend camping. Whilst the others stayed there, I returned home. It was here that an occasion arose for Satyagraha.

I approached the Commanding Officer and drew his attention to the complaints I had received. He wrote asking me to set out the complaints in writing, at the same time asking me 'to impress upon those who complain that the proper direction in which to make complaints is to me through their section commanders, now appointed, who will inform me through the instructors.' To this I replied saying that I claimed no authority, that in the military sense I was no more than any other private, but that I had believed that as Chairman of the Volunteer Corps, I should be allowed unofficially to act as their representative. I also set out the grievances and requests that had been brought to my notice.

This did not appeal to the Commanding Officer, who said it was repugnant to all military discipline that the section leaders should be elected by the Corps, and that the recall of appointments already made would be subversive of all discipline.

So we held a meeting and decided upon withdrawal. I brought home to the members the serious consequences of Satyagraha. But a very large majority voted for the resolution, which was to the effect that, unless the appointments of Corporals already made were recalled and the members of the Corps given an opportunity of electing their own Corporals, the members would be obliged to abstain from further drilling and weekend camping.

Hereupon I addressed a letter to the Secretary of State for India, acquainting him with all the facts and enclosing a copy of the resolution. He replied explaining that conditions in South Africa were different, and drawing my attention to the fact that under the rules the section commanders were appointed by the Commanding Officer, but assuring me that in future, when appointing section commanders, the

Commanding Officer would consider my recommendations.

About this time an unexpectedly large contingent of wounded soldiers arrived at the Netley Hospital, and the services of our Corps were requisitioned. Those whom the Commanding Officer could persuade went to Netley. The others refused to go. I was on my back, but was in communication with the members of the Corps. Mr. Roberts, the Under-Secretary of State, honoured me with many calls during those days. He insisted on my persuading the others to serve. He suggested that they should form a separate Corps and that at the Netley Hospital they could be responsible only to the Commanding Officer there, so that there would be no question of loss of self-respect, Government would be placated, and at the same time helpful service would be rendered to the large number of wounded received at the hospital This suggestion appealed both to my companions and to me, with the result that those who had stayed away also went to Netley.

Only I remained away, laying on my back and making the best of a bad job.

Gokhale returned to London soon after, Kallenbach and I used regularly to go to him. Our talks were mostly about the war, and as Kallenbach had the ecography of Germany at his finger tips, and had travelled much in Europe, he used to show him on the map the various places in connection with the war.

Meanwhile Gokhale left for home, as he could not stand the October fogs of London.

Homeward

Mr. Kallenbach had accompanied me to England with a view to going to India. We were staying together and of course wanted to sail by the same boat. Germans, however, were under such strict surveillance that we had our doubts about Mr. Kallenbach getting a passport. I did my best to get it, and Mr. Roberts, who was in favour of his getting his passport, sent a cable to the Viceroy in this behalf. But straight came Lord Hardinge's reply: 'Regret Government of India not prepared to take any such risk.' All of us understood the force of the reply.

It was a great wrench for me to part from Mr. Kallenbach, but I could see that his pang was greater. Could he have come to India, he would have been leading today the simple happy life of a farmer and weaver. Now he is in South Africa, leading his old life and doing brisk business as an architect.

We wanted a third class passage, but as there was none available on P. and O. boats, we had to go second.

Whether it was due to past experience or to any other reason, I do not know, but the kind of distance I noticed between the English and Indian passengers on the boat was something I had not observed even on my voyage from South Africa. I did talk to a few Englishmen, but the talk was mostly formal. The reason for this was, I think, to be found in the conscious or unconscious feeling at the back of the Englishman's mind that he belonged to the ruling race, and the feeling at the back of the Indian's mind that he belonged to the subject race.

I was eager to reach home and get free from this atmosphere.

On arriving at Aden we already began to feel somewhat at home.

A few days more and we reached Bombay. It was such a joy to get back to the homeland after an exile of ten years.

Gokhale had inspired a reception for me in Bombay, where he had come in spite of his delicate health. I had approached India in the ardent hope of merging myself in him, and thereby feeling free. But fate had willed it otherwise.

•••

9

Return to India with the Grand New Weapon of Satyagraha

Before I reached home, the party which had started from Phoenix had already arrived. According to our original plan I was to have preceded them, but my preoccupation in England with the war had upset all our calculations, and when I saw that I had to be detained in England indefinitely, I was faced with the question of finding a place for accommodating the Phoenix party. I wanted them all to stay together in India, if possible, and to live the life they had led at Phoenix. I did not know of any Ashram to which I could recommend them to go, and therefore cabled to them to meet Mr. Andrews and do as he advised.

So they were first put in the Gurukul Kangri, where Swami Shraddhanandji treated them as his own children. After this they were put in the Shantiniketan Ashram, where the Poet and his people showered similar love upon them. The experiences they gathered at both these places too stood them and me in good stead.

The Poet, Shraddhanandji and Principal Sushil Rudra, as I used to say to Andrews, composed his trinity. When in South Africa he was never tired of speaking of them, and of my many sweet memories of South Africa, Mr. Andrews' talks, day in and day out, *of* this great trinity, are amongst the sweetest and most vivid. Mr. Andrews naturally put the Phoenix party in touch also with Sushil Rudra. Principal Rudra had no

Ashram, but he had a home which he placed completely at the disposal *of* the Phoenix family. Within a day of their arrival, his people made them feel so thoroughly at home that they did not seem to miss Phoenix at all.

It was only when I landed in Bombay that I learnt that the Phoenix party was at Shantiniketan. I was therefore impatient to meet them as soon as I could after my meeting with Gokhale.

The receptions in Bombay gave me an occasion for offering what might be called a little Satyagraha. At the party given in my honour at Mr. Jehangir Petit's place, I did not dare to speak in Gujarati. **In those palatial surroundings of dazzling splendour I, who had lived my best life among indentured laboureds, felt myself a complete rustic.** With my Kathiawadi cloak, turban and dhoti, I tooked somewhat more civilized than I do today, but the pomp and splendour of Mr. Petit's mansion made me feel absolutely out of my element. However, I acquitted myself tolerably well, having taken shelter under Sir Pherozeshah's protecting wing.

Then there was the Gujarati function. The Gujaratis would not let me go without a reception, which was organized by Uttamlal Trivedi. I had acquainted myself with the programme beforehand. **Mr. Jinnah was present, being a Gujarati,** I forget whether as president or as the principal speaker. **He made a short and sweet little speech in English.** As far as I remember most of the other speeches were also in English. When my turn came, I expressed my thanks in Gujarati explaining my partiality for Gujarati and Hindustani, and entering my humble protest against the use of English in a Gujarati gathering. This I did, not without some hesitation, for I was afraid lest it should be considered discourteous for an inexperienced man, returned home after a long exile, to enter his protest against established practices. But no one seemed to misunderstand my insistence on replying in Gujarati. In fact I was glad to note that everyone seemed reconciled to my protest.

The meeting thus emboldened me to think that 1 should not find it difficult to place, **my new-fangled notions** before my countrymen.

After a brief stay in Bombay, full of these preliminary experiences, I went to Poona whither Gokhale had summoned me.

Meeting Lord Willingdon

The moment I reached Bombay Gokhale sent me word that the Governor was desirous of seeing me, and that it might be proper for me to respond before I left for Poona. Accordingly I called on His Excellency. After the usual inquiries, he said: 'I ask one thing of you. **I would like you to come and see me whenever you propose to take any steps connecting Government.**' (The government took note of Gandhi from day one.—Ed.)

I replied: 'I can very easily give the promise, inasmuch as it is my rule, as a Satyagrahi, to understand the viewpoint of the party I propose to deal with, and to try to agree with him as far as may be possible. I strictly observed the rule in South Africa and I mean to do the same here.'

Lord Willingdon thanked me and said: '**You may come to me whenever you like, and you will see that my Government do not wilfully, do anything wrong:**

To which I replied: 'It is that faith which sustains me.'

In Poona with Gokhale

After this I went to Poona. Gokhale and the members of the Servants of India Society overwhelmed me with affection. So far as I recollect, Gokhale had summoned all of them to meet me. I had a frank talk with them all on every sort of subject.

Gokhale was very keen that I should join the Society and so was I. But the members felt that, as there was a great difference between my ideals and methods of work and theirs, it might not be proper for me to join the Society. Gokhale believed that, in spite of my insistence on my own principles, I was ready and able to tolerate theirs.

'But,' he said, 'the members of the Society have not yet

understood your readiness for compromise. They are tenacious of their principles, and quite independent. But whether you are formally admitted as a member or not, I am going to look upon you as one.'

I informed Gokhale of my intentions. Whether I was admitted as a member or not, I wanted to have an Ashram where I could settle down with my Phoenix family, preferably somewhere in Gujarat, as, being a Gujarati, I thought I was best fitted to serve the country through serving Gujarat. Gokhale liked the idea. He said: 'You should certainly do so. Whatever may be the result of your talks with the members, **you must look to me for the expenses of the Ashram, which I will regard as my own.'**

My heart over flowed with joy. It was a pleasure to feel free from the responsibility of raising funds, and to realize that I should not be obliged to set about the work all on my own, but that I should be able to count on a sure guide whenever I was in difficulty. This took a great load off my mind.

So Dr. Dev was summoned and told to open an account for me in the Society's books and to give me whatever I might require for the Ashram and for public expenses.

I now prepared to go to Shantiniketan. On the eve of my departure Gokhale arranged a party of selected friends, taking good care to order refreshments of my liking, i.e., fruits and nuts. The party was held just a few paces from his room, and yet he was hardly in a condition to walk across and attend it. But his affection for me got the better of him and he insisted on coming. He came, but fainted and had to be carried away. Such fainting was not a new thing with him and so when he came to, he sent word that we must go on with the party.

This party was of course no more than a conversazione in the open space opposite the Society's guesthouse, during which friends had heart-to-heart chats over light refreshments of groundnuts, dates and fresh fruits of the season.

But the fainting fit was to be no common event in my life.

From Poona I went to Rajkot and Porbandar, where 1 had to meet my brother's widow and other relatives.

During the Satyagraha in South Africa I had altered my style of dress so as to make it more in keeping with that of the indentured labourers, and in England also I had adhered to the same style for indoor use. For landing in Bombay I had a Kathiawadi suit of clothes consisting of a shirt, a dhoti, a cloak and a white scarf, all made of Indian mill cloth. But as I was to travel third from Bombay, I regarded the scarf and the cloak as too much of an incumbrance, so I shed them, and invested in an eight-to-ten annas Kashmiri cap. One dressed in that fashion I was sure to pass muster as a poor man.

My First Satyagraha

On account of the plague prevailing at that time third class passengers were being medically inspected at Viramgam or Wadhwan—I forget which. I had slight fever. The inspector on finding that I had a temperature asked me to report myself to the Medical Officer at Rajkot and noted down my name.

Someone had perhaps sent the information that I was passing through Wadhwan, for the tailor Motilal, a noted public worker of the place, met me at the station. He told me about the Viramgam customs, and the hardships railway passengers had to suffer on account of it. I had little inclination to talk because of my fever, and tried to finish with a brief reply which took the form of a question: 'Are you prepared to go to jail?'

I had taken Motilal to be one of those impetuous youths who do not think before speaking. But not so Motilal. He replied with firm deliberation: 'We will certainly go to jail, provided you lead us. As Kathiawadis, we have the first right on you. Of course we do not mean to detain you now, but you must promise to halt here on your return.

Motilal captivated me. His comrade eulogizing him, said: 'Our friend is but a tailor. But he is such a master of his profession that he easily earns Rs. 15 a month—which is just what he needs—working an hour a day, and gives the rest of his time to public work. He leads us all, putting our education to shame.'

Later I came in close contact with Motilal, and I saw that there was no exaggeration in the eulogy. He made a point of spending some days in the then newly started Ashram every month to teach the children tailoring and to do some of the tailoring of the Ashram himself. He would talk to me every day of Viramgam, and the hardships of the passengers, which had become absolutely unbearable for him.

On reaching Rajkot, I reported myself to the Medical Officer the next morning. I was not unknown there. The doctor felt ashamed and was angry with the inspector.

Inspection of third class passengers for sanitary reasons is essential on such occasions. The officials, instead of looking upon third class passengers as fellowmen, regard them as so many sheep. They talk to them contemptuously, and may with impunity behave and blackmail him.

Wherever I went in Kathiawad I heard complaints about the Viramgam customs and hardships. I therefore decided immediately to make use of Lord Willingdon's offer. I connected and read all the literature available on the subject, convinced myself that the complaints were well-founded, and opened correspondence with the Bombay Government. I called on the Private Secretary to Lord Willingdon and waited on His Excellency also. The latter expressed his sympathy but shifted the blame on Delhi. If it had been in our hands, we should have removed the cordon long ago. You should approach the Government of India,' said the Secretary.

I communicated with the Government of India, but got no reply beyond an acknowledgment. It was only when I had an occasion to meet Lord Chelmsford later that redress could be had. When I placed the facts before him, he expressed his astonishment. He had known nothing of the matter. He gave me a patient hearing, telephoned that very moment for papers about Viramgam, and promised to remove the cordon if the authorities had no explanation or defence to offer.

Within a few days of this interview I read in the papers

that the Viramgam customs cordon had been removed.

I regarded this event as the advent of Satyagraha in India. For during my interview with the Bombay Government the Secretary had expressed his disapproval of a reference to Satyagraha in a speech which I had delivered in Bagasra.

'Is not this a threat?' he had asked. 'And do you think a powerful Government will yield to threats?'

'This was no threat,' I had replied. 'It was educating the people. **It is my duty to place before the people all the legitimate remedies for grievances. A nation that wants to come into its own ought to know all the ways and means to freedom. Usually they include violence as the last remedy. Satyagraha, on the other hand, is an absolutely non-violent weapon.** I regard it as my duty to explain its practice and its limitations._Government is a powerful Government, but I have no doubt also that **Satyagraha is sovereign remedy.'**

The clever Secretary sceptically nodded his head and said: 'We shall see.'

At Shantiniketan

From Rajkot I proceeded to Shantiniketan. The teachers and students overwhelmed me with affection. The reception was a beautiful combination of simplicity, art and love. It was here I met Kakasaheb Kalelkar for the first time.

The Phoenix family had been assigned separate quarters at Shantiniketan. Maganlal Gandhi was at their head, and he had made it his business to see that all the rules of the Phoenix Ashram should be scrupulously observed. Andrews was there, and also Pearson. Amongst the Bengali teachers with whom we came in fairly close contact were Jagadanandbabu, Nepalbabu, Santoshbabu, Kshitimohanbabu, Nagenbabu, Sharadbabu and Kalibabu.

As is my wont, I quickly mixed with the teachers and students, and engaged them in a discussion on self-help. I put it to the teachers that, if they and the boys dispensed with the service of paid cooks and cooked their food themselves, it would enable the teachers to control the kitchen from the point of view of the boys' physical and moral health, and it would afford to the students an object-lesson in self-help. One or two of them were inclined to shake their heads. Some of them strongly approved of the proposal. The boys welcomed it, if only because of their instinctive taste for novelty. So we launched the experiment. When I invited the Poet to express his opinion, he said that he did not mind it provided the teachers were favourable. To the boys he said, **'The experiment contains the key to Swaraj.'**

Pearson began to wear away his body in making the experiment a success. He threw himself into it with zest. A batch was formed to cut vegetables, another to clean the grain, and so on. Nagenbabu and others undertook to see to the sanitary cleaning of the kitchen and its surroundings. It was a delight to me to see them working spade in hand.

The experiment was, however, dropped after some time.

I had intended to stay at Shantiniketan for some time, but fate willed otherwise. I had hardly been there a week when I received from Poona a telegram announcing Gokhale's death. Shantiniketan was immersed in grief. All the members came over to me to express their condolences. A special meeting was called in the Ashram temple to mourn the national loss. It was a solemn function. The same day I left for Poona with my wife and Maganlal.

Andrews accompanied me up to Burdwan. 'Do you think,' he asked me, 'that a time will come for Satyagraha in India? And if so, have you any idea when it will come?'

'It is difficult to say,' said I. **'For one year I am to do nothing. For Gokhale took from me a promise that I should travel in India for gaining experience, and express no opinion on public questions until I have finished the period of probation.** Even after the year is over, I will be in no hurry to speak and pronounce opinions. And so **I do not suppose there will be any occasion for Satyagraha for five years or so.'**

I may note in this connection that Gokhale used to laugh at some of my ideas in *Hind Swaraj* or *Indian Home Rule* and say: 'After you have stayed a year in India, your views will correct themselves.'

Kumbha Mela

I next went to Rangoon to meet Dr. Mehta, and on my way I halted at Calcutta. I was the guest of Babu Bhupendranath Basu. Bengali hospitality reached its climax here. In those days I was a strict fruitarian, so all the fruits and nuts available in Calcutta were ordered for me. The ladies of the house kept awake all night skinning various nuts. Every possible care was taken in dressing fresh fruit in the Indian style. Numerous delicacies were prepared for my companions, amongst whom was my son Ramdas. Much as I could appreciate this affectionate hospitality, I could not bear the thought of a whole household being occupied in entertaining two or three guests. But as yet I saw no escape from such embarrassing attentions.

In Rangoon my fruitarian diet was again a source of additional trouble to the host. But since Dr. Mehta's home was as good as my own, I could control somewhat the lavishness of the menu.

In Hardwar

This year—1915—was the year of the Kumbha fair, which is held at Hardwar once every 12 years. I was by no means eager to attend the fair, but I was anxious to meet Mahatma Munshiramji who was in his Gurukul. Gokhale's Society had sent a big volunteer corps for service at the Kumbha. Pandit Hridayanath Kunzru was at the head, and Dr. Dev was the medical officer. I was invited to send the Phoenix party to assist them, and so Maganlal Gandhi had already preceded me. On my return from Rangoon, I joined the band.

Our stay in Shantiniketan had taught us that the scavenger's work would be our special function in India. Now for the volunteers in Hardwar tents had been pitched in a *dharmashala,* and Dr. Dev had dug some pits to be used as latrines. He had had to depend on paid scavengers for looking after these. Here was work for the Phoenix party. We offered to cover up the excreta with earth and to see to their disposal, and Dr. Dev gladly accepted our offer. My business was mostly to keep sitting in the tent giving *darshan* and holding religious and other discussions with numerous pilgrims who called on me. Thus it was in Hardwar that I realized what a deep impression my humble services in South Africa had made throughtout the whole of India.

An Unusual Vow

The day of the fair was now upon us. It proved a red-letter day for me. I had not gone to Hardwar with the sentiments of a pilgrim. I have never thought of frequenting places of pilgrimage in search of piety. But the seventeen lakhs of men that were reported to be there could not all be hypocrites or mere sightseers. I had no doubt that countless people amongst them had gone there to earn merit and for self-purification. It is difficult, if not impossible, to say to what extent this kind of faith uplifts the soul.

I therefore passed the whole night immersed in deep thought. If the visit to Hardwar was in itself a sin, I must publicly protest against it, and leave Hardwar on the day of Kumbha. If the pilgrimage to Hardwar and to the Kumbha fair was not sinful, I must impose some act of self-denial on myself in atonement for the iniquity prevailing there and purify myself.

This was quite natural for me. My life is based on disciplinary resolutions. I thought of the unnecessary trouble I had caused to my hosts at Calcutta and Rangoon, who had so lavishly entertained me. I therefore decided to limit the articles of my daily diet and to have my final meal before sunset. I was convinced that, if I did not impose these restrictions on myself, I should put my future hosts to considerable inconvenience and should engage them in serving me rather than engage myself in service. So **I pledged myself never whilst in India to take more than five articles in twenty-four hours, and never to eat after dark.** I wanted to leave no loophole. I rehearsed to myself what would happen during an illness, if I counted medicine among the five articles, and made no exception in favour of special articles of diet. I finally decided that there should be no exception on any account whatsoever.

It was a positive relief to reach the Gurukul and meet Mahatma Munshiramji with his giant frame. I at once felt the wonderful contrast between the peace of the Gurukul and the din and noise of Hardwar.

The Mahatma overwhelmed me with affection. The Brahmacharis were all attention. I had long discussions with Acharya Ramadevji and other professors about the necessity of introducing industrial training into the Gurukul. When the time came for going away it was a wrench to leave the place.

I had heard much in praise of the Lakshman Jhula (a hanging bridge over the Ganges) some distance from Rishikesh, and many friends pressed me not to leave Hardwar without having gone as far as the bridge. I wanted to do this pilgrimage on foot and so I did it in two stages.

Hindu without a Shikha

Many *sannyasis* called on me at Rishikesh. One of them was particularly attracted towards me. The Phoenix party was there and their presence drew from the Swami many questions.

We had discussions about religion and he realized that I felt deeply about matters of religion. He saw me bare-headed and shirtless as I had returned from my bath in the Ganges. He was pained to miss the *shikha* (tuft of hair) on my head and the sacred thread about my neck and said: 'It pains me to see you, a believing Hindu, going without a sacred thread and the *shikha.* These are the two external symbols of Hinduism and every Hindu ought to wear them.'

I made a clean breast of the whole matter to the Swami and said:

'I will not wear the sacred thread, for I see no necessity for it, when countless Hindus can go without it and yet remain Hindus. Moreover, the sacred thread should be a symbol of spiritual regeneration, presupposing a deliberate attempt on the part of the wearer at a higher and purer life. **I doubt whether in the present state of Hinduism and of India,**

Hindus can vindicate the right to wear a symbol charged with such a meaning. That right can come only after Hinduism has purged itself of untouchability, has removed all distinctions of superiority and inferiority, and shed a host of other evils and shams that have become rampant in it. My mind therefore rebels against the idea of wearing the sacred thread. But I am sure your suggestion about the *shikha* is worth considering. I once used to have it, and I discarded it from a false sense of shame. And so I feel that I should start growing it again. I shall discuss the matter with my comrades.'

I was charmed with the natural scenery about Rishikesh and the Lakshman Jhula, and bowed my head in reverence to our ancestors for their sense of the beautiful in Nature, and for their foresight in investing beautiful manifestations of Nature with a religious significance.

But the way in which men were using these beauty spots was far from giving me peace. As at Hardvar, so at Rishikesh, people dirtied the roads and the fair banks of the Ganges. They did not even hesitate to desecrate the sacred water of the Ganges. It filled me with agony to see people performing natural functions on the thoroughfares and river banks, when they could easily have gone a little farther away from public haunts.

The Svargashram which one reaches after crossing the bridge was a wretched place' being nothing but a number of shabby-looking sheds of galvanized iron sheets. These, I was told, were made for *sadhakas* (aspirants). There were hardly any one living there at the moment. Those who were in the main building gave one an unfavourable impression.

Founding of the Satyagraha Ashram to Spread the Movement

The Satyagraha Ashram was founded on the 25th of May, 1915. Shraddhanandji wanted me to settle in Hardwar. Some of my Calcutta friends recommended Vaidyanatha Dham. Others strongly urged me to choose Rajkot. But when I happened to pass through Ahmedabad, many friends pressed me to settle down there, and they volunteered to find the expenses of the Ashram, as well as a house for us to live in.

I had a predilection for Ahmedabad. Being a Gujarati I thought I should be able to render the greatest service to the country through the Gujarati language. And then, as Ahmedabad was an ancient centre of handloom weaving, it was likely to be the most favourable field for the revival of the cottage industry of hand-spinning. There was also the hope that, the city being the capital of Gujarat, monetary help from its wealthy citizens would be more available here than elsewhere.

The question of untouchability was naturally among the subjects discussed with the Ahmedabad friends. **I made it clear to them that I should take the first opportunity of admitting an untouchable candidate to the Ashram** if he was otherwise worthy.

So far as accommodation was concerned, Sjt. Jivanlal Desai, a barrister in Ahmedabad, was the principal man to help me. He offered to let, and we decided to hire, his Kochrab bungalow.

The first thing we had to settle was the name of the Ashram. I consulted friends. Amongst the names suggested were 'Sevashram' 'Tapovan' etc. I liked the name 'Sevashram' but for the absence of emphasis on the method of service. 'Tapovan' seemed to be a pretentious title, because though *tapas* was dear to us we could not presume to be *tapasvins*. Our creed was devotion to truth, and our business was the search for and insistence on truth. **I wanted to acquaint India with the method I had tried in South Africa, and I desired to test in India the extent to which its application might be possible. So my companions and I selected the name 'Satyagraha Ashram'.**

For the conduct of the Ashram a code of rules and observances was necessary. A draft was therefore prepared, and friends were invited to express their opinions on it. Amongst the many opinions that were received, that of Sir Gurudas Banerji is still in my memory. He liked the rules, but suggested that humility should be added as one of the observances, as he believed that the younger generation sadly lacked humility. Though I noticed this fault, I feared humility would cease to be humility the moment it became a matter of vow.

There were at this time about thirteen Tamilians in our party. Five Tamil youngsters had accompanied me from South Africa, and the rest came from different parts of the country. We were in all about twenty-five men and women.

This is how the Ashram was started. All had their meals in a common kitchen and strove to live as one family.

First Untouchable Family in the Ashram

The Ashram had been in existence only a few months when we were put to a test such as I had scarcely expected. I received a letter from Amritlal Thakkar to this effect: 'A humble and honest untouchable family is desirous of joining your Ashram. Will you accept them?'

I was perturbed. I had never expected that an untouchable family with an introduction from no less a man than Thakkar Bapa would so soon be seeking admission to the Ashram. I shared the letter with my companions. They welcomed it.

I wrote to Amritlal Thakkar expressing our willingness to accept the family, provided all the members were ready to abide by the rules of the Ashram.

The family consisted of Dudabhai, his wife Danibehn and their daughter Lakshmi, then a mere toddling babe. Dudabhai had been a teacher in Bombay. They all agreed to abide by the rules and were accepted.

But their admission created a flutter amongst the friends who had been helping the Ashram. The very first difficulty was found with regard to the use of the well, which was partly controlled by the owner of the bungalow. The man in charge of the water-lift objected that drops of water from our bucket would pollute him. So he took to swearing at us and molesting Dudabhai. I told everyone to put up with the abuse and continue drawing water at any cost. **When he saw that we did not return his abuse, the man became ashamed and**

ceased to bother us.

All monetary help, however, was stopped. Then came rumours of proposed social boycott. We were prepared for all this. I had told my companions that, if we were boycotted and denied the usual facilities, we would not leave Ahmedabad. We would rather go and stay in the untouchables' quarter and live on whatever we could get by manual labour. (This courage of conviction made him what for became: Mahatma Gandhi:— Ed.)

Matters came to such a pass that Maganlal Gandhi one day gave me this notice: 'We are out of funds and there is nothing for the next month.'

I quietly replied: 'Then we shall go to the untouchables' quarter.'

This was not the first time I had been faced with such a trial. On all such occasions God has sent help at the last moment. One morning, one of the children came and said that a Sheth who was waiting in a car outside wanted to see me. I went out to him. 'I want to give the Ashram some help. Will you accept it?' he asked.

'Most certainly,' said I. 'And I confess I am at the present moment at the end of my resources.'

'I shall come tomorrow at this time, he said. 'Will you be here?'

'Yes,' said I, and he left.

Next day, exactly at the appointed hour, the car drew up near our quarters, and the horn was blown. The children came with the news. The Sheth did not come in. I went out to see him. **He placed in my hands currency notes of the value of Rs. 13,000, and drove away.**

I had never expected this help, and what a novel way of rendering it! The gentleman had never before visited the Ashram. So far as I can remember, I had met him only once. No visit, no enquiries, simply rendering help and going away! This was a unique experience for me. The help deferred the exodus to the untouchables' quarter. We now felt quite safe for a year.

Just as there was a storm outside, so was there a storm in the Ashram itself. Though in South Africa untouchable friends used to come to my place and live and feed with me, my wife and other women did not seem quite to relish the admission into the Ashram of the untouchable friends. My eyes and ears easily detected their indifference, if not their dislike, towards Danibehn. The monetary difficulty had caused me no anxiety, but this internal storm was more than I could bear. Danibehn was an ordinary woman. Dudabhai was a man with slight education but of good understanding. I liked his patience. Sometimes he did flare up, but on the whole I was well impressed with his forbearance. I pleaded with him to swallow minor insults. He not only agreed, but prevailed upon his wife to do likewise.

The admission of this family proved a valuable lesson to the Ashram. In the very beginning we proclaimed to the world that the Ashram would not countenance untouchability. Those who wanted to help the Ashram were thus put on their guard, and the work of the Ashram in this direction was considerably simplified.

Another Success: Abolition of Indentured Emigration

Indentured labourers were those who had emigrated from India to labour under an indenture for five years or less. Under the Smuts-Gandhi Settlement of 1914, the £ 3 tax in respect of the indentured emigrants to Natal had been abolished, but the general emigration from India still needed treatment.

In March 1916 Pandit Madan Mohan Malaviya moved a resolution in the Imperial Legislative Council for the abolition of the indenture system. In accepting the motion Lord Hardinge announced that he had 'obtained from His Majesty's Government the promise of the abolition in due course' of the system. I felt, however, that India could not be satisfied with so very vague an assurance, but ought to agitate for immediate abolition. India had tolerated the system through sheer negligence, and I believed the time had come when people could successfully agitate for this redress. I met some of the leaders, wrote in the press, and saw that public opinion was solidly in favour of immediate abolition. Might this be a fit subject for Satyagraha? I had no doubt that it was, but I did not know the *modus operandi.*

So in February 1917, Pandit Malaviyaji asked for leave to introduce a bill for the immediate abolition of the system. Lord Chelmsford refused permission. It was time for me to tour the country for an all-India agitation.

Before I started the agitation I thought it proper to wait upon the Viceroy. So I applied for an interview. He immediately granted it. Mr. Maffey, now Sir John Maffey, was his private secretary. I came in close contact with him. I had a satisfactory talk with Lord Chelmsford who, without being definite, promised to be helpful.

I began my tour from Bombay. Mr. Jehangir Petit undertook to convene the meeting under the auspices of the Imperial Citizenship Association. The Executive Committee of the Association met first for framing the resolutions to be moved at the meeting. The discussion centred round the fixing of the period within which the Government was to be asked to abolish the system. We adopted the 31st July as the latest date by which the abolition should be announced, a resolution to that effect was passed at the public meeting, and meetings throughout India resolved accordingly.

Mrs. Jaiji Petit put all her energies into the organization of a ladies' deputation to the Viceroy. Amongst the ladies from Bombay who formed the deputation I remember the names of Lady Tata and the late Dilshad Begam. The deputation had a great effect. The Viceroy gave an encouraging reply.

I visited Karachi, Calcutta and various other places. There were fine meetings everywhere, and there was unbounded enthusiasm. I had not expected anything like it when the agitation was launched.

In those days I used to travel alone, and had therefore wonderful experiences. The C.I.D. men were always after me.

But as I had nothing to conceal, they did not molest me, nor did I cause them any trouble. Fortunately, I had not then received the stamp of Mahatmaship, though the shout of that name was quite common where people knew me.

I somehow reached Delhi and thence Calcutta. The Maharaja of Cassimbazaar, the president of the Calcutta meeting, was my host. Just as in Karachi, here also there was unbounded enthusiasm. The meeting was attended by several Englishmen.

Before the 31st July the Government announced that indentured emigration from India was stopped.

It was in 1894 that I drafted the first petition protesting against the system, and I had then hold that this 'semi-slavery', as Sir W. W. Hunter used to call the system, would some day be brought to an end.

There were many who aided in the agitation which was started in 1894, but **I cannot help saying that potential Satyagraha hastened the end.**

Champaran: A Major Satyagraha

Champaran is the land of King Janaka. Just as it abounds in mango groves, so used it to be full of indigo plantations until the year 1917. The Champaran tenant was bound by law to plant three out of every twenty parts of his land with indigo for his landlord. This system was known as the *tinkathia* system.

I did not then know even the name, much less the geographical position of Champaran, and I had hardly any notion of indigo plantations. I had seen packets of indigo, but little dreamed that it was grown and manufactured in Champaran at great hardship to thousands of agriculturists.

Rajkumar Shukla was one of the agriculturists who had been under this harrow and he was filled with a passion to wash away the stain of indigo for the thousand who were suffering, as he has suffered.

This man caught hold of me at Lucknow, where I had gone for the Congress of 1916. 'Vakil Babu will tell you everything about our distress,' he said, and urged me to go to Champaran. 'Vakil Babu' was none other than Babu Brajkishore Prasad, who became my esteemed co-worker in Champaran, and who is the soul of public work in Bihar. Rajkumar Shukla brought him to my tent. He was dressed in a black alpaca *achkan* and trousers.

Brajkishore Babu failed then to make an impression on me. I took it that he must be some vakil exploiting the simple agriculturists. Having heard from him something of Champaran, I replied as was my wont: 'I can give no opinion without seeing the condition with my own eyes. You will please move the resolution in the Congress, but leave me free for the present.' Rajkumar Shukla of course wanted some help from the Congress. Babu Brajkishore Prasad moved the resolution, expressing sympathy for the people of Champaran, and it was unanimously passed.

Rajkumar Shukla wanted me personally to visit Champaran and witness the miseries of the ryots there: I told him that I would include Champaran in the tour which I had contemplated and give it a day or two.

From Lucknow I went to Kanpur. Rajkumar Shukla followed me there. 'Champaran is very near here. Please give a day,' he insisted. 'Pray excuse me this time. But I promise that I will come,' said I, further committing myself.

I returned to the Ashram. The ubiquitous Rajkumar was there too. 'Pray fix the day now,' he said. 'Well,' said I, 'I have to be in Calcutta on such and such a date, come and meet me then, and take me from there.'

Before I reached Bhupen Babu's place in Calcutta, Rajkumar Shukla had gone and established himself there. Thus this ignorant, unsophisticated but resolute agriculturist captured me.

So early in 1917, we left Calcutta for Champaran, looking just like fellow rustics. I did not even know the train. He took me to it, and we travelled together, reaching Patna in the morning.

This was my first visit to Patna. I had no friend or acquaintance with whom I could think of putting up.

Rajkumar Shukla took me to Rajendra Babu's place in Patna. Rajendra Babu had gone to Puri or some other place, I now forget which. There were one or two servants at the bungalow who paid us no attention. I had with me something to eat. I wanted dates which my companion procured for me from the bazaar.

I saw now that Rajkumar Shukla could not guide me, and that I must take the reins in my own hands.

I knew Maulana Mazharul Haq in London when he was studying for the bar, and when I met him at the Bombay Congress in 1915—the year in which he was President of the Muslim League—he had renewed the acquaintance, and extended me an invitation to stay with him whenever I happened to go to Patna. I bethought myself of this invitation and sent him a note indicating the purpose of my visit. He immediately came in his car, and pressed me to accept his hospitality. I thanked him and requested him to guide me to my destination by the first available train. He had a talk with Rajkumar Shukla and suggested that I should first go to Muzaffarpur. There was a train for that place the same evening, and he sent me off by it.

Principal Kripalani was then in Muzaffarpur. I had known of him ever since my visit to Hyderabad. Dr. Choithram had told me of his great sacrifice, of his simple life, and of the Ashram that Dr. Choithram was running out of funds provided by Prof. Kripalani. He used to be a professor in the Government College, Muzaffarpur, and had just resigned the post when I went there. I had sent a telegram informing him of my arrival, and he met me at the station with a crowd of students, though the train reached there at midnight. He had no rooms of his own, and was staying with Professor Malkani who therefore virtually became my host. It was an extraordinary thing in those days for a Government professor to harbour a man like me.

Professor Kripalani spoke to me about the desperate condition of Bihar, particularly of the Tirhut division and gave me an idea of the difficulty of my task. He had established very close contact with the Biharis, and had already spoken to them about the mission that took me to Bihar.

In the morning a small group of vakils called on me. I still remember Ramnavmi Prasad among them, as his earnestness specially appealed to me.

'It is not possible,' he said, 'for you to do the kind of work you have come for, if you stay here (meaning Prof. Malkani's, quarters). You must come and stay with one of us. Gaya Babu is a well-known vakil here. I have come on his behalf to invite you to stay with him. I confess we are all afraid of Government, but we shall render what help we can. Most of the things Rajkumar Shukla had told you are true. It is a pity our leaders are not here today. I have, however, wired to them both, Babu Brajkishore Prasad and Babu Rajendra Prasad. I expect them to arrive shortly, and they are sure to be able to give you all the information you want and to help you considerably. Pray come over to Gaya Babu's place.'

This was a request that I could not resist, so I went over to stay with him. He and his people showered all their affection on me.

Brajkishorebabu now arrived from Darbhanga and Rajendra Babu from Puri. Brajkishorebabu was not the Babu Brajkishore Prasad I had met in Lucknow. He impressed me this time with his humility, simplicity, goodness and extraordinary faith, so characteristic of the Biharis, and my heart was joyous over it. The Bihar vakils' regard for him was an agreeable surprise to me.

'Having studied these cases,' said I, 'I have come to the conclusion that we should stop going to law courts. Taking such cases to the courts does little good. Where the ryots are so crushed and fear-stricken, law courts are useless. The real relief for them is to be free from fear. We cannot sit still until we have driven *tinkathia* out of Bihar. I had thought that I should be able to leave here in two days, but I now realize that the work might take even two years. I am prepared to give that time, if necessary. I am now feeling my ground, but I want your help.'

I found Brajkishorebabu exceptionally coolheaded. 'We shall render all the help we can,' he said quietly, 'but pray tell us what kind of help you will need.'

And thus we sat talking until midnight.

'I shall have little use for your legal knowledge,' I said to them. 'I want clerical assistance and help in interpretation. It may be necessary to face imprisonment, but, much as I would love you to run that risk, you would go only so far as you feel yourselves capable of going. Even turning yourselves into clerks and giving up your profession for an indefinite period is no small thing. I find it difficult to understand the local dialect of Hindi, and I shall not be able to read papers written in Kaithi or Urdu. I shall want you to translate them for me. We cannot afford to pay for this work. It should all be done for love and out of a spirit of service.'

Brajkishorebabu understood this immediately, and he now cross examined me and his companions by turns. He tried to ascertain the implications of all that I had said—how long their service would be required, how many of them would be needed, whether they might serve by turns and so on. Then he asked the vakils the capacity of their sacrifice.

Ultimately they gave me this assurance. 'Such and such a number of us will do whatever you may ask. Some of us will be with you for so much time as you may require. The idea of accommodating oneself to imprisonment is a novel thing for us. (Gandhis major contribution to Indian polity:—Ed.) We will try to assimilate it.'

Ordered to Leave Champaran

My object was to inquire into the condition of the Champaran agriculturists and understand their grievances against the indigo planters. For this purpose it was necessary that I should meet thousands of the ryots. But I deemed it essential, before starting on my inquiry, to know the planters' side of the case and see the Commissioner of the Division. I sought and was granted appointments with both.

The Secretary of the Planters' Association told me plainly that I was an outsider and that I had no business to come between the planters and their tenants, but if I had any representation to make, I might submit it in writing. I politely told him that I did not regard myself as an outsider, and that I had every right to inquire into the condition of the attendants if they desired me to do so. **The Commissioner, on whom I called, proceeded to bully me, and advised me forthwith to leave Tirhut.**

I acquainted my co-workers with all this, and told them that there was a likelihood of Government stopping me from proceeding further, and that I might have to go to jail earlier than I had expected, and that, if I was to be arrested, it would be best that the arrest should take place in Motihari or if possible in Bettiah. It was advisable, therefore, that I should go to those places as early as possible. Champaran is a district of the Tirhut division and Motihari is its headquarters.

I started with my co-workers for Motihari the same day. Babu Gorakh Prasad harboured us in his home, which became a caravanserai. It could hardly contain us all. The very same day we heard that about five miles from Motihari a tenant had been ill-treated. It was decided that, in company with Babu Dharanidhar Prasad, I should go and see him the next morning, and we accordingly set off for the place on elephant's back. (An elephant, by the way, is about as common in Champaran as a bullock-cart in Gujarat.)

We had scarcely gone half way when a messenger from the Police Superintendent overtook us and said that the latter had sent his compliments. I saw what he meant. Having left Dharanidharbabu to proceed to the original destination, I got into the third carriage which the messenger had brought. He then served on me a notice to leave Champaran, and drove me to my place. On his asking me to acknowledge the service of the notice, I wrote to the effect that I did not propose to comply with it and leave Champaran till my inquiry was finished. Thereupon I received a summons to take my trial the next day for disobeying the order to leave Champaran.

I kept awake that whole night writing letters and giving necessary instructions to Babu Brajkishore Prasad.

The news of the notice and the summons spread like wildfire, and I was told that Motihari that day witnessed unprecedented scenes. Gorakhbabu's house and the court house overflowed with men. Fortunately, I had finished all my work during the night and so was able to cope with the crowds.

A sort of friendliness sprang up between the officials—Collector, Magistrate, Police Superintendent—and myself. I might have legally resisted the notices served on me. Instead I accepted them all, and my conduct towards the officials was correct. **They thus say that I did not want to offend them personally, but that I wanted to offer civil resistance to their orders.** In this way they were put at ease, and instead of harassing me they gladly availed themselves of my and my co-workers' co-operation in regulating the crowds. But it was an ocular demonstration to them of the fact that their authority was shaken. The people had for the moment lost all fear of punishment and yielded obedience to the power of love which their new friend exercised.

That day in Champaran was an unforgettable event in my life and and a red-letter day for the peasants and for me. According to this law, I was to be on my trial, but truly speaking, Government was to be on its trial. The Commissioner only succeeded in trapping Government in the net which he had spread for me.

Case Withdrawn

The trial began. The Government pleader, the Magistrate and other officials were on tenterhooks. They were at a loss *to* know what to do. The Government pleader was pressing the Magistrate to postpone the case. But **I interfered and requested the Magistrate not to postpone the case, as I wanted to plead guilty to having disobeyed the order to leave Champaran,** and read a brief statement.

There was now no occasion to postpone the hearing, but as both the Magistrate and the Government pleader had been taken by surprise, the Magistrate postponed judgment. Meanwhile, I had wired full details to the Viceroy, to Patna friends, as also to Pandit Madan Mohan Malaviya and others.

Before I could appear before the Court to receive the sentence, the Magistrate sent a written message that the Lieutenant Governor had ordered the case against me to be withdrawn, and the Collector wrote to me saying that I was at liberty to conduct the proposed inquiry, and that I might count on whatever help I needed from the officials. None of us was prepared for this prompt and happy issue.

I called on the Collector Mr. Heycock. He seemed to be a good man, anxious to do justice. He told me that I might ask for whatever papers I desired to see, and that I was at liberty to see him whenever I liked.

The country thus had its first direct object-lesson in Civil Disobedience. The affair was freely discussed both locally and in the press, and my inquiry got unexpected publicity.

The Champaran struggle was a proof of the fact that disinterested service of the people in any sphere ultimately helps the country politically.

Social Work in Champaran

As I gained more experience of Bihar, I became convinced that a work of a permanent nature was impossible without proper village education. The ryots' ignorance was pathetic. They either allowed their children to roam about, or made them toil on indigo plantations from morning to night for a couple of coppers a day. In those days a male labourer's wage did not exceed ten pice, a female's did not exceed six, and a child's three. He who succeeded in earning four annas a day was considered most fortunate.

In consultation with my companions I decided to open primary schools in six villages. One of our conditions with the villagers was that they should provide the teachers with board and lodging while we would see to the other expenses. The village folk had hardly any cash in their hands, but they could well afford to provide foodstuffs.

From where to get the teachers was a great problem. It was difficult to find local teachers who would work for a bare allowance or without remuneration. So I issued a public appeal for voluntary teachers. It received a ready response. Sjt. Gangadharrao Deshpande sent Babasaheb Soman and Pundalik. Shrimati Avantikabai Gokhale came from Bombay and Mrs. Anandibai Vaishampayan from Poona. I sent to the Ashram for Chhotala, Surendranath and my son Devdas. About this time Mahadev Desai and Narahari Parikh with their wives cast in their lot with me. Kasturbai was also summoned for the work. This was a fairly strong contingent. Shrimati Avantikabai and Shrimati Anandibai were educated enough, but Shrimati Durga Desai and Shrimati Manibehn Parikh had nothing more than a bare knowledge: of Gujarati, and Kasturbai not even that.

I explained to them that they were expected to teach the children not grammar and the three R's so much as cleanliness and good manners. I further explained that even as regards letters there was not so great a difference between Gujarati, Hindi and Marathi as they imagined, and in the primary classes, at any rate, the teaching of the rudiments of the alphabet and numerals was not a difficult matter. The result was that the classes taken by these ladies were found to be most successful. Avantikabai's became a model school. Through these ladies we could, to some extent, reach the village women.

But I did not want to stop at providing for primary education. The villages were insanitary, the lanes full of filth, the wells surrounded by mud and stink and the courtyards unbearably untidy. The elder people badly needed education in cleanliness. They were all suffering from various skin diseases. So it was decided to do as much sanitary work as possible and to penetrate every department of their lives.

Doctors were needed for this work. I requested the Servants of India Society to lend us the services of Dr. Dev. He readily offered his services for six months. The teachers—men and women—had all to work under him.

All of them had express instructions not to concern

themselves with grievances against planters or with politics. People who had any complaints to make were to be referred to me. No one was to venture out of his beat. The friends carried out these instructions with wonderful fidelity. I do not remember a single occasion of indiscipline.

Thus the volunteers with their schools, sanitation work and medical relief gained the confidence and respect of the village folk, and were able to bring good influence to bear upon them.

But I must confess with regret that my hope of putting this constructive work on a permanent footing was not fulfilled. The volunteers had come for temporary periods, I could not secure any more from outside, and permanent honorary workers from Bihar were not available. As soon as my work in Champaran was finished, work outside, which had been preparing in the meantime, drew me away.

Indigo Plantation Abolished

The work of recording statements of the ryots' grievances was progressing apace. Thousands of such statements were taken, and they could not but have their effect. The ever growing number of ryots coming to make their statements increased the planters' wrath, and they moved heaven and earth to counteract my inquiry.

One day I received a letter from the Bihar Government to the following effect: 'Your inquiry has been sufficiently prolonged, should you not now bring it to an end and leave Bihar?' The letter was couched in polite language, but its meaning was obvious.

I wrote in reply that the inquiry was bound to be prolonged, and unless and until it resulted in bringing relief to the people, I had no intention of leaving Bihar. I pointed out that it was open to Government to terminate my inquiry by accepting the ryots' grievances as genuine and redressing them, or by recognizing that the ryots had made out a *prima facie* case for an official inquiry which should be immediately instituted.

Sir Edward Gait, the Lieutenant Governor, asked me to see him, expressed his willingness to appoint an inquiry and invited me to be a member of the Committee.

Sir Frank Sly was appointed Chairman of the Committee.

The Committee' found in favour of the ryots, and recommended that the planters should refund a portion of the exactions made by them which the Committee had found to be unlawful, and that the *tinkathia* system should be abolished by law.

Sir Edward Gait had a large share in getting the Committee to make a unanimous report and in getting the agrarian bill passed in accordance with the Committee's recommendations. The planters wielded extraordinary power. They offered strenuous opposition to the bill in spite of the report, but Sir Edward Gait remained firm up to the last and fully carried out the recommendations of the Committee.

The *tinkathia* system which had been in existence for about a century was thus abolished, and with it the planters' *raj* came to an end. The ryots, who had all along remained crushed, now somewhat came to their own, and the superstition that the stain of indigo could never be washed out was exploded.

Millworkers Strike in Ahmedabad

Whilst I was yet winding up my work on the Committee, I received a letter from Sjt. Mohanlal Pandya and Shankarlal Parikh telling me of the failure of grops in the Kheda district, and asking me to guide the peasants, who were unable to pay the assessment. I had not the inclination, the ability or the courage to advise without an inquiry on the spot.

At the same time there came a letter from Shrimati Anasuyabai about the condition of labour in Ahmedabad. Wages were low, the labourers had long been agitating for an increment, and I had a desire to guide them if I could. But I had not the confidence to direct even this comparatively small affair from that long distance. So I seized the first opportunity to go to Ahmedabad. I had hoped that I should be able to finish both these matters quickly and get back to Champaran to supervise the constructive work that had been inaugurated there.

But things did not move as swiftly as I had wished, and I was unable to return to Champaran, with the result that the schools closed down one by one. My co-workers and I had built many castles in the air, but they all vanished for the time being.

One of these was cow protection work in Champaran, besides rural sanitation and education. Cow protection, in my opinion, included cattle-breeding, improvement of the stock, humane treatment of bullocks, formation of model dairies, etc. The Marwadi friends had promised full co-operation in this work, but as I could not fix myself up in Champaran, the scheme could not be carried out.

Whilst the Kheda peasants' question was still being discussed, I had already taken up the question of the mill-hands in Ahmedabad.

I was in a most delicate situation. The mill-hands' case was strong. Shrimati Anasuyabai had to battle against her own brother, Sjt. Ambalal Sarabhai, who led the fray on behalf of the mill-owners. My relations with them were friendly, and that made fighting with them the more difficult. I had consultations with them, and requested them to refer the dispute to arbitration, but they refused to recognize the principle of arbitration.

I had therefore to advise the labourers to go on strike. Before I did so, I came in very close contact with them and their leaders, and explained to them the conditions of a successful strike:

1. never to resort to violence,

2. never to molest blacklegs,

3. never to depend upon alms, and

4. to remain firm, no matter how long the strike continued, and to earn bread during the strike, by any other honest labour.

The leaders of the strike understood and accepted the conditions, and the labourers pledged themselves at a general meeting not to resume work until either their terms were accepted or the mill-owners agreed to refer the dispute to arbitration.

It was during this strike that I came to know intimately. Vallabhbhai Patel and Shankarlal Banker.

We had daily meetings of the strikers under the shade of a tree on the bank of the Sabarmati. They attended the meeting in their thousands and I reminded them in my speeches of their pledge and of the duty to maintain peace and self-respect. They daily paraded the streets of the city in peaceful procession, carrying their banner bearing the inscription *'Ek Tek'* (keep the pledge).

The strike went on for twenty-one days. During the continuance of the strike I consulted the mill-owners from time to time and entreated them to do justice to the labourers. 'We have our pledge too,' they used to say. 'Our relations with the labourers are those of parents and children. . . . How can we brook the interference of a third party? Where is the room for arbitration?'

A Fast Solved the Problem

For the first two weeks the mill-hands exhibited great courage and self-restraint and daily held monster meetings. But at last they began to show signs of flagging. Just as physical weakness in men manifests itself in irascibilityæ their attitude towards the blacklegs became more and more menacing as the strike seemed to weaken, and I began to fear an outbreak of rowdyism on their part. The attendance at their daily meetings also began to dwindle by degrees, and despondency and despair were writ large on the faces of those who did attend. Finally, the information was brought to me that the strikers had begun to totter. I felt deeply troubled and set to thinking furiously as to what my duty was in the circumstances. I had had experience of a gigantic strike in South Africa, but the situation that confronted me here was different. The mill-hands had taken the pledge at my suggestion.

One morning—it was at a mill-hands' meeting—while I was still groping and unable to see my way clearly, the light came to me. Unbidden and all by themselves the words came to my lips: 'Unless the strikers rally,' I declared to the meeting, 'and continue the strike till a settlement is reached, or till they leave the mills altogether, I will not touch any food.'

The labourers were thunderstruck. Tears began to course down Anasuyabehn's cheeks. The labourers broke out, 'Not you but we shall fast. It would be monstrous if you were to fast. Please forgive us for our lapse, we will now remain faithful to our pledge to the end.'

'There is no need for you to fast,' I replied. 'It would be enough if you could remain true to your pledge. As you know we are without funds, and we do not want to continue our strike by living on public charity . You should therefore try to eke out a bare existence by some kind of labour, so that you may be able to remain unconcerned, no matter how long the strike may continue. As for my fast, it will be broken only after the strike is settled.'

In the meantime Vallabhbhai was trying to find some employment for the strikers under the Municipality, but there was not much hope of success there. Maganlal Gandhi suggested that, as we needed sand for filling the foundation of our weaving school in the Ashram, a number of them might be employed for that purpose. The labourers welcomed the proposal. Anasuyabehn led the way with a basket on her head and soon an endless stream of labourers carrying baskets of sand on their heads could be seen issuing out of the hollow of the river-bed. It was a sight worth seeing.

My fast was not free from a grave defect. For as I have already mentioned in a previous chapter, I enjoyed very close and cordial relations with the mill-owners, and my fast could not but affect their decision. As a Satyagrahi I knew that I might not fast against them, but ought to leave them free to be influenced by the mill-hands' strike alone. My fast was undertaken not on account of lapse of the mill-owners, but on account of that of the labourers in which, as their representative, I felt I had a share. With the mill-owners, I could only plead; to fast against them would amount to coercion. Yet in spite of my knowledge that my fast was bound to put pressure on them, as in fact it did, I felt I could not help it.

I tried to set the mill-owners at ease. 'There is not the slightest necessity for you to withdraw from your position,' I said to them. But they received my words coldly and even flung keen, delicate bits of sarcasm at me, as indeed they had a perfect right to do.

The principal man at the back of the mill-owners' unbending attitude towards the strike was Sheth Ambalal. The strain produced by my fast upon the opposition, of which he was the head, cut me, therefore, to the quick. And then, Sarladevi, his wife, was attached to me with the affection of a blood-sister and I could not bear to see her anguish on account of my action.

Anasuyabehn and a number of other friends and labourers shared the fast with me on the first day. But after some difficulty I was able to dissuade them from continuing it further.

The net result of it was that an atmosphere of goodwill was created all round. The hearts of the mill-owners were touched, and they set about discovering some means for a settlement. Anasuyabehn's house became the venue of their discussions. Sjt. Anandshankar Dhruva intervened and was in the end appointed arbitrator, and the strike was called off after I had fasted only for three days. The mill-owners commemorated the event by distributing sweets among the labourers, and thus a settlement was reached after 21 days' strike.

At the meeting held to celebrate the settlement, both the mill-owners and the Commissioner were present. The advice which the latter gave to the mill-hands on this occasion was: 'You should always act as Mr. Gandhi advise you.'

Kheda Satyagraha

No breathing time was, however, in store for me. Hardly

was the Ahmedabad mill-hands' strike over, when I had to plunge into the Kheda Satyagraha struggle.

A condition approaching famine had arisen in the Kheda district owing to a widespered failure of crops, and the Patidars of Kheda were considering the question of getting the revenue assessment for the year suspended.

Sjt. Amritlal Thakkar had already inquired into the situation and personally discussed the question with the Commissinor, before I gave definite advice to the cultivators. Sjts. Mohanlal Pandya and Shankarlal Parikh had also thrown themselves into the fight, and had set up an agitation in the Bombay Legislative Council through Sjt. Vithalbhai Patel and Sir. Gokuldas Kahandas Parekh. More than one deputation had waited upon the Governor in that connection.

I was at this time President of the Gujarat Sabha. The Sabha sent petitions and telegrams to the Government and even patiently swallowed the insults and threats of the Commissioner. The conduct of the officials on this occasion was so ridiculous and undignified as to be almost incredible now.

The cultivators' demand was as clear as daylight, and so moderate as to make out a strong case for its acceptance. Under the Land Revenue Rules, if the crop was four annas or under, the cultivators could claim full suspension of the revenue assessment for the year. According to the official figures the crop was said to be over four annas. The contention of the cultivators, on the other hand, was that it was less than four annas. But the Government was in no mood to listen and regarded the popular demand for arbitration as *lese majeste*. At last all petitioning and prayer having failed, after taking counsel with co-workers, I advised the Patidars to resort to Satyagraha.

Besides the volunteers of Kheda, my principal comrades in this struggle were Sjt. Vallabhbhai Patel, Shankarlal Banker, Shrimati Anasuyabehn, Sjts. Indulal Yajnik, Mahadev Desai and others. Sjt. Vallabhbhai, in joining the struggle, had to suspend a splendid and growing practice at the bar, which for all practical purpose he was never able to resume.

We fixed up our headquarters at the Nadiad Anathashram, no other place being available which would have been large enough to accommodate all of us.

A pledge was signed by the Satyagrahis.

Champaran being in a far away corner of India, and the press having been kept out of the campaign, it did not attract visitors from outside. Not so with the Kheda campaign, of which the happenings were reported in the press from day to day.

The Gujaratis were deeply interested in the fight, which was to them a novel experiment. They were ready to pour forth their riches for the success of the cause. It was not easy for them to see that Satyagraha could not be conducted simply by means of money. Money is the thing that it least needs. In spite of my remonstrance, the Bombay merchants sent us more money than necessary, so that we had some balance left at the end of the campaign.

At the same time the Satyagrahi volunteers had to learn the new lesson of simplicity. I cannot say that they imbibed it fully, but they considerably changed their ways of life. For the Patidar farmers, too, the fight was quite a new thing. We had, therefore, to go about from village to village explaining the principles of Satyagraha.

The main thing was to rid the agriculturists of their fear by making them realize that the officials were not the masters but the servants of the people, inasmuch as they received their salaries from the tax-payer. And then it seemed well nigh impossible to make them realize the duty of combining civility with fearlessness. If they resorted to incivility it would spoil their Satyagraha, like a drop of arsenic in milk. I realized later that they had less fully learnt the lesson of civility than I had expected. **Experience has taught me that civility is the most difficult part of Satyagraha.**

In the initial stages, though the people exhibited much courage, the Government did not seem inclined to take strong action. But as the people's firmness showed no signs of wavering, the Government began coercion. The attachment officers sold people's cattle and seized whatever movables they could lay hand, on. Penalty notices were served, and in some cases standing crops were attached. This unnerved the peasants, some of whom paid up the dues, while others desired to place safe movables in the way of the officials so that they might attach them to realize the dues.

While these things were going on, one of Sjt. Shankarlal Parikh's tenants paid up the assessment in respect of his land. This created a sensation. Sjt. Shankarlal Parikh immediately made amends for his tenants' mistake by giving away for charitable purposes the land for which the assessment had been paid. He thus saved his honour and set a good example to others.

With a view to stealing the hearts of those who were frightened, I advised the people, under the leadership of Sjt. Mohanlal Pandya, to remove the crop of onion, from a field which had been, in my opinion wrongly attached. I did not regard this as civil disobedience, but even if it was, I suggested that this attachment of standing crops, though it might be in accordance with law, was morally wrong, and was nothing short of looting, and that therefore it was the people's duty to remove the onion in spite of the order of attachment. This was a good opportunity for the people to learn a lesson in courting fines or imprisonment, which was the necessary consequence of such disobedience. For Sjt. Mohanlal Pandya it was a thing after his heart. So he volunteered to remove the onion crop from the field, and in this seven or eight friends joined him.

It was impossible for the Government to leave them free. The arrest of Sjt. Mohanlal and his companions added to the people's enthusiasm. When the fear of jail disappears, repression puts heart into the people. Crowds of them besieged the court-house on the day of the hearing. Pandya and his companions were convicted and sentenced to a brief term of imprisonment. A procession escorted the 'convicts' to jail, and on that day Sjt. Mohanlal Pandya earned from the people the honoured title of *'dungli chor'* (onion thief).

The campaign came to an unexpected end. It was clear that the people were exhausted, and I hesitated to let the unbending be driven to utter ruin. I was casting about for some graceful way of terminating the struggle which would be acceptable to a Satyagrahi. Such a one appeared quite unexpectedly. The Mamlatdar of the Nadiad Taluka sent me word that, if well-to-do Patidars paid up, the poorer ones would be granted suspension. I asked for a written undertaking to that effect, which was given. But as a Mamlatdar could be responsible only for his Taluka, I inquired of the Collector, who alone could give an undertaking in respect of the whole district. He replied that orders declaring suspension in terms of the Mamlatdar's letter had been already issued. I was not aware of it, but if it was a fact, the people's pledge had been fulfilled.

The Kheda Satyagraha marks the beginning of an awakening among the peasants of Gujarat, the beginning of their true political education. That Vallabhbhai found himself during this campaign was by itself no small achievement. We could realize its measure during the flood relief operations last year and the Bardoli Satyagraha. Public life in Gujarat became instinct with a new energy and a new vigour. The lesson was indelibly imprinted on the public mind that the salvation of the people depends upon themselves, upon their capacity for suffering and sacrifice. Through the Kheda campaign Satyagraha took firm root in the soil of Gujarat.

Shifting the Ashram

At that time the Ashram was in Kochrab, a small village near Ahmedabad. Plague broke out in this village, and I saw evident danger to the safety of the Ashram children. It was impossible to keep ourselves immune from the effects of the surrounding insanitation, however scrupulously we might observe the rules of cleanliness within the Ashram walls. We were not then equal either to getting the Kochrab people to observe these rules nor to serving the village otherwise.

Punjabhai Hirachand, a merchant in Ahmedabad, had come in close contact with the Ashram, and used to serve us in a number of matters in a pure and selfless spirit. He had a wide experience of things in Ahmedabad, and he volunteered to procure us suitable land. I went about with him north and south of Kochrab in search of land, and then suggested to him to find out a piece of land three or four miles to the north. He hit upon the present site. Its vicinity to the Sabarmati Central Jail was for me a special attraction. As jail-going was understood to be the normal lot of Satyagrahis, I liked this position. And I knew that the sites selected for jails have generally clean surroundings.

In about eight days the sale was executed. There was no building on the land and no tree. But its situation on the bank of the river and its solitude were great advantages. We decided to start by living under canvas, and having a tin shed for a kitchen, till permanent houses were built.

The Ashram had been slowly growing. We were now over forty souls, men, women and children, having our meals at a common kitchen. The whole conception about the removal was mine, the execution was as usual left to Maganlal.

Hindu-Muslim Unity

The Kheda campaign was launched while the deadly war in Europe was still going on. Now a crisis had arrived, and the Viceroy had invited various leaders to a war conference in Delhi. I had also been urged to attend the conference. I have already referred to the cordial relations between Lord Chelmsford, the Viceroy, and myself.

In response to the invitation I went to Delhi. I had, however, objections to taking part in the conference, the principal one being the exclusion from it of leaders like the Ali Brothers. They were then in jail. I had met them only once or twice, though I had heard much about them. Everyone had spoken highly of their services and their courage. I had not then come in close touch with Hakim Saheb, but Principal Rudra and Dinabandhu Andrews had told me a deal in his praise. I had met Mr. Shuaib Qureshi and Mr. Khwaja at the Muslim League in Calcutta. I had also come in contact with Drs. Ansari and Abdur Rahman. I was seeking the friendship of good Musalmans, and was eager to understand the

Musalman mind through contact with their purest and most patriotic representatives. I therefore never needed any pressure to go with them, wherever they took me, in order to get into intimate touch with them.

I had realized early enough in South Africa that there was no genuine friendship between the Hindus and the Musalmans. I never missed a single opportunity to remove obstacles in the way of unity. It was not in my nature to placate anyone by adulation, or at the cost of self-respect. **But my South African experiences had convinced me that it would be on the question of Hindu-Muslim unity that my Ahimsa would be put to its severest test,** and that the question presented the widest field for my experiments in Ahimsa. Every moment of my life I realize that God is putting me on my trial.

Having such strong convictions on the question when I returned from South Africa, I prized the contact with the Brothers. But before closer touch could be established they were isolated. Maulana Mahomed Ali used to write long letters to me from Betul and Chhindwada whenever his jailers allowed him to do so. I applied for permission to visit the Brothers, but to no purpose.

It was after the imprisonment of the Ali Brothers that I was invited by Muslim friends to attend the session of the Muslim League at Calcutta. Being requested to speak, I addressed them on the duty of the Muslims to secure the Brothers' release. A little while after this I was taken by these friends to the Muslim College at Aligarh. **There I invited the young men to be fakirs for the service of the motherland.**

Next I opened correspondence with the Government for the release of the Brothers. In that connection I studied the Brothers' views and activities about the Khilafat. I had discussions with Musalman friends. I felt that, if I would become a true friend of the Muslims, I must render all possible help in securing the release of the Brothers, and a just settlement of the Khilafat question. It was not for me to enter into the absolute merits of the question, provided there was nothing immoral in their demands. **In matters of religion beliefs**

differ, and each one's is supreme for himself. If all had the same belief about all matters of religion, there would be only one religion in the world. As time progressed I found that the Muslim demand about the Khilafat was not only not against any ethical principle, but that the British Prime Minister had admitted the justice of the Muslim demand. I felt, therefore, bound to render what help I could in securing a due fulfilment of the Prime Minister's pledge. The pledge had been given in such clear terms that the examination of the Muslim demand on the merits was needed only to satisfy my own conscience.

Friends and critics have criticized my attitude regarding the Khilafat question. In spite of the criticism I feel that I have no reason to revise it or to regret my cooperation with the Muslims. I should adopt the same attitude, should a similar occasion arise.

When, therefore, I went to Delhi, I had fully intended to submit the Muslim case to the Viceroy. The Khilafat question had not then assumed the shape it did subsequently.

Recruiting for the War

So I attended the conference. The Viceroy was very keen on my supporting the resolution about recruiting. I asked for permission to speak in Hindi-Hindustani. They Viceroy acceded to my request, but suggested that I should speak also in English. I had no speech to make. I spoke but one sentence to this effect: 'With a full sense of my responsibility I beg to support the resolution.'

Many congratulated me on my having spoken in Hindustani. That was, they said, the first instance within living memory of anyone having spoken in Hindustani at such a meeting. The congratulations and the discovery that I was to first to speak in Hindustani at a Viceregal meeting hurt my national pride. I felt like shrinking into myself.

There was one undertaking that I had to fulfil while yet in Delhi. I had to write a letter to the Viceroy. This was no easy thing for me. I felt it my duty both in the interests of the Government and of the people to explain therein how and why

I attended the conference, and to state clearly what the people expected from Government.

In the letter I expressed my regret for the exclusion from the conference of leaders like Lokamanya Tilak and the Ali Brothers, and stated the people's minimum political demand as also the demands of the Muslims on account of the situation created by the war. I asked for permission to publish the letter, and the Viceroy gladly gave it.

The other part of my obligation consisted in raising recruits. Where could I make a beginning except in Kheda? And whom could I invite to be the first recruits except my own coworkers? So as soon as I reached Nadiad, I had a conference with Vallabhbhai and other friends. Some of them could not easily take to the proposal. Those who liked the proposal had misgivings about its success. There was no love lost between the Government and the classes to which I wanted to make my appeal. The bitter experience they had had of the Government officials was still fresh in their memory.

And yet they were in favour of starting work. As soon as I set about my task, my eyes were opened. My optimism received a rude shock. Whereas during the revenue campaign the people readily offered their carts free of charge, and two volunteers came forth when one was needed, it was difficult now to get a cart even on hire, to say nothing of volunteers. We decided to dispense with the use of carts and to do our journeys on foot. At this rate we had to trudge about 20 miles a day. If carts were not forthcoming, it was idle to expect people to feed us. So it was decided that every volunteer must carry his food in his satchel. No bedding or sheet was necessary as it was summer.

We had meetings wherever we went. People did attend, but hardly one or two would offer themselves as recruits. 'You are a votary of Ahimsa, how can you ask us to take up arms?' 'What good has Government done for India to deserve our cooperation?' These and similar questions used to be put to us.

However, our steady work began to tell. Quite a number

of names were registered, and we hoped that we should be able to have a regular supply as soon as the first batch was sent. I had already begun to confer with the Commissioner as to where the recruits were to be accommodated.

The Commissioners in every division were holding conferences on the Delhi model. One such was held in Gujarat. My coworkers and I were invited to it. We attended, but I felt there was even less place for me here than at Delhi. In this atmosphere of servile submission I felt ill at ease. I spoke somewhat at length. I could say nothing to please the officials, and had certainly one or two hard things to say.

I used to issue leaflets asking people to enlist as recruits. One of the arguments I had used was distasteful to the Commissioner: 'Among the many misdeeds of the British rule in India, history will look upon the Act depriving a whole nation of arms as the blackest. If we want the Arms Act to be repealed, if we want to learn the use of arms, here is a golden opportunity. If the middle classes render voluntary help to Government in the hour of its trial, distrust will disappear, and the ban on possessing arms will be withdrawn.' The Commissioner referred to this and said that he appreciated my presence in the conference in spite of the differences between us. And I had to justify my standpoint as courteously as I could.

Attack of Dysentery

I very nearly ruined my constitution during the recruiting campaign. In those days my food principally consisted of groundnut, butter and lemons. I knew that it was possible to eat too much butter and injure one's health, and yet I allowed myself to do so. This gave me a slight attack of dysentery. I did not take serious notice of this, and went that evening to the Ashram, as was my wont every now and then. I scarcely took any medicine in those days. I thought I should get well if I skipped a meal, and indeed I felt fairly free from trouble as I omitted the morning meal next day. I knew, however, that to be entirely free I must prolong my fast and, if I eat anything at all, I should have nothing but fruit juices.

There was some festival that day, and although I had told Kasturbai that I should have nothing for my midday meal, she tempted me and I succumbed. Instead of eating very little I had my fill of the meal. This was sufficient invitation to the angel of death. Within an hour the dysentery appeared in acute form.

The same evening I had to go back to Nadiad. I walked with very great difficulty to the Sabarmati station, a distance of only ten furlongs. Sjt. Vallabhbhai, who joined me at Ahmedabad, saw that I was unwell, but I did not allow him to guess how unbearable the pain was.

We reached Nadiad at about ten o'clock. The Hindu Anathashram where we had our headquarters was only half a mile from the station; but it was as good as ten for me. I somehow managed to reach the quarters, but the griping pain was steadily increasing. Instead of using the usual latrine which was a long way off, I asked for a commode to be placed in the adjoining room. I was ashamed to have to ask for this, but there was no escape. Sjt. Fulchand immediately procured a commode. All the friends surrounded me deeply concerned. They were all love and attention, but they could not relieve my pain. And my obstinacy added to their helplessness. I refused all medical aid. I would take no medicine, but preferred to suffer the penalty for my folly. So they looked on in helpless dismay. I must have had thirty to forty motions in twenty-four hours. I fasted, not taking even fruit juices in the beginning. The appetite had all gone. I had thought all along that I had an iron frame, but I found that my body had now become a lump of clay. It had lost all power of resistance. Dr. Kanuga came and pleaded with me to take medicine. I declined. He offered to give me an injection. I declined that too.

My ignorance about injections was in those days quite ridiculous. I believed that an injection must be some kind of serum. Later I discovered that the injection that the doctor suggested was a vegetable substance, but the discovery was too late to be of use. The motions still continued, leaving me completely exhausted. The exhaustion brought on a delirious fever. The friends got more nervous, and called in more doctors. But what could they do with a patient who would not listen to them?

Sheth Ambalal with his good wife came down to Nadiad, conferred with my co-workers and removed me with the greatest care to his Mirzapur bungalow in Ahmedabad. But a sort of low fever persisted, wearing away my body from day to day. I felt that the illness was bound to be prolonged and possibly fatal. I began to get restless and urged him to remove me to the Ashram. He had to yield to my importunity.

Whilst I was thus tossing on the bed of pain in the Ashram, Sjt. Vallabhbhai brought the news that Germany had been completely defeated, and that the Commissioner had sent word that recruiting was no longer necessary. The news that I had no longer to worry myself about recruiting came as a very great relief.

I had now been trying hydropathy which gave some relief, but it was a hard job to build up the body. The many medical advisers over whelmed me with advice, but I could not persuade myself to take anything.

This protracted and first long illness in my life thus afforded me a unique opportunity to examine my principles and to test them. One night I gave myself up to despair. I felt that I was at death's door. I sent word to Anasuyabehn. She ran down to the Ashram. Vallabhbhai came up with Dr. Kanuga, who felt my pulse and said, 'Your pulse is quite good. I see absolutely no danger. This is a nervous breakdown due to extreme weakness.'

The morning broke without death coming. But I could not get rid of the feeling that the end was near, and so I began to devote all my waking hours to listening to the Gita being read to me by the inmates of the Ashram. All interest in living had ceased, as I have never liked to live for the sake of living.

Whilst I lay thus very expectant of death Dr. Talvalkar came one day with a strange creature. He hailed from Maharashtra. He was not known to fame, but **the moment I**

saw him I found that he was a crank like myself. He had come to try his treatment on me. He had almost finished his course of studies in the Grant Medical College without taking the degree. Later I came to know that he was a member of the Brahmo Samaj. Sjt. Kelkar, for that is his name, is a man of an independent and obstinate temperament. He swears by the ice treatment, which he wanted to try on me. We gave him the name of 'Ice Doctor'.

I allowed him to experiment on my body. I did not mind external treatment. The treatment consisted in the application of ice all over the body. Whilst I am unable to endorse his claim about the effect his treatment had on me, it certainly infused in me a new hope and a new energy, and the mind naturally reacted on the body. I began to have an appetite, and to have a gentle walk for five to ten minutes. He now suggested a reform in my diet. Said he: 'I assure you that you will have more energy and regain your strength quicker if you take raw eggs. Eggs are as harmless as milk. They certainly cannot come under the category of meat. And do you know that all eggs are not fertilized? There are sterilized eggs on the market.' I was not, however, prepared to take even the sterilized eggs. But the improvement was enough to give me interest in public activities.

Friends and doctors assured me that I should recuperate quicker by a change to Matheran, so I went there. But the water at Matheran being very hard, it made my stay there extremely difficult. As a result of the attack of the dysentery that I had, my anal tract had become extremely tender, and owing to fissures, I felt an excruciating pain at the time of evacuation, so that the very idea of eating filled me with dread. Before the week was over, I had to flee from Matheran. Shankarlal Banker now constituted himself the guardian of my health, and pressed me to consult Dr. Dalal. Dr. Dalai was called accordingly. His capacity for taking instantaneous decisions captured me.

He said: 'I cannot rebuild your body unless you take milk. If in addition you would take iron and arsenic injections, I would guarantee fully to renovate your constitution.'

'You can give me the injections,' I replied, 'but milk is a different question; I have a vow against it.'

'What exactly is the nature of your vow?' the doctor inquired.

I told him the whole history and the reasons behind my vow.

'But surely you cannot have any objection to goat's milk then,' Kasturbai interposed.

The doctor too took up the strain. 'If you will take goat's milk, it will be enough for me,' he said.

I succumbed. My intense eagerness to take up the Satyagraha fight had created in me a strong desire to live, and so I contented myself with adhering to the letter of my vow only, and sacrificed its spirit. The will to live proved stronger than the devotion to truth, and for once the votary of truth compromised his sacred ideal by his eagerness to take up the Satyagraha fight.

Soon after I began taking goat's milk, Dr. Dalal performed on me a successful operation for fissures. As I recuperated, my desire to life revived, especially because God had kept work in store for me.

The Rowlatt Bills

I had hardly begun to feel my way towards recovery, when I happened casually to read in the papers the Rowlatt Committee's report which had just been published. Its recommendations startled me. Shankarlal Banker and Umar Sobani approached me with the suggestion that I should take some prompt action in the matter. In about a month I went to Ahmedabad. I mentioned my apprehensions to Vallabhbhai, who used to come to see me almost daily. 'Something must be done,' said I to him. 'But what can we do in the circumstances?' he asked in reply. I answered, 'If even a handful of men can be found to sign the pledge of resistance, and the proposed measure is passed into law in defiance of it, we ought to offer Satyagraha at once. If I was not laid up like this, I should give battle against it all alone, and expect others to follow suit. But in my present helpless condition I feel myself to be altogether unequal to the task.'

As a result of this talk, it was decided to call a small meeting of such persons as were in touch with me. The recommendations of the Rowlatt Committee seemed to me to be altogether unwarranted by the evidence published in its report, and were, I felt, such that no self-respecting people could submit to them.

The proposed conference was at last held at the Ashram. Hardly a score of persons had been invited to it. So far as I remember, among those who attended were, besides Vallabhbhai, Sarojini Naidu, Mr. Horniman, Mr. Umar Sobani, Sjt. Shankarlal Banker and Shrimati Anasuyabehn. The Satyagraha pledge was drafted at this meeting, and was signed by all present. I was not editing any journal at that time, but I used occasionally to ventilate my views through the daily press. I followed the practice on this occasion. Shankarlal Banker took up the agitation in right earnest, and for the first time I got an idea of his wonderful capacity for organization and sustained work.

As all hope of any of the existing institutions adopting a novel weapon like Satyagraha seemed to me to be in vain, a separate body called the Satyagraha Sabha was established at my instance. Its principal members were drawn from Bombay where therefore, its headquarters were fixed. The intending convenanters began to sign the Satyagraha pledge in large numbers, bulletins were issued, and popular meetings began to be held everywhere recalling all the familiar features of the Kheda campaign.

I became the president of the Satyagraha Sabha. I soon found that there was not likely to be much chance of agreement between myself and the intelligentsia composing this Sabha. My insistence on the use of Gujarati in the Sabha, as also some of my other methods of work that would appear to be peculiar, caused them not small worry and embarrassment. I must say to their credit, however, that most of them generously put up with my idiosyncrasies.

But from the very beginning it seemed clear to me that the Sabha was not likely to live long. I could see that already my emphasis on truth and Ahimsa had begun to be disliked by some of its members. Nevertheless in its early stages our new activity went on at full blast, and the movement gathered head rapidly.

The First All-India Satyagraha

Thus, while on the one hand, the agitation against the Rowlatt Committee's report gathered volume and intensity, on the other, the Government grew more and more determined to give effect to its recommendations, and the Rowlatt Bill was published. I have attended the proceedings of India's legislative chamber only once in my life, and that was on the occasion of the debate on this Bill. Shastriji delivered an impassioned speech, in which he uttered a solemn note of warning to the Government. The Viceroy seemed to be listening spell-bound, his eyes rivetted on Shastriji as the latter poured forth the hot stream of his eloquence. For the moment it seemed to me as if the Viceroy could not but be deeply moved by it, it was so true and so full of feeling.

But you can wake a man only if he is really asleep; no effort that you may make will produce any effect upon him if he is merely pretending sleep. That was precisely the Government's position. It was anxious only to go through the farce of legal formality. Its decision had already been made. Shastriji's solemn warning was, therefore, entirely lost upon the Government.

In these circumstances mine could only be a cry in the wilderness. I earnestly pleaded with the Viceroy. I addressed him private letters as also public letters, in the course of which I clearly told him that the Government's action left me no other course except to resort to Satyagraha. But it was all in vain.

The Bill had not yet been gazetted as an Act. I was in a very weak condition, but when I received an invitation from Madras I decided to take the risk of the long journey. I could not at that time sufficiently raise my voice at meetings. My entire frame would shake, and heavy throbbing would start on an attempt to speak standing for any length of time.

I have ever felt at home in the south. Thanks to my South African work I felt I had some sort of special rights over the Tamils and Telugus, and the good people of the south have never belied my belief. The invitation had come over the signature of Sjt. Kasturi Ranga Iyengar. But the man behind the invitation, as I subsequently learnt on my way to Madras, was Rajagopalachari. This might be said to be my first acquaintance with him; at any rate this was the first time that we came to know each other personally.

Rajagopalachari had then only recently left Salem to settle down for legal practice in Madras at the pressing invitation of friends like Sjt. Kasturi Ranga Iyengar, and that with a view to taking a more active part in public life. It was with him that we had put up in Madras.

We daily discussed together plans of the fight, **but beyond the holding of public meetings I could not then think of any other programme.** I felt myself at a loss to discover how to offer civil disobedience against the Rowlatt Bill if it was finally passed into law.

Sjt. Kasturi Ranga Iyengar called together a small conference of leaders to thrash out the matter. Among those who took a conspicuous part in it was Sjt. Vijayaraghavachari. **He suggested that I should draw up a comprehensive manual of the science of Satyagraha,** embodying even minute details. I felt the task to be beyond my capacity, and I confessed as much to him.

The Idea Came in a Dream

While these cogitations were still going on, news was received that the Rowlatt Bill had been published as an Act. That night I fell asleep while thinking over the question. Towards the small hours of the morning I woke up somewhat earlier than usual. **I was still in that twilight condition between sleep and consciousness when suddenly the idea**

broke upon me—it was as if in a dream. Early in the morning I related the whole story to Rajagopalachari.

'The idea came to me last night in a dream that we should call upon the country to observe a general *hartal.* Satyagraha is a process of self-purification, and ours is a sacred fight, and it seems to me to be in the fitness of things that it should be commenced with an act of self-purification. **Let all the people of India, therefore suspend their business on that day and observe the day as one of fasting and prayer.** The Musalmans may not fast for more than one day; so the duration of the fast should be 24 hours. It is very difficult to say whether all the provinces would respond to this appeal of ours or not, but I feel fairly sure of Bombay, Madras, Bihar and Sindh. I think we should have every reason to feel satisfied even if all these places observe the hartal fittingly.'

Rajagopalachari was at once taken up with my suggestion. Other friends too welcomed it when it was communicated to them later. I drafted a brief appeal. The date of the *hartal* was first fixed on the 30th March 1919, but was subsequently changed to 6th April. The people thus had only a short notice of the *hartal.* As the work had to be started at once, it was hardly possible to give longer notice.

But who knows how it all came about? **The whole of India from one end to the other, towns as well as villages, observed a complete *hartal* on that day. It was a most wonderful spectacle.**

After a short tour in South India I reached Bombay, I think on the 4th April, having received a wire from Sjt. Shankarlal Banker asking me to be present there for the 6th of April celebrations.

In Delhi and Bombay

But in the meanwhile Delhi had already observed the *hartal* on the 30th March. The word of Swami Shraddhanandji and Hakim Ajmal Khan Saheb was law there. The wire about the postponement of the *hartal* till the 6th of April had reached there too late. **Delhi had never witnessed a *hartal* like that**

before. Hindus and Musalmans seemed united like one man. Swami Shraddhanandji was invited to deliver a speech in the Jumma Masjid which he did. All this was more than the authorities could bear. The police checked the *hartal* procession as it was proceeding towards the railway station and opened fire, causing a number of casualties, and the reign of repression commened in Delhi.

Shraddhanandji urgently summoned me to Delhi. I wired back, saying I would start for Delhi immediately after the 6th of April celebrations were over in Bombay.

The story of happenings in Delhi was repeated with variations in Lahore and Amritsar. From Amritsar Drs. Satyapal and Kitchlu had sent me a pressing invitation to go there. I was altogether unacquainted with them at that time, but I communicated to them my intention to visit Amritsar after Delhi.

On the morning of the 6th the citizens of Bombay flocked in their thousands to the Chaupati for a bath in the sea, after which they moved on in a procession to Madhavbag. The procession included a fair sprinkling of women and children while the Musalmans joined it in large numbers. From Madhavbag some of us who were in the procession were taken by the Musalman friends to a mosque, where Mrs. Naidu and myself were persuaded to deliver speeches. Sjt. Vithaldas Jerajani proposed that we should then and there administer the Swadeshi and Hindu-Muslim unity pledges to the people, but I resisted the proposal on the ground that pledges should not be administered or taken in precipitate hurry, and that we should be satisfied with what was already being done by the people.

Needless to say the *hartal* in Bombay was a complete success. Full preparation had been made for starting civil disobedience. Two or three things had been discussed in this connection. It was decided that civil disobedience might be offered in respect of such laws only as easily lent themselves to being disobeyed by the masses. The salt tax was extremely unpopular and a powerful movement had been for some time past going on to secure its repeal. **I therefore suggested that the people might prepare salt from sea-water in their own houses in disregard of the salt laws. My other suggestion, was about the sale of proscribed literature.** Two of my books, *Hind Swaraj* and *Sarvodaya* (Gujarati adaptation of Ruskin's *Unto This Last),* which had been already proscribed, came handy for this purpose. A sufficient number of copies of the books was therefore printed, and it was arranged to sell them at the end of the monster meeting that was to be held that evening after the breaking of the fast.

On the evening of the 6th an army of volunteers issued forth accordingly with this prohibited literature to sell it among the people. Both Sarojini Devi and I went out in cars. All the copies were soon sold out. Both these books were priced at four annas per copy, but I hardly remember anybody having purchased them from me at their face value merely. Quite a large number of people simply poured out all the cash that was in their pockets to purchase their copy. Five and ten rupee notes just flew out to cover the price of a single copy, while in one case I remember having sold a copy for fifty rupees! It was duly explained to the people that they were liable to be arrested and imprisoned for purchasing the proscribed literature. But for the moment they has shed all fear of jail-going.

It was subsequently learnt that the Government had conveniently taken the view that the books that had been proscribed by it had not in fact been sold, and that what we had sold was not held as coming under the definition of proscribed literature. The reprint was held by the Government to be a new edition of the books that had been proscribed, and to sell them did not constitute an offence under the law. This news caused general disappointment.

The next morning another meeting was held for the administration of the pledges with regard to Swadeshi and Hindu-Muslim unity. Vithaldas Jerajani for the first time realized that all is not gold that glitters. Only a handful of persons came. I distinctly remember some of the sisters who were present on that occasion. The men who attended were also very few. I had already drafted the pledge and brought it with me. I thoroughly explained its meaning to those present before I administered it to them. The paucity of the attendance neither pained nor surprised me, **for I have noticed this characteristic difference in the popular attitude—partiality for exciting work and dislike for quite constructive effort.**

On the night of the 7th I started for Delhi and Amritsar. On reaching Mathura on the 8th I first heard rumours about my probable arrest. At the next stoppage after Mathura, Acharya Gidvani came to meet me, and gave me definite news that I was to be arrested, and offered his service to me if I should need them. I thanked him for the offer, assuring him that I would not fail to avail myself of it, if and when I felt it necessary.

Before the train had reached Palwal railway station, I was served with a written order to the effect that I was prohibited from entering the boundary of the Punjab, as my presence there was likely to result in a disturbance of the peace. I was asked by the police to get down from the train. I refused to do so saying, 'I want to go to the Punjab in response to a pressing invitation, not to foment unrest, but to allay it. I am therefore sorry that it is not possible for me to comply with this order.'

At last the train reached Palwal. Mahadev was with me. I asked him to proceed to Delhi to convey to Swami Shraddhanandji the news about what had happened and to ask the people to remain calm. He was to explain why I had decided to disobey the order served upon me and suffer the penalty for disobeying it, and also why it would spell victory for our side if we could maintain perfect peace in spite of any punishment that might be inflicted upon me.

Arrest at Palwal

At Palwal railway station I was taken out of the train and put under police custody. A train from Delhi came in a short time. I was made to enter a third class carriage, the police party accompanying. On reaching Mathura, I was taken to the police barracks, but no police official could tell me as to what they proposed to do with me or where I was to be taken next. **Early at 4 o'clock the next morning I was waked up and put in a goods train that was going towards Bombay.** At noon I was again made to get down at Sawai Madhopur. Mr. Bowring, Inspector of Police, who arrived by the mail train from Lahore, now took charge of me. I was put in a first class compartment with him **and from an ordinary prisoner I became a 'gentleman' prisoner.**

The officer commenced a long panegyric of Sir Michael O'Dwyer. Sir Michael had nothing against me personally, he went on, only he apprehended a disturbance of the peace if I entered the Punjab and so on. In the end he requested me to return to Bombay of my own accord and agree not to cross the frontier of the Punjab. I replied that I could not possibly comply with the order, and that I was not prepared of my own accord to go back. Whereupon the officer, seeing no other course, told me that he would have to enforce the law against me. 'But what do you want to do with me?' I asked him. He replied that he himself did not know, but was awaiting further orders. 'For the present,' he said,' I am taking you to Bombay.'

We reached Surat. Here I was made over to the charge of another police officer. 'You are now free,' the officer told me when we had reached Bombay. 'It would however be better,' he added, 'if you get down near the Marine Lines where I shall get the train stopped for you. At Colaba there is likely to be a big crowd.' I told him that I would be glad to follow his wish. He was pleased and thanked me for it. Accordingly I alighted at the Marine Lines. The carriage of a friend just happened to be passing by. It took me and left me at Revashankar Jhaveri's place. The friend told me that **the news of my arrest had incensed the people and roused them to a pitch of mad frenzy.** 'An outbreak is apprehended every minute near Pydhuni, the Magistrate and the police have already arrived there,' he added.

Scarcely had I reached my destination, when Umar Sobani and Anasuyabehn arrived and asked me to motor to Pydhuni at once. The people have become impatient, and are very much excited,' they said, 'we cannot pacify them. Your presence alone can do it.'

People's Demonstration

I got into the car. Near Pydhuni I saw that a huge crowd had gathered. On seeing me the people went mad with joy. A procession was immediately formed, and the sky was rent with the shouts of *Vande Mataram* and *Allaho Akbar.* At Pydhuni we sighted a body of mounted police. Brickbats were raining down from above. I besought the crowd to be calm, but it seemed as if we should not be able to escape the shower of brickbats. As the procession issued out of Abdur Rahman Street and was about to proceed towards the Crawford Market, it suddenly found itself confronted by a body of the mounted police, who had arrived there to prevent it from proceeding further in the direction of the Fort.

The crowd was densely packed. It had almost broken through the police cordon. There was hardly any chance of my voice being heard in that vast concourse. Just then the officer in charge of the mounted police gave the order to disperse the crowd, and at once the mounted party charged upon the crowd brandishing their lances as they went. For a moment I felt that I would be hurt. But my apprehension was groundless, the lances just grazed the car as the lancers swiftly passed by. The ranks of the people were soon broken, and they were thrown into utter confusion, which was soon converted into a rout. Some got trampled under foot, others were badly mauled and crushed. In that seething mass of humanity there was hardly any room for the horses to pass, nor was there any exit by which the people could disperse. So the lancers blindly cut their way through the crowd. I hardly imagine they could see what they were doing. The whole thing presented a most dreadful spectacle. The horsemen and the people were mixed together in mad confusion.

Thus the crowd was dispersed and its progress checked. Our motor was allowed to proceed. I had it stopped before the Commissioner's office, and got down to complain to him about the conduct of the police.

Meeting the Commissioner

So I went to the Commissioner Mr. Griffith's office. All about the staircase leading to the office I saw soldiers armed from top to toe, as though for military action. The verandah was all astir. When I was admitted to the office, I saw Mr. Bowring sitting with Mr. Griffith.

I described to the Commissioner the scenes I had witnessed. He replied briefly: 'I did not want the procession to proceed to the Fort as a disturbance was inevitable there. And as I saw that the people would not listen to persuasion, I could not help ordering the mounted police to charge through the crowd.'

'But,' said I, 'you knew what the consequences must be. The horses were bound to trample on the people. I think it was quite unnecessary to send that contingent of mounted men.'

'You cannot judge that': said Mr. Griffith. 'We police officers know better than you the effect of your teaching on the people. If we did not start with drastic measures, the situation would pass out of our hands. I tell you that the people are sure to go out of your control. Disobedience of law will quickly appeal to them; it is beyond them to understand the duty of keeping peaceful. I have no doubt about your intentions, but the people will not understand them. They will follow their natural instinct.'

'It is there that I join issue with you,' I replied. 'The people are not by nature violent but peaceful.'

And thus we argued at length. Ultimately, Mr. Griffith said, 'But suppose you were convinced that your teaching had been lost on the people, what would you do?'

'I should suspend civil disobedience if I were so convinced.'

'What do you mean? You told Mr. Bowring that you would proceed to the Punjab the moment you are released.'

'Yes, I wanted to do so by the next available train. But it is out of the question today.'

'If you will be patient, the conviction is sure to grow on you. Do you know what is happening in Ahmedabad? And what has happened in Amritsar? People have everywhere gone nearly mad. I am not yet in possession of all the facts. The telegraph wires have been cut in come places. I put it to you that the responsibility for all these disturbances lies on you.'

'I assure you I should readily take it upon myself wherever I discovered it. But I should be deeply pained and surprised, if I found that there were disturbances in Ahmedabad. I cannot answer for Amritsar. I have never been there, no one knows me there. But even about the Punjab I am certain of this much that, had not the Punjab Government prevented my entry into the Punjab, I should have been considerably helpful in keeping the peace there. By preventing me they gave the people unnecessary provocation.'

And so we argued on and on. It was impossible for us to agree. I told him that I intended to address a meeting on Chaupati and to ask the people to keep the peace, and took leave of him. The meeting was held on the Chaupati sands. I spoke at length on the duty of non-violence and on the limitations of Satyagraha, and said: 'Satyagraha is essentially a weapon of the truthful. A Satyagrahi is pledged to non-violence, and, unless people observe it in thought, word and deed, I cannot offer mass Satyagraha.'

Anasuyabehn, too, had received news of disturbances in Ahmedabad. Someone had spread a rumour that she also had been arrested. The mill-hands had gone mad over her rumoured arrest, struck work and committed acts of violence, and a sergeant had been done to death.

Visit to Ahmedabad

I proceeded to Ahmedabad. I learnt that an attempt had been made to pull up the rails near the Nadiad railway station, that **a Government officer had been murdered in Viramgam and that Ahmedabad was under martial law.** The people were terror-stricken. They had indulged in acts of violence and were being made to pay for them with interest.

A police officer was waiting at the station to escort me to Mr. Pratt, the Commissioner. I found him in a state of rage. I spoke to him gently, and expressed my regret for the disturbances. I suggested that martial law was unnecessary, and declared my readiness to co-operate in all efforts to restore peace. I asked for permission to hold a public meeting on the grounds of the Sabarmati Ashram. The proposal appealed to him, and the meeting was held, I think on Sunday, the 13th of April, and martial law was withdrawn the same day or the day after. Addressing the meeting, I tried to bring home to the people the sense of their wrong, **declared a penitential fast of three days for myself, appealed to the people to go on a similar fast for a day,** and suggested to those who had been guilty of acts of violence to confess their guilt.

I saw my duty as clear as daylight. It was unbearable for me to find that the labourers, amongst whom I had spent a good deal of my time, whom I had served, and from whom I had expected better things, had taken part in the riots, and I felt I was a sharer in their guilt.

Just as I suggested to the people to confess their guilt, I suggested to the Government to condone the crimes. Neither accepted my suggestion.

Sir Ramanbhai and other citizens of Ahmedabad came to me with an appeal to suspend Satyagraha. The appeal was needless, for **I had already made up my mind to suspend Satyagraha so long as people had not learnt the lesson of peace.** The friends went away happy.

There were, however, others who were unhappy over the decision. They felt that, if I expected peace. everywhere and regarded it as a condition precedent to launching Satyagraha, mass Satyagraha would be an impossibility. I was sorry to disagree with them. If those amongst whom I worked, and whom I expected to be prepared for non-violence and self-suffering, could not be non-violent, Satyagraha was certainly impossible. I was firmly of opinion that those who wanted to lead the people to Satyagraha ought to be able to keep the people within the limited non-violence expected of them.

A Himalayan Miscalculation

Almost immediately after the Ahmedabad meeting I went to Nadiad. It was here that I first used the expression 'Himalayan miscalculation' which obtained such a wide currency afterwards. Even at Ahmedabad I had begun to have a dim perception of my mistake. But when I reached Nadiad and saw the actual state of things there and heard reports about a large number of people from Kheda district having been arrested, it suddenly dawned upon me that I had committed a grave error in calling upon the people in the Kheda district and elsewhere to launch upon civil disobedience prematurely, as it now seemed to me. I was addressing a public meeting. My confession brought down upon me no small amount of ridicule. But I have never regretted having made that confession. For I have always held that it is only when one sees one's own mistakes with a convex lens, and does just the reverse in the case of the others, that one is able to arrive at a just relative estimate of the two. I further believe that a scrupulous and conscientious observance of this rule is necessary for one who wants to be a Satyagrahi.

Before one can be fit for the practice of civil disobedience one must have rendered a willing and respectful obedience to the State laws. For the most part we obey such laws out of fear of the penalty for their breach, and this holds good particularly in respect of such laws as do not involve a moral principle. Such compliance is not, however, the willing and spontaneous obedience that is required of a Satyagrahi. A Satyagrahi obeys the laws of society intelligently and of his own free will, because he considers it to be his sacred duty to do so. Only then does the right accrue to him to the civil disobedience of certain laws in well-defined circumstances. My error lay in my failure to observe this necessary limitation. I had called on the people to launch upon civil disobedience before they had thus qualified themselves for it, and this mistake seemed to me of Himalayan magnitude. I realized that before a people could be fit for offering civil disobedience, they should thoroughly understand its deeper implications. That being so, before restarting civil disobedience on a mass scale, it would be necessary to create a band of well-tried, pure-hearted volunteers who thoroughly understood the strict conditions of Satyagraha. They could explain these to the people, and by sleepless vigilance keep them on the right path.

Training the Satyagrahis

With these thoughts filling my mind I reached Bombay, raised a corps of Satyagrahi volunteers through the Satyagraha Sabha there, and with their help commenced the work of educating the people with regard to the meaning and inner significance of Satyagraha.

But whilst this work was going on, I could see that it was a difficult task to interest the people in the peaceful side of Satyagraha. The volunteers too failed to enlist themselves in large numbers. Nor did all those who actually enlisted take anything like a regular systematic training, and as the days passed by, the number of fresh recruits began gradually to dwindle instead of to grow. I realized that the progress of the training in civil disobedience was not going to be as rapid as I had at first expected.

Situation in Punjab

Thus, whilst this movement for the preservation of non-violence was making steady though slow progress on the one hand, Government's policy of lawless repression was in full career on the other, and was manifesting itself in the Punjab in all its nakedness. Leaders were put under arrest, martial law, which in other words meant no law, was proclaimed, special tribunals were set up. These tribunals were not courts of justice but instruments for carrying out the arbitrary will of an autocrat. Sentences were passed unwarranted by evidence and in flagrant violation of justice. In Amritsar innocent men and women were made to crawl like worms on their bellies. Before this outrage the Jalianwala Bagh tragedy paled into insignificance in my eyes, though it was this massacre principally that attracted the attention of the people of India and the world.

I was pressed to proceed to the Punjab immediately in disregard of consequences. I wrote and also telegraphed to the Viceroy asking for permission to go there, but in vain. If I proceeded without the necessary permission, I should not be allowed to cross the boundary of the Punjab, but left to find what satisfaction I could from civil disobedience. I was thus confronted by a serious dilemma. As things stood, to break the order against my entry into the Punjab could, it seemed to me, hardly be classed as civil disobedience, for I did not see around me the kind of peaceful atmosphere that I wanted, and the unbridled repression in the Punjab had further served to aggravate and deepen the feelings of resentment. For me, therefore, to offer civil disobedience at such a time, even if it were possible, would have been like fanning the flame. I therefore decided not to proceed to the Punjab in spite of the suggestion of friends. It was a bitter pill for me to swallow. Tales of rank injustice and oppression came pouring in daily from the Punjab, but all I could do was to sit helplessly by and gnash my teeth.

'Navajivan' and 'Young India'

Just then Mr. Horniman, in whose hands *The Bombay Chronicle* had become a formidable force, was suddenly spirited away by the authorities. This act of the Government seemed to me to be surrounded by a foulness which still stinks in my nostrils. I was asked by the directior of *The Bombay Chronicle* to take up the responsibility of conducting that paper. Mr. Brelvi was already there on the staff, so not much remained to be done by me, but as usual with my nature, the responsibility would have become an additional tax. But the Government came as it were to my rescue, for by its order the publication of *The Chronicle* had to be suspended.

The friends who were directing the management of *The Chronicle* Messrs. Umar Sobani and Shankarlal Banker, were at this time also controlling *Young India*. They suggested that, in view of the suppression of *The Chronicle,* I should now take up the editorship of *Young India* and that, in order to fill the gap left by the former, *Young India* should be converted from a weekly into a biweekly organ. This was what I felt also.

But how could the general public be trained in Satyagraha through the medium of English? My principal field of work lay in Gujarat. Sjt. Indulal Yajnik was at that time associated with the group of Messrs. Sobani and Banker. He was conducting the Gujarati monthly *Navajivan* which had the financial backing of these friends. They placed the monthly at my disposal, and further, Sjt. Indulal offered to work on it. This monthly was converted into a weekly.

In the meantime *The Chronicle* was resuscitated. *Young India* was therefore restored to its original weekly form. As *Navajivan* was already being published from Ahmedabad, *Young India* was also removed there at my suggestion. Through these journals I now commenced to the best of my ability the work of educating the reading public in Satyagraha. Both of them had reached a very wide circulation, which at one time rose to the neighbourhood of forty thousand each.

These journals helped me also to some extent to remain at peace with myself for, whilst immediate resort to civil disobedience was out of the question, they enabled me freely to ventilate my views and to put heart into the people. Thus I feel that both the journals rendered good service to the people in this hour of trial, and did their humble bit towards lightening the tyranny of the material law.

Visit to Punjab

Sir Michael O'Dwyer held me responsible for all that had happened in the Punjab, and some irate young Punjabis held me responsible for the martial law. They asserted that, if only I had not suspended civil disobedience, there would have been no Jalianwala Bagh massacre. Some of them even went to the length of threatening me with assassination if I went to the Punjab.

I was impatient to go to the Punjab. I had never been there before, and that made me all the more anxious to see things for myself. Dr. Satyapal, Dr. Kitchlu and Pandit Rambhaj Dutt Chowdhari who had invited me to the Punjab, were at this time in jail. A large number of Punjabis used to come and see me whenever I was in Bombay. I ministered to them a word of cheer on these occasions, and that would comfort them. My self-confidence of that time was infectious.

But my going to the Punjab had to be postponed again and again. The Viceroy would say, 'not yet', every time I asked for permission to go there.

In the meantime, the Hunter Committee was announced to hold an inquiry in connection with the Punjab Government's doings under the martial law. Mr. C. F. Andrews had now reached the Punjab. His letters gave a heart-rending description of the state of things there, and I formed the impression that the martial law atrocities were in fact even worse than the press reports had showed. He pressed me urgently to come and join him. At the same time Malaviyaji sent telegrams asking me to proceed to the Punjab at once. I once more telegraphed to the Viceroy asking whether I could now go to the Punjab. He wired back in reply that I could go there after a certain date. I cannot exactly recollect now, but I think it was 17th of October.

The scene that I witnessed on my arrival at Lahore can never be effaced from my memory. **The railway station was from end to end one seething mass of humanity. The entire populace had turned out of doors in eager expectation, as if to meet a dear relation after a long separation, and was delirious with joy.** I was put up at Pandit Rambhaj Dutt's bungalow, and the burden of entertaining me fell on the shoulders of Shrimati Sarala Devi. A burden it truely was, for even then, as now, the place where I was accommodated became a veritable caravanserai.

Owing to the principal Punjab leaders being in jail, their place, I found, had been properly taken up by Pandit Malaviyaji, Pandit Motilalji and Swami Shraddhanandji. This was the first occasion on which I came in close personal contact with Motilalji. All these leaders, as also such local leaders as had escaped the privilege of going to jail, at once made me feel perfectly at home amongst them.

How we unanimously decided not to lead evidence before

the Hunter Committee is now a matter of history. Looking back upon these events from this distance of time, I still feel that our decision to boycott the Committee was absolutely correct and proper.

Inquiry and Report

It was decided to appoint a non-official Inquiry Committee to hold almost a parallel inquiry on behalf of the Congress. Pandit Motilal Nehru, Deshbandhu C.R. Das, Sjt. Abbas Tyabji, Sjt. M.R. Jayakar and myself were appointed to this Committee, virtually by Pandit Malaviyaji. We distributed ourselves over various places for purpose of inquiry. The responsibility for organizing the work of the Committee devovled on me.

In the course of my inquiry I made acquittance with the women of the Punjab also. It was as if we had known one another for ages. Whenever I went they came flocking, and laid before me their heaps of yarn. My work in connection with the inquiry brought home to me the fact that the Punjab could become a great field for Khadi work.

The task of drafting the report of this Committee was also entrusted to me. This report, prepared as it was solely with a view to bringing out the truth and nothing but the truth, will enable the reader to see to what lengths the British Government is capable of going, and what inhumanities and barbarities it is capable of perpetrating in order to maintain its power. So far as I am aware, not a single statement made in this report has ever been disproved.

Khilafat and Cow Protection

The Congress inquiry into Dyerism in the Punjab had just commenced, when I received a letter of invitation to be present at a joint conference of Hindus and Musalmans that was to meet at Delhi to deliberate on the Khilafat question. Among the signatories to it were Hakim Ajmal Khan Saheb and Mr. Asaf Ali. Swami Shraddhanandji, it was stated, would be attending and, if I remember right, he was to be the vice-president of the conference, which, so far as I can recollect, was to be held in the November of that year. The conference was to deliberate on the situation arising out of the Khilafat betrayal, and on the question as to whether the Hindus and Musalmans should take any part in the peace celebrations. The letter of invitation went on to say, among other things, that not only the Khilafat question but the question of cow protection as well would be discussed at the conference, and it would, therefore, afford a golden opportunity for a settlement of the cow question. I did not like this reference to the cow question. In my letter in reply to the invitation, therefore, whilst promising to do my best to attend, I suggested that the two questions should not be mixed up together or considered in the spirit of a bargain, but should be decided on their own merits and treated separately.

With these thoughts filling my mind, I went to the conference. It was a very well attended gathering, though it did not present the spectacle of later gatherings that were attended by tens of thousands. I discussed the question referred to above with Swami Shraddhanandji, who was present at the conference. He appreciated my argument and left it to me to place it before the conference. I likewise discussed it with Hakim Saheb. Before the conference I contended that, if the Khilafat question had a just and legitimate basis, as I believe it had, and if the Government had really committed a gross injustice, the Hindus were bound to stand by the Musalmans in their demand for the redress of the Khilafat wrong. It would ill become them to bring in the cow question in this connection, or to use the occasion to make terms with the Musalmans, just as it would ill become the Musalmans to offer to stop cow slaughter as a price for the Hindus' support on the Khilafat question. But it would be another matter and quite graceful and reflect great credit on them, if the Musalmans of their own free will stopped cow slaughter out of regard for the religious sentiments of the Hindus, and from a sense of duty towards them as neighbours had children of the same soil. To take up such an independent attitude was, I contended, their duty, and would enhance the dignity of their conduct.

But in spite of my warning Maulana Abdul Bari Saheb said: 'No matter whether the Hindus help us or not, the Musalmans ought, as the countrymen of the Hindus, out of regard for the latter's susceptibilities, to give up cow slaughter.' And at one time it almost looked as if they would really put an end to it.

There was a suggestion from some quarters that the Punjab question should be tacked on to that of the Khilafat wrong. I opposed the proposal. The Punjab question, I said, was a local affair and could not therefore weigh with us in our decision to participate or not in the peace celebrations. If we mixed up the local question with the Khilafat question, which arose directly out of the peace terms, we should be guilty of a serious indiscretion. My argument easily carried conviction.

Among the numerous resolutions that were passed at this conference, **one called upon both Hindus and Musalmans to take the Swadeshi vow, and as a natural corollary to it, to boycott foreign goods.** Khadi had not as yet found its proper peace. This was not a resolution that Hasrat Mohani Saheb would accept. His object was to wreak vengeance on the British Empire, in case justice was denied in the matter of the Khilafat. Accordingly, he brought in a counter proposal for the "boycott purely of British goods so far as practicable." I opposed it on the score of principle, as also of practicability. I also put before the conference my viewpoint of non-violence. I noticed that my arguments made a deep impression on the audience.

Before me, Hasrat Mohani's speech had been received with such loud acclamations that I was afraid that mine would only be a cry in wilderness. But, to my agreeable surprise, my speech was followed with the closest attention by those present, and evoked a full measure of support among those on the platform, and speaker after speaker rose to deliver speeches in support of my views. The leaders were able to see that not only would the boycott of British goods fail in its purpose, but would, if adopted, make of them a laughing stock.

I felt that something new, over and above boycott of foreign cloth, would be necessary. An immediate boycott of foreign cloth seemed to me also to be a clear impossibility at that time. I did not then know that we could, if we liked, produce enough Khadi for all our clothing requirements; this was only a later discovery.

I was handicapped for want of suitable Hindi or Urdu words. This was my first occasion for delivering an argumentative speech before an audience especially composed of Musalmans of the North. Here, I was faced with a critical, if not hostile, audience, to whom I had to explain and bring home my viewpoint. But I had cast aside all shyness. I was not there to deliver an address in the faultless, polished Urdu of the Delhi Muslims, but to place before the gathering my views in such broken Hindi as I could command. And in this I was successful. This meeting afforded me a direct proof of the fact that Hindi-Urdu alone could become the *lingua franca* of India. Had I spoken in English, I could not have produced the impression that I did of the audience.

Amritsar Congress

The Punjab Government could not keep in confinement the hundreds of Punjabis who, under the martial law regime, had been clapped into jail on the strength of the most meagre evidence by tribunals that were courts only in name. There was such an outcry all round against this flagrant piece of injustice that their further incarceration became impossible. Most of the prisoners were released before the Congress opened. Lala Harkishanlal and the other leaders were all released while the session of the Congress was still in progress. The Ali Brothers too arrived then straight from jail. The people's joy knew no bounds. Pandit Motilal Nehru, who, at the sacrifice of his splendid practice, had made the Punjab his headquarters and had done great service, was the President of the Congress; Swami Shraddhanandji was the Chairman of the Reception Committee.

Up to this time my share in the annual proceedings of the Congress was confined only to the constructive advocacy of Hindi by making my speech in the national language, and to presenting in that speech the case of the Indians overseas.

Nor did I expect to be called upon to do anything more this year. But, as had happened on many a previous occasion, responsible work came to me all of a sudden.

The King's announcement on the new reforms had just been issued. It was not wholly satisfactory even to me, and was unsatisfactory to everyone else. But I felt at that time that the reforms, though defective, could still be accepted. I felt in the King's announcement and its language the hand of Lord Sinha, and it lent a ray of hope. But experienced stalwarts like Lokamanya and Deshabandhu Chittaranjan Das shook their heads. Pandit Malaviyaji was neutral.

Pandit Malaviyaji had harboured me in his own room. I had a glimpse of the simplicity of his life on the occasion of the foundation ceremony of the Hindu University; but on this occasion, being in the same room with him, I was able to observe his daily routine in the closest detail, and what I saw filled me with joyful surprise. His room presented the appearance of a free inn for all the poor. You could hardly cross from one end to the other. It was so crowded. In a corner of this crib lay my *charpai* in all its dignity.

Initiation in the Congress

I must regard my participation in Congress proceedings at Amritsar as my real entrance into the Congress politics. My attendance at the previous Congresses was nothing more perhaps than an annual renewal of allegiance to the Congress. I never felt on these occasions that I had any other work cut out for me except that of a mere private, nor did I desire more.

My experience of Amritsar had shown that there were one or two things for which perhaps I had some aptitude and which could be useful to the Congress. I could already see that Lokamanya, the Deshabandhu, Pandit Motilalji and other leaders were pleased with my work in connection with the Punjab inquiry. They used to invite me to their informal gatherings where, as I found, resolutions for the Subjects Committee were conceived. At these gatherings only those persons were invited who enjoyed the special confidence of the leaders and whose services were needed by them.

There were, for the coming year, two things which interested me, as I had some aptitude for them. One of these was the memorial of the Jalianwala Bagh Massacre. The Congress had passed a resolution for it amid great enthusiasm. A fund of about five lakhs had to be collected for it. I was appointed one of the trustees. Pandit Malaviyaji enjoyed the reputation of being the prince among beggars for the public cause. But I knew that I was not far behind him in that respect. I had not the unrivalled magic of Malaviyaji for commanding princely donations from the potentates of India. But I knew that there was no question of approaching the Rajas and Maharajas for donations for the Jalianwala Bagh memorial. The main responsibility for the collection thus fell, as I had expected, on my shoulders. The generous citizens of Bombay subscribed most liberally.

Making the Constitution

My other aptitude which the Congress could utilize was as a draftsman. The Congress leaders had found that I had a faculty for condensed expression, which I had acquired by long practice. The then existing constitution of the Congress was Gokhale's legacy. He had framed a few rules which served as a basis for running the Congress machinery. The interesting history of the framing of these rules had learnt from Gokhale's own lips. But everybody had now come to feel that these rules were no longer adequate for the ever increasing business of the Congress. The question had been coming up year after year. The Congress at that time had practically no machinery functioning during the interval between session and session, or for dealing with fresh contingencies that might arise in the course of the year.

The existing rules provided for three secretaries, but as a matter of fact only one of them was a functioning secretary, and even he was not a wholetimer. How was he, single-handed, to run the Congress office, to think of the future, or to discharge during the current year the obligations contracted by the Congress in the past? During that year, therefore, everybody felt that this question would assume all the more importance. The Congress was too unwieldy a body for the discussion of public affairs. There was no limit set to the number of delegates in the Congress or to the number of delegates that each province could return.

I undertook the responsibility of framing a constitution on one condition. I saw that there were two leaders, Lokamanya and Deshabandhu who had the greatest hold on the public. I requested that they, as the representatives of the people, should be associated with me on the Committee for framing the constitution. But since it was obvious that they would not have the time personally to participate in the constitution-making work, I suggested that two persons enjoying their confidence should be appointed along with me on the Constitution Committee, and that the number of its personnel should be limited to three. This suggestion was accepted by Lokamanya and Deshabandhu, who suggested the names of Sjts. Kelkar and I. B. Sen respectively as their proxies.

The Constitution Committee could not even once come together, but we were able to consult with each other by correspondence, and in the end presented a unanimous report. I regard this constitution with a certain measure of pride. I hold that, if we could fully work out this constitution, the mere fact of working it out would bring us Swaraj. With the assumption of this responsibility I may be said to have made my real entrance into the Congress politics.

The Khadi Story

I do not remember to have seen a handloom or a spinning wheel when in 1908 I described it in *Hind Swaraj* as the panacea for the growing pauperism of India. In that book I took it as understood that anything that helped India to get rid of the grinding poverty of her masses would in the same process also establish Swaraj. Even in 1915, when I returned to India from South Africa, I had not actually seen a spinning wheel. When the Satyagraha Ashram was founded at Sabarmati, we introduced a few handlooms there. But no sooner had we done this than we found ourselves up against a difficulty. All of us belonged either to the liberal professions or to business; not one of us was an artisan. We needed a weaving expert to teach us to weave before we could work the looms. One was at last procured from Palanpur, but he did not communicate to us the whole of his art. But Maganlal Gandhi was not to be easily baffled. Possessed of a natural talent for mechanics, he was able fully to master the art before long, and one after another several new weavers were trained up in the Ashram.

The object that we set before ourselves was to be able to clothe ourselves entirely in cloth manufactured by our own hands. We therefore forthwith discarded the use of mill-woven cloth, and all the members of the Ashram resolved to wear handwoven cloth made from Indian yarn only. The adoption of this practice brought us a world of experience. It enabled us to know, from direct contact, the conditions of life among the weavers, the extent of their production, the handicaps in the way of their obtaining their yarn supply, the way in which they were being made victims of fraud, and, lastly, their ever growing indebtedness. We were not in a position immediately to manufacture all the cloth for our needs. The alternative therefore was to get our cloth supply from handloom weavers. But ready-made cloth from Indian mill-yarn was not easily obtainable either from the cloth-dealers or from the weavers themselves. All the fine cloth woven by the weavers was from foreign yarn, since Indian mills did not spin fine counts.

So the time passed on, and my impatience grew with the time. I plied every chance visitor to the Ashram who was likely to possess some information about handspinning with questions about the art. But the art being confined to women and having been all but exterminated, if there was some stray spinner still surviving in some obscure corner, only a member of that sex was likely to find out her whereabouts.

In the year 1917 I was taken by my Gujarati friends to preside at the Broach Educational Conference. It was here that I discovered that remarkable lady Gangabehn Majmudar. She was a widow, but her enterprising spirit knew no bounds. In courage and commonsense she easily surpassed the general run of our educated women. She had means of her own, and her needs were few. She had a well seasoned constitution, and went about everywhere without an escort. She felt quite at home on horseback. To her I poured out my grief about the charkha, and she lightened my burden by a promise to prosecute an earnest and incessant search for the spinning wheel.

At last, after no end of wandering in Gujarat, Gangabehn found the spinning wheel in Vijapur in the Baroda State. Quite a number of people there had spinning wheels in their homes, but had long since consigned them to the lofts as useless lumber. They expressed to Gangabehn their readiness to resume spinning, if someone promised to provide them with a regular supply of slivers, and to buy the yarn spun by them. Gangabehn communicated the joyful news to me. The providing of slivers was found to be a difficult task. On my mentioning the thing to Umar Sobani, he solved the difficulty by immediately undertaking to send a sufficient supply of slivers from his mill. I sent to Gangabehn the slivers received from Umar Sobani; and soon yarn began to pour in at such a rate that it became quite a problem how to cope with it.

The spinning wheel gained a rapid footing in the Ashram. Maganlal Gandhi, by bringing to bear all his splendid mechanical talent on the wheel, made many improvements in it, and wheels and their accessories began to be manufactured at the Ashram. The first piece of Khadi manufactured in the Ashram cost 17 annas per yard. I did not hesitate to commend this very coarse Khadi at that rate to friends.

I was laid up in bed at Bombay. But I was fit enough to make searches for the wheel there. At last I chanced upon two spinners. They charged one rupee for a seer of yarn, i.e., 28 *tolas* or nearly three quarters of a pound. I was then ignorant of the economics of Khadi. On comparing the rates paid by me with those paid in Vijapur I found that I was being cheated. The spinners refused to agree to any reduction in their rates.

I now grew impatient for the exclusive adoption of Khadi for my dress. My *dhoti* was still of Indian mill cloth. The coarse

Khadi manufactured in the Ashram and at Vijapur was only 30 inches in width. I gave notice to Gangabehn that, unless she provided me with a Khadi *dhoti* of 45 inches width within a month, I would do with coarse, short Khadi *dhoti*. The ultimatum came upon her as a shock. But she proved equal to the demand made upon her. Well within the month she sent me a pair of Khadi *dhotis* of 45 inches width, and thus relieved me from what would then have been a difficult situation for me.

At about the same time Sjt. Lakshmidas brought Sjt. Ramji, the weaver, with his wife from Lathi to the Ashram and got Khadi *dhotis* woven at the Ashram. The part played by this couple in the spread of Khadi was by no means insignificant. They initiated a host of persons in Gujarat and also outside into the art of weaving handspun yarn.

Whilst the powerful Khilafat agitation set up by the Ali Brothers was in full progress, I had long discussions on the subject with Maulana Abdul Bari and the other UleÉa, especially, with regard to the extent to which a Musalman could observe the rule of non-violence. In the end **they all agreed that Islam did not forbid its followers from following non-violence as a policy, and further, that, they were bound faithfully to carry it out.** At last non-co-operation resolution was moved in the Khilafat Conference, and carried after prolonged deliberations. I have a vivid recollection how once at Allahabad a committee sat all night deliberating upon the subject. In the beginning Hakim Saheb was sceptical as to the practicability of non-violent non-co-operation. But after his scepticism was overcome he threw himself into it heart and soul, and his help proved invaluable to the movement.

Next, the non-co-operation resolution was moved by me at the Gujarat political conference that was held shortly afterwards. The preliminary contention raised by the opposition was that it was not competent to a provincial conference to adopt a resolution in advance of the Congress. As against this, I suggested that the restriction could apply only to a backward movement; but as for going forward, the subordinate organizations were not only fully competent, but were in duty bound to do so, if they had in them the necessary grit and confidence. The proposition was then discussed on its merits, the debate being marked by its keeness no less than the atmosphere of 'sweet reasonableness' in which it was conducted. On the ballot being taken the resolution was declared carried by an overwhelming majority. The successful passage of the resolution was due not a little to the personality of Sjt. Vallabhbhai and Abbas Tyabji. The latter was the president, and his leanings were all in favour of the non-co-operation resolution.

The All-India Congress Committee resolved to hold a special session of the Congress in September 1920 at Calcutta to deliberate on this question. Preparations were made for it on a large scale. Lala Lajpatrai was elected President. Congress and Khilafat specials were run to Calcutta from Bombay. At Calcutta there was a mammoth gathering of delegates and visitors.

At the request of Maulana Shaukat Ali I prepared a draft of the non-co-operation resolution in the train. Up to this time I had more or less avoided the use of the word non-violent in my drafts. I invariably made use of this word in my speeches. My vocabulary on the subject was still in process of formation. I found that I could not bring home my meaning to purely Moslem audiences with the help of the Samskrit equivalent for non-violent. I therefore asked Maulana Abul Kalam Azad to give me some other equivalent for it. He suggested the word *ba-aman;* similarly, for non-co-operation he suggested the phrase *tark-i-mavalat.*

My plight was pitiable indeed. I was absolutely at sea as to who would support the resolution and who would oppose it. Nor had I any idea as to the attitude that Lalaji would adopt. I only saw an imposing phalanx of veteran warriors assembled for the fray at Calcutta, Dr. Besant, Pandit Malaviyaji, Sjt. Vijayaraghavachari, Pandit Motilalji and the Deshabandhu being some of them.

In my resolution non-co-operation was postulated only

with a view to obtaining redress of the Punjab and the Khilafat wrongs. That, however, did not appeal to Sjt. Vijayaraghavachari. 'If non-co-operation was to be declared, why should it be with reference to particular wrongs? The absence of Swaraj was the biggest wrong that the country was labouring under; it should be against that that non-co-operation should be directed,' he argued. Pandit Motilalji also wanted the demand for Swaraj to be included in the resolution. I readily accepted the suggestion and incorporated the demand for Swaraj in my resolution, which was passed after an exhaustive, serious and somewhat stormy discussion.

Motilalji was the first to join the movement. I still remember the sweet discussion that I had with him on the resolution. He suggested some changes in its phraseology which I adopted. He undertook to win the Deshabandhu for the movement. The Deshabandhu's heart was inclined towards it, but he felt sceptical as to the capacity of the people to carry out the programme. It was only at the Nagpur Congress that he and Lalaji accepted it wholeheartedly.

I felt the loss of Lokamanya very deeply at the special session. It has been my firm faith to this day that, had the Lokamanya been then alive, he would have given his benedictions to me on that occasion. But even if it had been otherwise, and he had opposed the movement, I should still have esteemed his opposition as a privilege and an education for myself. We had our differences of opinion always, but they never led to bitterness. He always allowed me to believe that the ties between us were of the closest.

Even as I write these lines, the circumstances of his death stand forth vividly before my mind's eye. It was about the hour of midnight, when Patwardhan, who was then working with me, conveyed over the telephone the news of his death. I was at that time surrounded by my companions. Spontaneously the exclamation escaped my lips, 'My strongest bulwark is gone.' The non-co-operation movement was then in full swing, and I was eagerly looking forward to encouragement and insperation from him. What his attitude would have been with regard to the final phase of non-co-operation will always be a matter of speculation, and an idle one at that. But this much is certain—that the deep void left by his death weighed heavily upon everybody present at Calcutta. Everyone felt the absence of his counsels in that hour of crisis in the nation's history.

Nagpur Congress

At Nagpur, as at Calcutta, there was a great rush of visitors and delegates. **The number of delegates in the Congress had not been limited yet. As a result, the figure on this occasion reached about fourteen thousand.** Lalaji pressed for a slight amendment to the clause about the boycott of schools, which I accepted. Similarly, some amendments were made at the instance of the Deshabandhu, after which the non-co-operation resolution was passed unanimously.

The resolution regarding the revision of the Congress constitution too was to be taken up at this session of the Congress. The sub-committee's draft was presented at the Calcutta special session. The matter had therefore been thoroughly ventilated and thrashed out. At the Nagpur session, where it came up for final disposal, Sjt. C. Vijayaraghavachariar was the President. The Subjects Committee passed the draft with only one important change. In my draft the number of delegates had been fixed, I think, at 1,500; the Subjects Committee substituted in its place the figure 6,000. In my opinion this increase was the result of hasty judgment, and experience of all these years has only confirmed me in my view. I hold it to be an utter delusion to believe that a large number of delegates is in any way a help to the better conduct of the business, or that it safeguards the principle of democracy.

The question of the goal of the Congress formed a subject for keen discussion. **In the constitution that I had resented, the goal of the Congress was the attainment of Swaraj within the British Empire if possible and without if necessary.** A party in the Congress wanted to limit the goal to Swaraj within the British Empire only. Its viewpoint was put forth by Pandit Malaviyaji. and Mr. Jinnah. But they were not able to get many votes. Again the draft constitution provided that the means for the attainment were to be peaceful and legitimate. This condition too came in for opposition, it being contended that there should be no restriction upon the means to be adopted. But the Congress adopted the original draft after an instructive and frank discussion. I am of opinion that, if this constitution had been worked out by the people honestly, intelligently and zealously, it would have become a potent instrument of mass education, and the very process of working it out would have brought us Swaraj.

Resolutions about Hindu-Muslim unity, the removal of untouchability and Khadi too were passed in this Congress, and since then the Hindu members of the Congress have taken upon themselves the responsibility of ridding Hinduism of the curse of untouchability, and the Congress has established a living bond of relationship with the 'skeletons' of India through Khadi. The adoption of non-co-operation for the sake of the Khilafat was itself a great practical attempt made by the Congress to bring about Hindu-Muslim unity.

Farewell

The time has now come to bring these chapters to a close. My life from this point onward has been so public that there is hardly anything about it that people do not know. Moreover, since 1921 I have worked in such close association with the Congress leaders that I can hardly describe any episode in my life since then without referring to my relations with them. For though Shraddhanandji, the Deshabandhu, Hakim Saheb and Lalaji are no more with us today, we have the good luck to have a host of other veteran Congress leaders still living and working in our midst. The history of the Congress, since the great changes in it that I have described above, it still in the making. And my principal experiments during the past seven years have all been made through the Congress. Lastly, my conclusions from my current experiments can hardly as yet be regarded as decisive. It therefore seems to me to be my plain duty to close this narrative here. In fact my pen instinctively refuses to proceed further.

•••

About the Book

INDIA BOOKVARSITY provides the best of philosophy, religion, arts and history of the most ancient, essentially thought-oriented, secular-democratic, federative and peace-loving community and culture-India-for the new generation now spread all over the world, looking for their roots, identity, and seeking authentic knowledge about it.

This is in part a revival of already published works of great quality by Western scholars over a century ago, thoroughly edited, keeping in view the mindset and requirements of the present-day fast progressing youth, and the globalization of life in all its aspects.

Any ideas and suggestions, as well as support, would be welcome. Over 50 volumes by several publishers have so far been published.

About the Author

The Series-Editor, Mahendra Kulasrestha, educated in India and Japan, has been the first editor of the well known Orient Paperbacks, and has been associated with the Bharatiya Vidya Bhawan, Mumbai; V. Vedic Research Inst., Hoshiarpur, Pb.; Vision Books; Hind Pocket Books; Rajpal and Sons; Indira Gandhi Memorial Trust; HUDCO; DDA(Slum Wing); SEWA Delhi, etc. He has planned and edited the much useful Public Concerns Series, and been Consultant Editor of International Books Update.

His works include: Japan-An Enigma, An Anthology of Japanese Literature in Hindi, Tagore Centenary Volume, The Genius of Tagore, Aspects of Indian Culture, World Poetry Number of a Hindi literary magazine, An Anthology of Hindi Short Stories, Existence and Other Poems (English translations of Amrita Pritam's poems), a study of 14 Western philosophers in Hindi, etc.

Other Books on

PHILOSOPHY, RELIGION & CULTURE

1. Gandhi Global For The New Gen (New) 175/-
2. The Golden Book of World Religions (New) 395/-
3. Hindu Social System First Famous Study (New) 295/-
4. The Lotus Sutra Saddharma Pundarika (New) 295/-
5. The Master Swami Vivekananda (New) 250/-
6. Everyman's Book of Hindu Religion & Mythology (New) 295/-
7. The ABC of Hindu Culture (New) 295/-
8. India In China The Gift of Buddha (New) 295/-
9. The Vital Truths of Hinduism (New) 250/-
10. Philosophy India (New) 350/-
11. The Dhammapada 295/-
12. The Last Days of Lord Buddha 295/-
13. Complete Book of Hindu Gods And Goddesses 395/-
14. Vatsyayana's Kamasutra Select and his Times 125/-
15. The Kama Sutra of Mallinaga Vatsyayana 125/-
16. Judgment No Aircrash No Death 350/-
17. Patriot Netaji Subhas Chandra Bose 350/-
18. The Life of Lord Buddha 295/-
19. The Discourses of Lord Buddha 395/-
20. The Golden Book of Buddhism 395/-
21. The Golden Book of Hinduism 395/-
22. The Golden Book of Islam (New) 395/-
23. The Golden Book of Rigveda 395/-
24. The Golden Book of Jainism 395/-
25. The Golden Book of Upanishads 395/-

26. Learn Rajayoga From Vivekananda 250/-
27. Colossus Vivekananda Select 350/-
28. Intellect India 250/-
29. Culture India 250/-
30. My Experiments with Truth 250/-
31. Mahatma Gandhi The Bhagavadgita 250/-
32. Shirdi Sai Baba 80/-
33. The Ramayana For Every Home 150/-
34. The Mahabharata For Every Home 150/-
35. Sai - The Age of Cosmic Family 80/-
36. Sathya Sai and His Miraculous Powers 150/-
37. To Bloom Like a Lotus 225/-
38. The History of Sikh Gurus 225/-
39. Indian Mythology 195/-

Lotus PRESS

Unit No. 220, Second Floor, 4735/22,
Prakash Deep Building, Ansari Road, Darya Ganj,
New Delhi - 110002, Ph.: 32903912, 23280047, 09811594448
E-mail: lotuspress1984@gmail.com, www.lotuspress.co.in